To Mummy,
For Mother's d[...]
& Birthday[...]
with love, peter & Eunice.

CW00968421

2

IN SEARCH OF MY FATHER

IN SEARCH
OF MY FATHER

A Portrait of Leslie Howard

RONALD HOWARD

WILLIAM KIMBER·LONDON

First published in 1981 by
WILLIAM KIMBER & CO. LIMITED
Goldophin House, 22a Queen Anne's Gate,
London, SW1H 9AE

© Ronald Howard, 1981
ISBN 0-7183-0168-4

Photoset by Robcroft Ltd, London WC1
and printed and bound in Great Britain by
The Garden City Press Limited
Letchworth, Hertfordshire. SG6 1JS

Contents

List of Illustrations

TO JEAN
for her help, tolerance and stamina

Acknowledgements

For reference and research work I should like to thank The British Council (Archivist J.L.H. Webster), The Foreign and Commonwealth Office, the BBC Written Archives Centre, Caversham (Mrs Jacqueline Kavanagh), the Public Record Office, the British Film Institute and the Supervisor Archives British Airways (Mrs M. Lakritz).

For the use of personal letters, reminiscences and other records I am most grateful to Dr James Wightman, Mrs John Silkin (Rosamund John) Mary Morris, Gwyneth Williams, MBE, the late the Hon Anthony Asquith, the late Ian Colvin, the late Professor Walter Starkie, CMG, George West, OBE, Lord Miles, Sir Michael Stewart, KCMG, Samuel Mervyn Herbert, W.C. Collett, Derek Partridge, Sir John Ward, GCMG, Sidney Cole, Geoffrey Stow, Phillip C. Samuel, the late Roland Pertwee, Robert de Steiger, Stephen Watts, Hurford Janes, the late Maurice Elvey – and finally, my aunt Irene Howard and my sister Doodie (Mrs Dale-Harris).

I am also grateful to those authors and publishers who have permitted me to quote from material within their copyright: to Mr J.B. Priestley, OM, for a quotation from one of his *Postscript* broadcasts; to Studio Vista for *Politics and Film* by Furhammar and Isaksson; to Macmillan Ltd for *Special Relationships* by Sir John Wheeler Bennett; to the author's agent A.M. Heath & Co Ltd for *Flight 777* by Ian Colvin; to Collins Publishers for *Opportunity Knocks Once* by Sir Campbell Stuart and *Ambassador on Special Mission* by Sir Samuel Hoare and to the Oxford University Press for the *Dictionary of National Biography*.

R.H.

THE UNDERSTANDING

To come to terms, to grips, to an acceptance of grief,
To force oneself, against oneself, to a last understanding
With truth, no matter how bitter – the thin end of belief:
This for the heart is the hardest, the cruellest thing.

That there will sound no more upon the landing
The creak of the returning feet, the stumbling oath
Upon the stairs, the laughing last 'good night'. The heart stops
Upon a frontier of unbelief that love may be no more
Of substance than the far sea wind that spreads the wave-tops
Frigid as sheets on an empty bed. A sudden shutting door
Startles with false hope: On edge we comb the restless track
Of ocean as if our hearts had eyes to seek him out,
And ears to hear him call . . .

      But love brings him not back;
Not all our love or our unstinted prayers are stout
Enough to shield his candle from the wind. The flame is out.
And this our hearts must understand, this hardest thing:
No more for his home-coming may our love be listening,
But here, within his fading dark, as the last stars dim,
Listen, as the wind lifts on your cheek, for the wind shall tell of him.

          In memory – 1st June, 1943.

Introduction

When the shooting down, on 1st June 1943, of the civil air-liner bringing my father back from a lecture tour in Spain and Portugal was first announced, his close friend and associate, Anthony Asquith, said: 'If he is really lost, we have lost one of the greatest men in British films. People thought of Howard as a film star – but he was infinitely more than that; he was a brilliant technician. He had the art of the cinema at his finger tips. I have never worked with anyone more understanding, more courteous or more sincere. He was the best of colleagues, the best of friends.'

Leslie was only fifty when he died – and he had been a star actor of both stage and screen for many years – but the last four were the diamond years when he reached the heights. Looking back one senses a strong element of destiny about them – almost of predestination. Those four years were to lift him to his creative apogee and then, suddenly, snuff him out like a candle in the wind. If one believes in a destiny one might say that his life had been a preparation for this time – for it was to be in these years that he finally found himself under the strange stimulus of war. I say strange because he was very much a man of peace – a quiet, leisurely man whose very mode of life found violence abhorrent. Suddenly, in a time of extreme violence, he found a new role wider than simply interpretive artist, a fulfilment of ambitions in the more creative fields of director and producer and last, but not least, subtle propagandist culminating in his final bow to the gods on that June day in 1943. And, perhaps, this was the final act of destiny that drew the moth, unerringly, to the flame. To such a gentle man the leave-taking was unexpectedly violent and out of character: to Leslie, who had consistently underplayed most of his life, his death seemed in the wrong style – too bizarre, too melodramatic – in the blazing inferno of a plane. Indeed, his instinctive reaction to his own demise would have been to distrust it. It was, altogether, too overplayed.

As a primarily creative person he certainly distrusted war as a time for artists of all types – particularly film and theatre people – not only because of the inherent difficulties of war-time entertainment and film production, but also because of the psychological deterrents. Broadcasting in July 1940 – after the fall of France and just before the battle of Britain – he said:

'. . . Aside from all this, there are two profound psychological deterrents: the first is the inertia which strikes artists of all kinds in times of violence and destruction because creative work requires tranquillity in which to thrive, and the second is the conviction that film entertainment is a trivial occupation in times where there are such tremendous and historic tasks to be done.'*

I think, at first, he genuinely doubted what could be achieved in these disruptive times by mere entertainment. To begin with, as far as he was concerned, it was a daunting battle – frequently fought against apathy. Later he was to learn how much, surprisingly, could be done by the spoken word and visual image – as part of the war effort – once the scattered forces of entertainment were drawn together and mobilised. Though shaken, the efforts of artists would not be negligible or trivial. And Leslie would learn that artistry could survive – even without tranquillity – jolted by new dangers and adversities to unexpected fruition. It survived, like the rest of the embattled country, to flower with new vigour and pertinacity.

Leslie was to contribute a great deal to this flowering in adversity not only by the stylish individuality of the films he produced, directed and acted in, but by his quiet, distinctive voice in the many broadcasts he made. If Leslie's best work was propaganda, it was propaganda in its most palatable form, sweetened with his selective intelligence and unerring taste.

Leslie matured considerably during the war. I think people were surprised how well he adapted his normally reticent and retiring personality to the needs of war. He created in himself a personality far more positive and assured than any of the fictional characters in which he had earlier excelled. And, somehow, despite a deceptive appearance of fragility, he had an enduring and endearing obstinacy of purpose which well-reflected the condition of his beleaguered country. He mirrored, in his own way, much of the humour in adversity, frequently misguided optimism and foolish courage with which his countrymen fought alone against the massed weight of the dictatorships. Surprisingly, in a way, for he had none of the

* 'English Films and the War': *Radio Newsreel*, July 1940.

bulldog tenacity or natural belligerence of Churchill, being a withdrawn, mystical sort of man.

When Leslie came home on the edge of war – against the (carefully reasoned) advice of many English and American friends in Hollywood – he found his professional activities suddenly reduced to a complete standstill. It was all as they said. No one was in the least interested in making films, and there seemed little Leslie could do to get them interested. The prospects were indeed bleak. Yet at the time of his death, four years later, he had established himself as a major force in a flourishing industry – which was something of an achievement for a man who had set out for America twenty years earlier as the lightest of light comedians to appear on the American stage in a frolic called *Just Suppose*.

Had Leslie been spared he might well have consolidated his position, as producer and director, in a post-war British film industry. His survival was not to be so it is an academic question. I am inclined to believe that his moment had come then – the moment for which he may well have been destined. I have always felt that Leslie was a man who discovered his metier, his raison d'etre, by a combination of great artistic intuition, a practical genius for seeing essentials and impeccable timing. If he was neither a great actor nor showman he made up for it by high technical skill and shrewd judgement of what he could do best. Above all, he found not only himself in the right place at the right moment but a new purpose in the few remaining years of his life. As a result his innate professional skill was able to bear its best fruit.

In this respect he was not alone – but, perhaps, one of the few. Others were to find themselves – some after long periods of isolation and indifference – and in the next four years were to be finally forged and annealed for a special purpose. I believe Leslie's purpose was no less destined.

CHAPTER ONE

Farewell Hollywood
1939

It was curious, and paradoxical in a way, that when Leslie boarded the SS *Aquitania* in New York on 22nd August 1939 in company with my mother, Ruth, and sister, Doodie, he should have been preparing a film script of a story by H. de Vere Stacpoole called *The Man Who Lost Himself*. In reply to questions by reporters as to what he intended to do when he reached England, he told them he planned to make a film of that story, both directing and acting in it. It at once amused and surprised them – for they regarded Leslie almost as American property – that he should be going to England to film such an incongruous-sounding, and somewhat exotic subject when war, which had stalked the wings for some time, seemed about to make its entrance on the European stage.

Leslie, demurring on the question of timing, suggested tentatively that entertainment was meant to take people's minds off unpleasant subjects, and, besides, war was far from certain with Mr Chamberlain in the wings! Was he not probably about to make another entrance, preferably ahead of Herr Hitler?

The reporters good-humouredly accepted this possibility, then, pressed Leslie on the point of his 'Americanisation'. They indicated that he had spent over half his life in the United States, prospered there, had a home there and was, as far as they were concerned, almost an American citizen. He didn't disagree with that – it was certainly half the truth of the matter – but admitted that, despite it, he had still, perhaps somewhat foolishly, retained his British passport, that he had a second home in Surrey which he rather enjoyed retreating to at odd moments of exasperation with Hollywood and, more importantly, there were some Americans living in the county of Surrey he was looking forward to meeting again. This surprised and intrigued the reporters and when they asked him who these Americans were he confessed that they were, in fact, a dozen Texas polo-ponies. Was that not a good reason for going to England? Anyway, he reassured them, being a foot-loose sort of fellow he was bound to be back if David Selznick would find something else for him to do. 'But, God forbid, not another Ashley!'

In fact 1939, despite Ashley Wilkes (his part in *Gone With The Wind*), had been a good year for him and had followed a previously successful one when he had co-directed and played Higgins in the film *Pygmalion*. Leslie might well have been at the zenith of his career. Not only had he played 'the abominable Ashley' opposite Vivien Leigh's Scarlett O'Hara, he had been bribed to keep his tongue in his cheek and 'not be too bored' by David Selznick offering him the film *Intermezzo* as principal actor and associate producer.

One might have said that he had been altogether fortunate in landing the part of Ashley in *Gone With The Wind*, but Leslie did not quite see it in that light. He found Ashley 'a dreadful milk-sop, totally spineless and negative'. Leslie was churlish about Ashley because he found the character unsure and vacillating, uncertain as a moth fluttering between lamps – the done-to instead of the doing man, torn between the opposing polarities of two equally determined women, Scarlett and Melanie. But in life there were, indeed, many men in exactly this sort of position, and if Leslie had looked into his heart he might well have seen the face of Ashley mirrored there. For Leslie was a man endlessly torn between opposites, if only he would admit it. He pursued will-o'-the-wisps like a man with a butterfly net. But, in the case of Ashley, he was not confusing life with fiction. He only saw Ashley as the man he neither respected nor wanted to be – a divided man trapped in emotional treacle and, however true to its author's intentions, a character that when presented on the screen always came off worst.

'I don't really think I can do much with him,' he admitted, in some alarm, to Selznick. And Selznick, who had cast him, gave him sound enough advice: 'Don't *do* anything, Leslie. Just be yourself.'

Certainly, there were many other actors who would have given their eye-teeth to do something with him – for the role had been eagerly sought after by most of the *jeunes premiers* of Hollywood. With a touch of sarcasm, Leslie admitted it might well be considered some sort of achievement for 'an old fossil of forty-six' to have beaten the youngsters to it. After all, Ashley in the book was supposed to be no more than twenty-eight. Leslie's youthful hormones were the source of much professional leg-pulling – Bogart once asked him what he took as he would like to try it – and, certainly, the ability to belie his years was frequently his trump-card. But it annoyed him intensely if people thought he traded on it.

As to his physical qualifications for the role of Ashley he once remarked to me: 'Well, Wink, I suppose it must have been because I could sit on a horse. The other actors they tested fell off!'

Speaking of the technicalities of the film, and his part in it, Leslie had this to say: 'From my own point of view, it was the most – what can I say? – violent film I've ever played in. Just one climax after another. That's what happens when you try to compress a story of that size and that virulence into a film. All the bits between the high-spots have got to go. It's full of deaths and murders and passions and jealousies and fighting – oh, and fires, lots of Technicolor fires.

'The Technicolor cameras made me break one tradition of a life-time. I had to wear make-up for the first time on the screen. My own hair photographed reddish-brown in Technicolor and Ashley, you know, was definitely "tow-coloured". So I had my hair bleached and had to use a greyish-white make-up on my face to get a natural pale skin tone.'

Though Leslie seldom met Clark Gable during the filming 'as our scenes seldom coincided and we used to work alternate shifts' he had a very clear, and very strong, impression of Vivien Leigh.

'Vivien Leigh, of course, was on duty all the time. I shall never forget the first time I heard her doing her stuff. Curiously enough we never met in England though we had both worked for Korda at one time. I had wanted her to come out to New York to play Ophelia for me in the theatre, but she was tied up with her film work and with a play in London. The first tests I made for Ashley in Hollywood were with another actress altogether. Just as I was coming off the floor from the test, thoroughly disheartened, I heard the most terrific Southern accent on the next set. It was the best Southern I'd heard yet – talking to the coloured Mammy in the scene where she pulls up Scarlett's stay-laces. I asked who it was, and they told me it was an English actress, Vivien Leigh, just come over to Hollywood on a visit. She had worked up her Southern accent in about five days, but she must have stuck at it like a Trojan. It was perfect. I believe she got the job on that scene. You realised in a flash why David Selznick believed he'd got just the right girl for Scarlett at last.'

I think another contributory factor to Leslie's boredom with Ashley were the interminable longueurs and delays attendant upon the production. He sat about Hollywood for over two months for the purpose of make-up tests and costume-fittings before he got near a rehearsal, let alone a camera. And when he referred to his performance afterwards as 'If you sneeze, you miss me' he wasn't

completely joking for it was essentially a small part that took
months to film. However, he did manage to turn the waiting time to
advantage, for he was not only able to squeeze in the part of Holgar
in the David Selznick film of *Intermezzo* (known in England as *Escape
to Happiness*) but was also able to work on the production side of the
film as associate producer.

Though the role of associate producer sounds a lot more than it is
– being a generalised term to cover a number of functions, like
being a buffer state between producer and director – Leslie did have
the satisfaction of being closely involved with the scenario and
preparation of the film for production. In fact, in a quiet way, his
brief was wider and he did considerably influence the way the film
was made. He was also a steadying influence on the somewhat
Ruritanian technique of his old Russian friend, Gregory Ratoff, the
director. Ratoff, if left to his own devices, was subject to flights of
fancy and 'ginger bread' reminiscent of *Grand Guignol*. Such
tendencies to elaborate had to be contained for the innately
sentimental nature of the film would have been exploited even
more but for Leslie's restraining influence and restrained performance. The inherent danger was that it could so easily become a
'handkerchief' film and spill over into bathos. To achieve this a very
fine line had to be steered and the girl's and the wife's part to be
credible, could, in no sense, be lachrymose or sugary.

A great deal of the effectiveness of *Intermezzo* was due to a
performance of touching simplicity by Ingrid Bergman, at the time
a comparatively unknown young Swedish actress, who had played
the role in the original version a year earlier. Here she was to score
again – and, perhaps, more affectingly with Leslie opposite her in
that delicate relationship, almost of master and pupil, gradually
deepening into love, which owed so much of its reality and
tenderness to the playing of their joint scenes. And the choice of
Edna Best as the wife was one of the triumphs of the film – for she
made Holgar's wife completely sympathetic by a performance of
great sweetness and sensitive understanding.

Without doubt, Ingrid Bergman was one of the rarest finds
Hollywood ever made, which I think was mainly due to Selznick
who brought her over for the film. Far from the somewhat
adulterated blooms that burst upon the world from the Hollywood
'hot-house', she had an innocence and candour that had never been
seen out there before, and I don't think has since. Entirely unsullied
and tremendously beautiful, she took everyone's breath away, even
though the casting people were unsure how this girl would go down

in America by comparative standards of the local product.

Leslie was enchanted by her unaffectedness – as indeed was Gregory Ratoff – and they both encouraged her to do absolutely nothing that was not entirely natural to her. She must not be forced, in any way, to accommodate or 'Americanise'. Indeed, one's impression of her performance is of a rare, almost alpine flower opening its petals for the first time at the onset of spring. It had a quality of being almost in slow-motion, as if the pace of the film had been consciously slowed down to capture each detail of its flowering. I suppose by the more astringent standards of today *Intermezzo* must seem old-fashioned, almost a product of the 'Vienna school' of unabashed sentimentality. Its musical score and theme song perhaps make it more so. Fortunately much of its sentimental nature was successfully suspended by its intelligent interpretation.

Leslie had always been very conscious of the perils and pitfalls of Hollywood – and its hardness – and he had carefully avoided falling into the mill and being ground to the uniform size. But he was honest enough to say, 'For some it works, for me it doesn't.' If, earlier in his career, he had complained about the Hollywood product because he, personally, had been involved in some bad films and had referred to them as 'typical effusions of the conveyor mentality', he did also realise it was the one place in the world where the set-up was economically sound enough for films to be made ad nauseam, ad infinitum. Here was an industry, and a machine that worked efficiently, which constantly employed thousands of people.

Leslie had certainly had all the advantages of that viable Hollywood machinery however he may have carped at its regimentation, its naif pragmatism of studio 'bosses', and general slickness and impersonality of output. It had enabled him to become a well-paid actor, living comfortably in Beverly Hills, instead of struggling with the vagaries and uncertainties of film production back home in England. It may have seemed at times like a cell to Leslie, but it was a comfortably padded one. He was well aware, by comparison, that the English film industry had, so far, never been able to do this sort of thing, or compete with it. He was later to say in a BBC broadcast:

'The result of our peculiar situation is that, in spite of every kind of ingenious legislation and notwithstanding an occasional highly untrustworthy boom, the English film industry has never in its history been able to cast off the shackles of an inescapable competition within its own domain, or to put itself into a condition of artistic and economic health. The problems of British film

production are varied and many . . . It is sufficient to say that most
of the methods employed to promote film-making here are mainly
makeshift and unsound.*

I don't think Leslie's attitude to Hollywood was coloured by any
sense of inferiority or imbalance in these filmic horse-trading
arrangements. Hollywood had captured our markets long before
Leslie got there by a combination of superior products and canny
business methods which even our 'quota' restrictions could not
stem – and he could only admire Hollywood for it. Of course, he
was frequently to be accused of being too aloof and critical of what
he once called 'Holy Hollywood'. If he disapproved of their
methods, yet took advantage of them, this was felt by some to be a
rather snide way of biting the hand that fed him. But I think his
respect for what Hollywood could do and we in England couldn't,
discounted this. It just nettled him to think that we, as a film
producing centre, were so unequal.

As far as living in Hollywood was concerned Leslie had always
kept a pretty low profile, not from any innate hostility to the place,
but simply because he was not a very social animal. He was rarely
seen 'around and about' whether in London, New York or
Hollywood and carefully avoided gatherings of large numbers of
people, suffering from a genuine agoraphobia – crowds really
frightened him – and having, as he admitted, 'no head for parties'.
In fact, elusive as was his nature, he generally got out of Hollywood
as quickly as he could, if only to the nearby desert at La Quinta
where he could ride or lie about in the sun without feeling he was
under inspection. It was in no sense a 'Howard exclusivity cult' but
simply that he needed to escape from time to time, was basically
solitary and shy and only really wanted the company of a very few
intimate friends.

The late Roland Pertwee, playwright, novelist, screen-writer and
sometime actor, who knew Leslie well from early days until just
before his death wrote this of him in that Hollywood-setting of the
nineteen-thirties:

> I have very tender, soft-edged memories of Leslie who, untouched
> by success, moved gently through life and always contrived to
> appear just a scrap out of focus. Unlike the majority of stars in
> that particular firmament he never made the slightest effort to
> excite publicity and, indeed, if your mother had not adjured him

* *Radio Newsreel*: 'English Films and the War'

to take off his glasses, put his shoulders back and smile when passing through the lion-hunting crowds at the premiere of a film, nobody would have known he was in the theatre.

I cannot recall a single occasion on which he said anything deliberately quotable or performed any capers to attract attention. It is, nevertheless, a fact that his natural self-effacement in a community of exhibitionists made him as conspicuous as the Empire State Building on the New York skyline. One night when he and I were dining at the Vendome someone exclaimed excitedly as we moved towards our table: 'Why look! It's Leslie Howard!' Catching the excitement in the woman's tone Leslie looked about him short-sightedly and demanded: 'Where?'

Yet despite the mildness of his demeanour, he was a terror to pin down and with half the leading producers in Hollywood tumbling over each other to secure his services, he smiled his way out of their clutches and brushing off astronomical offers resolutely avoided doing anything but please himself. He did not find pleasing himself easy, for he was his most severe critic and before deciding upon a future assignment he suffered long periods of sighful contemplation.

Once when he and I were stopping at the fabulous Hearst Ranch (San Simeon) that great pundit of the press followed him from room to room and terrace to terrace trying to persuade him to appear with Marion Davies in some subject the name of which I have forgotten. No bloodhound could have been more persistent than W.R.H. but in spite of the growls and threats and pleadings Leslie preserved his artistic virginity and made good his escape without even so much as a promise to think things over.

*

When Leslie finally left Hollywood in August 1939, he was, as I said, on his way home to England to produce, direct and act in the film *The Man Who Lost Himself*. Despite his light-hearted exchanges with reporters in New York, it must obviously have occurred to him that if there was a war in Europe that film might have to be postponed, if not indefinitely shelved.

His friends in Hollywood, particularly the English ones, had been listening to the more recent rantings of Hitler with increasing alarm. The majority felt that England might be in a state of war within weeks, some felt days. Wasn't it a bit pointless, they felt, going back to a country where film production – never particularly brisk – might soon come to a complete standstill? Not only that, he might even be conscripted.

Many of these friends spoke as perpetual exiles living contentedly in a place where the oranges were the biggest in the world and the sun shone almost every day of the year, summer or winter. They were emigrés in a lotus-land to whom the call of King and Country must have sounded like the distant exhortations of Lord Kitchener. The English in Hollywood – or the British Raj as they were sometimes called – could reasonably regard themselves as landed colonists who now paid taxes to the Republic and not the King. Their allegiance lay where their bread was buttered. Wasn't Leslie being unnecessarily chauvinistic, going back and putting his head in the Lion's mouth?

He had to listen to a lot of this persuasive talk. And very reasonable it sounded coming from the older brigade who had, like himself, seen service in that other 'war to end all wars'. I imagine that he had probably argued that they were being over-pessimistic and that, after the Austrian Anschluss and the Czecho-Slovak crisis, Munich – and the Man With The Umbrella – had opened the door to 'Peace in our Time'. Let them take heart from that. Appeasement seemed the order of the day and, as long as people were sensible and kept their heads, there really need be no war. He did his best to reassure them that he would be back next year – knowing it was highly unlikely – and bid them *au revoir*.

As the *Aquitania* bore him further and further from the United States Leslie felt his exhilaration grow with each eastward mile of the pulsating ship. He was freer, happier than for a long time and thought no more of those friends on the west coast, except, perhaps, to feel sorry for them stuck there, incarcerated in Hollywood, saddened and fearful at what might happen. Whatever happened Leslie was looking forward to it – glad, if there was a war, to be going towards it. The uncertainties, and the dangers, fitted well with his current mood. He only prayed there would be time for his film.

Periodically, Leslie left Ruth and Doodie in their chairs on the sun-deck, and put his head into the Smoke Room where a number of men sat about with anxious faces listening to the news as it was relayed from Europe. Hitler, not satisfied with the agreement at Munich, seemed on the verge of adding another bit of *Lebensraum* to the Reich, this time Danzig and the Polish Corridor. Our Ambassador in Berlin, Henderson, was endeavouring to persuade the Poles not to provoke Hitler whose patience was, as usual, becoming 'rapidly exhausted'. Was this to be another 'carve-up', another scuttling settlement? Unless Hitler modified his demands our Treaty terms made it inevitable that we come to the aid of Poland. Surely we could not back down this time. The consensus in the Smoke Room seemed to favour a compromise, satisfaction of German 'minorities' and a 'free area' with an Autobahn to the port of Gdynia. If the Polish government was prepared to make concessions then Chamberlain could sleep easily, his policy of brinkmanship once more justified.

Leslie returned to his deckchair wondering if Henderson might pull it off and, even if 'Peace in our Time' was just a noble-sounding, politician's phrase, might we not gain peace in time to re-arm, to prepare ourselves. He stood a moment looking down at the pile of notes he had been making. The scenario of *The Man Who Lost Himself* lay beside them in the deck-chair, the pages fluttering to and fro in the wind. He wondered if there might be time for that, too – it was a subject that intrigued him – but it desperately needed peace in which to do it. If war came it might well have to wait. He sat down and began to read through his notes.

The story of *The Man Who Lost Himself* concerns two men who change places, one assuming the identity of the other. The switch takes place after a bout of drinking and the fact that one man is the twin image of the other scarcely makes for simplicity of plot and disbelief is, at times, suspended with some difficulty. The author, H. de Vere Stacpoole, tells us that his hero, Victor Jones, has come to London to negotiate a vital contract but it has fallen through and he is left virtually bankrupt. Jones is disconsolately drowning his sorrows in a bar when he sees reflected in a mirror the face of his twin image, Lord Rochester, a man in even greater pecuniary straits whose marriage and domestic life are in chaos. Rochester forces the inebriated Jones not only into his clothes but into his disastrous identity. Shortly afterwards, Rochester commits suicide leaving Jones, as his stand-in, to live out the domestic and financial complications of his somewhat sordid life. This is, I'm afraid, a trite resumé of an ingenious and highly complicated story by an author who had many stories adapted for the screen, none more successfully, perhaps, than *The Blue Lagoon*.

What quite attracted Leslie to the story I do not know, apart from the switching of identities which obviously appealed to his filmic imagination. The idea of playing two more or less identical yet different characters, by a technique known as 'split-screen', has always appealed, as something of a tour de force, to actors. My mother, I remember, having read the script did not think either the story or the character of Victor Jones would do much to enhance Leslie's reputation, and she used the argument that he would be somewhat out of character in the part. Knowing Leslie's obstinacy, and how he leapt to the defence of his ideas, he probably replied that they must be beyond her understanding if she insisted on taking such a limited view! Perhaps, at heart, he suspected she was right about this one – she often was – and simply thought, with the war coming, he might have more important things to do. Time was to prove her right. (As I recount later, Leslie never did the film. It reverted to Hollywood and Universal made it in 1941, starring Brian Aherne.)

Two days later, by the time the *Aquitania* docked at Southampton, Hitler's patience seemed finally exhausted. Nevile Henderson had his bags packed and the lights were beginning to dim in the British Embassy, Berlin. It really seemed the piping days of peace were over.

I remember I had driven down to Southampton in my small two-seater car to welcome them home – father, mother and kid-sister, Doodie. In those days one could drive straight onto the dock beside the liner and there, amid the deafening blasts of the ship's sirens, I stood peering up hopefully, my fingers in my ears. Then, I saw them – the three of them standing together on the boat-deck – looking straight down at me. But why were they laughing and shaking their heads in such a disparaging way? And why was my mother gesturing at me in her imperious way and shouting inaudibly? I couldn't understand what it was all about.

As the final echo of the sirens died away, I unplugged my ears, cupped my hands round my mouth and shouted up: 'What's so funny?'

They heard me well enough for my mother made one of her large, dismissive gestures, this time directed straight at my car. Then, she said in a voice loud enough to be heard in the middle of Southampton. 'You don't think we're all going to drive home in that little death-trap, do you?'

It was not the unfair description of my car as a death-trap that worried me (it was normally described, in a more affectionate way, as the flying bed-pan) but the thought that Leslie's eight-cylinder Cadillac, chauffeur-driven, might have broken down on the way from Westcott. I need not have worried. By the time the ship was berthed the Cadillac emerged, gleamingly immaculate, and rolled impressively onto the dock. All it needed was a flag and it would have done for the President of the United States. Soon we were all reunited. Everyone seemed to be there on the dockside – the Chief Steward, Purser and so on. A Customs Officer, scarcely glancing at Leslie's assortment of brass-bound cabin-trunks, seemed more interested in *Gone With The Wind* – and getting Leslie's autograph.

'Delighted,' Leslie said. 'If you wouldn't mind putting yours on my luggage!' And they duly exchanged signatures while the chauffeur loaded the suitcases into the Cadillac – the portmanteaux were entrusted to the care of Carter Paterson – and Leslie and Ruth, with final waves to the assembled ship's company, were on their way.

My sister, who had elected to drive home with me in 'the death-trap', studied the little car for a moment and said: 'Nothing like this in Hollywood, Wink. This is a *real* car – I mean, you can step into it without even opening the door!' Despite this, I opened it for her – thanking her for the patriotism of her remark – and we set off, in hot pursuit, determined to overtake the Cadillac.

As we drove along I glanced covertly at this extraordinary creature who sat beside me. She was, undoubtedly, my sister and, equally undoubtedly, no more than fifteen years old. But she was scarcely my *kid*-sister any more. A startling metamorphosis had taken place which had turned her into more than the customary piece of Hollywood confectionery. She seemed to have anticipated Baby-Doll and Blanche du Bois at one bound – and become the composite prototype of each. Who was this sophisticated child-woman who sat there draped in a silver fox fur, wearing a sexy dress with far too much cleavage, silver-painted finger nails, silk stockings, high-heeled shoes. Was this really my baby-sister or some bedizened creature from the 'Sunset Strip'? She caught me looking at her and turned, giving me suddenly a little girl's pout through all the make-up.

'Why are you looking at me like that?'

'I'm trying to figure out what's become of my little sister.'

'Probably buried under all this!' Doodie laughed. 'Don't worry, it'll come off!'

'Good. I was looking forward to meeting her again – you know, the kid in jodhpurs with the dirty face!'

'Oh, poo to you!' was her only comment.

At this moment we saw the Cadillac ahead and, on a clear stretch, drove alongside it waving in some triumph. The triumph was short-lived. A rear window was wound down and my mother leaned out, making a fierce, dismissive gesture.

'Get back, you fool. Get back! You'll kill your sister!' This was enough to make me promptly accelerate and pass them. Mother's remark completely collapsed Doodie into hysterics and floored her son who was now, more than ever, convinced that she didn't love him. A little crestfallen, I remarked to Doodie:

'Isn't that typical? She wouldn't mind if *I* was killed. I mean, she might have said "us" or even "yourselves" – but not just "your sister"!' This convulsed Doodie even more. Between hoots of laughter, she turned to me.

'She's probably remembering the day you hit me with a baseball-bat and broke my nose. She thinks you're wildly reckless.' Doodie glanced back at the receding Cadillac. 'And she probably thought you did that on purpose just to upset her.'

If not quite a half-wit, it was certainly evident my mother had long regarded me as a kind of *enfant perdu*, not to be trusted riding a bike let alone driving a sports car. In that shared knowledge, giving my sister a gleeful smile, I sped on in my usual reckless fashion.

Now, that the laughter had subsided, we sat reflectively silent. We were somewhere along the Hog's Back – the wind tugging at the car, disarranging my sister's elaborately coiffeured curls – before I said: 'It doesn't make sense.'

'What doesn't?' Doodie leaned towards me, clutching her fur.

'You all coming back like this – at the eleventh hour. There's bound to be a war. You should have stayed in Hollywood till things were a bit clearer. Why didn't you?'

'Because we didn't want to. We weren't that passionately attached to the place. Anyway, who knows, we might have got stuck there. Besides, Wink, it wasn't all that pleasant.'

'Why not?' I said blankly.

Doodie gave me a wide-eyed, slightly ambivalent look.

'Well, for Mother, you nut – with Daddy leading his double life with-you-know-who.'

'Oh, God, I'd forgotten . . . ' Or did I really know?

'Living here one might. Out there we couldn't very well.'

I certainly wasn't aware of the latest developments. Anyway, the details of Leslie's somewhat bisected existence were rarely, if ever, discussed. A kind of family taboo surrounded his emotional life. It was a grey area, a *terra incognita* and certainly one I preferred not to explore. In a kind of male chauvinist way I thought his private life was his own business. In any case, I'd convinced myself long ago that his behaviour was the inevitable norm – par for the Howard course, as it were – and not wanting to be too closely involved buried my head in the sand.

'Must have been rather awkward,' I said lamely.

'You *could* say that,' said Doodie. 'Bit like Chinese torture – exquisite in its way – with Daddy slipping down from Beverly Drive to pay us irregular visits, looking rather like the condemned man.'

I confessed to having been rather out of the picture. Perhaps I was being dense but the few postcards I'd received of views of Hollywood had not exactly been explicit. Though Leslie had, apparently, been full of his usual solicitude and kindness, doing his best to be charming, though regrettably divided, self, things had, naturally, been rather upsetting for Mother. *She* found it a little difficult to have a sense of humour about.

'It had its funny moments, mind you – even the travel plans were like a comic opera. I'll tell you the whole story sometime.' Doodie smiled, shaking her head a little sadly. 'That's why we wanted to leave – quite apart from the war situation. Anyway, Stowe Maries is *home*, Wink, not 606, North Camden Drive, Beverly Hills. That was just an arrangement.'

If it was difficult to think about, it was even harder to talk about with the wind tearing the words from our lips – and I sped on fast, though not exactly furious, towards Westcott and Stowe Maries. If my sister found the situation somewhat more trying than I did, it was understandable. She had to live with it. In the present situation I felt a little helpless – even though the questions that formed in my mind were not new ones. But in a male way I pushed them away from me. Anyway, they could wait. I only hoped the air inside the Cadillac had not been as pungent as the aside to the driver of the sports car, and that any recrimination had been silent.

Stopping for a drink at our local pub we steered the conversation along lighter lines, discussing the film Leslie was apparently so keen on but Doodie wondered whether he would ever make with the threat of war so close. She also explained, with ironic humour, the crowning subtleties of their departure from Hollywood, their reunion with Leslie in New York and the journey home *en famille* across the Atlantic. I imagined the situation could have been quite funny – like the plot of a farcical, triangular movie – to someone not too closely involved.

When we arrived home half an hour later we saw the Cadillac parked by the garage and hurried indoors where my sister was greeted with hugs and kisses by Miss Gospel, our old nanny-housekeeper, who deserves a book to herself. She had, more or less, brought us up – and was always known, affectionately, as 'Gargy'. Of Ruth and Leslie there was no sign save their luggage in the hall. I was a little worried that they might have got the cudgels out, or even the duelling pistols, and looked enquiringly at 'Gargy'. But she didn't bat an eyelid, being a wise woman with a gift for keeping her own brand of quiet counsel. She simply remarked that they had gone to the stables to see the horses.

When Doodie and I, setting off across the garden, reached the corner by the loose-boxes there was no blood-bath to greet us, in fact, the reverse. There was Leslie, in the best of spirits, chatting away with Jack Hessey, the groom, while rubbing the noses of his polo-ponies as he fed them lumps of sugar. He was getting acquainted with his Texan friends again, almost as if he'd never been away. Nearby stood my mother, watching this scene of reunion, without a hint of recrimination in her face. It was a look of almost tender approval. Was it forgiveness, reconciliation I read there – or simply benign resignation? I wasn't, at first, at all sure.

CHAPTER TWO

A Glance Back
1920-1939

Despite the emotional complexities that Leslie brought back on the
eve of war, I am convinced that he would never have stayed on in
America after the completion of *Gone With The Wind* and *Intermezzo*
had even the chance presented itself. Whatever the circumstances
of his private or professional life his first instinct would have been to
return – particularly with the threat of war so close at hand. In spite
of his almost dual nationality, and the fact that he had homes in
both countries, England was his real home at heart and he
remained, for all his long absences, essentially English and England-
loving.

Though this is somewhat at variance with the fact that his father
was born a Hungarian, possibly accounting for a certain volatility in
Leslie's temperament, his mother and his environment were
entirely English and he had been born and brought up in London.
The Europeanness never loomed very large in his nature and the
hybridity was difficult to detect. Again, though he owed a great deal
to America, he had little of America about him save in the
superficialities of clothes and a liking for certain types of American
food. Though he had spent two thirds of his working life in the
United States he remained at heart stoically, almost insularly
English.

Of course, in those earlier days of the twenties and thirties, actors
were great travellers – far more peripatetic than they are now – and
Leslie was no exception. Chevalier or von Stroheim or Barrymore
moved freely from country to country, from one artistic capital to
another – their loyalties professional rather than national. These
citizens of the playhouse or film studio were internationally
interchangeable. To the great actor-illusionists there were no
frontiers that could not be penetrated by artistry and professional
skill. In fact, it was this international convertibility – almost like a
convertible currency – that was in those days the most important
part of successful acting.

At that time, leading actors who had ultimately escaped the repertoire system were, I suppose, infinitely less adaptable – as actors – than their counterparts today. The assumption of a convincing disguise was far less important than the presentation of a personality, more or less identifiable in all they did. This was the basis of the old 'star-system', the magic by which audiences became attracted and which established an actor at the box-office. They could identify their favourite actors immediately – no matter how heavy the make-up – for the actors, by and large, remained comfortingly themselves. Both theatre impresarios and cinema moguls, hawking their wares in the world market, adhered slavishly to this principle. Once the actor's 'trade-mark' – his style – was established he was called upon to do very little else but to keep on reduplicating himself. It was, thus, easier for managements and, particularly, film companies to sell him. If it was boring for the actor, at least you knew precisely what you were getting for your money.

Though still practised, it is out of favour today with directors of the newer persuasions who frown upon this sort of establishment where the product is packaged and pre-sold on the names of the stars. They prefer to create their own raw materials – often using virtually unknown actors – and retain control by putting their own 'trade-mark' on the product. It is an important switch of emphasis – away from the actor to the director.

If Leslie was, inevitably, to become a star of this older system of the personality cult he was not really of it – nor had he any attraction to it – in fact, the reverse. He deplored the absurd postures of some successful actors and their vanity about themselves which frequently affected production adversely. He was always modest about himself and disliked affectations in others, or any pretence of grandeur. He expected actors to take advice and listen to the director's interpretation – not supply their own. On the other hand, he didn't think actors should be moulded slavishly like plasticine. They should be encouraged to contribute their own personalities – that is what they were employed and paid for – to an intelligent illumination of the roles they were assigned. Primarily actors were interpretive – not creative – though they could create in their plastic natures very vivid effects. But they must not try to capture audiences out of context by being encouraged to perform 'star-turns'. They must remain a disciplined part of the pattern.

Unfortunately, the basic trouble with many plays and films of the twenties and thirties was that they were constructed for just that

Proud father with new son, Winkie.

Leslie, Ruth and Wink (at Chicago en route Hollywood-London, 1937).

(*Left*) Father and son – at home – Great Neck, Long Island. (*Right*) Roller-skating craze – Doodie and Wink, Beverly Hills in 1932.

Script conference with family dogs – Stowe Maries.

purpose – to show off one or two stars to effect and the producers, playwrights and script-writers connived at it, so that the director simply became the tool of the 'star-system'. And of this Leslie strongly disapproved for he knew, instinctively, that actors should not control the system in this way.

When Leslie, as a young actor, first arrived in America Jack Barrymore was already a Broadway star – if of somewhat eccentric proportions. He had also made a number of silent movies – including *Dr Jekyll and Mr Hyde*, a bizarre tour de force for his bravura style. Barrymore's roots were very much in the older acting tradition and his exotic, flamboyant personality dominated the plays and films he appeared in. The acting called for in silent movies was an extension of the old, theatrical fortissimo style and Barrymore had no difficulty in adapting himself to the technique, with its inescapable echoes of the barn-stormer. The roles he played from the era of the first world war into that of talkies very much reflected this style and were generally tailor-made to accommodate his burgeoning, larger-than-life personality. Suffice to say he remained true to himself, an ageing *enfant terrible* of whom directors were suitably terrified. Certainly his domination was eminently successful and he capered and roared his way through a number of pieces that without him would have been dull fare indeed. But his presence did involve the setting up of special scenes – to show him off to effect – and a certain amount of actor-direction whereby these scenes could be coaxed to accommodate 'bits of business' peculiar to his genius. If a change of style to a less theatrical type of personality and performance was now becoming evident, Barrymore remained aloof and resolutely refused to succumb to what he referred to as 'the mouse in the match-box school of acting'.

Leslie at the other end of the spectrum was the least flamboyant actor and, in the Barrymore sense, quite unmagnetic. (He could, indeed, have been Barrymore's 'mouse'!) Never a traditional actor – yet certainly a transitional one – he was to be identified more with a way of life that was shaping outside the entertainment world rather than what was still being presented in it. If younger audiences, in the twenties, were looking for something more typical of the new society they were creating and identified with, then Leslie's more 'naturalistic', under-playing style of acting accurately reflected it. In this transitional sense Leslie represented the changing scene where subjects and characters from everyday life were beginning to find a place in the theatre however ephemeral they appeared. But the change in the film world with the advent of the talkies had not yet

arrived – though the revolution was not far off – and the silent movie
remained grossly mimic, exaggerated and tied to the older theatre
tradition.

By 1929, however, these hastily-improvised, star-dominated,
mimic-screenplays had a contrived and artificial look and with the
birth of the sound-track Hollywood for the first time began to
employ dialogue-writers, many of them playwrights of 'the new
wave' emerging in New York. The off-the-cuff improvisations
cobbled together by directors and actors for silent movies would no
longer serve and studio heads looked east buying film-rights in
plays that had achieved success on Broadway. Once these plays had
completed their theatrical runs they were imported lock, stock and
barrel to Hollywood. In the early days, of course, a play would be
transferred to film more or less as it stood, the actors by and large
repeating their Broadway performances. To begin with the sound
film was in essence a photographed stage play.

It was by this lock, stock and barrel process that Leslie reached
Hollywood in 1930 to star in the film version of a New York play
called *Outward Bound*. This was an extremely subtle play and, with
its theme of the possibility of life after death and migration of souls,
a surprising and daring choice for a film in this somewhat rough
and tumble era of Hollywood's first transition to sound. But it
certainly marked a watershed – one of Hollywood's earliest
attempts to grapple with an intellectual theme of great sensitivity.
Alfred Lunt had in the New York production played the lead role
and Leslie the juvenile. Now, Leslie was to play Lunt's part in the
film and Doug Fairbanks, Jr, Leslie's.

Outward Bound had first been produced at the Everyman Theatre,
Hampstead; its author was a young, new dramatist by the name of
Sutton Vane. It was referred to in its initial production as 'a subtle
and imaginative play on the question of survival – which was so
acceptable that it was successfully transferred to the Garrick
Theatre.' It was the sort of play in its idea that Leslie always
responded to strongly – the survival of the mind after death. And it
was certainly a better, and far more original, play than those current
pastiches that passed as entertainment on either Broadway or
Shaftesbury Avenue in the nineteen-twenties. Despite its photographed stage-play technique the film must have seemed a daring
breakaway in the Hollywood of *The Singing Fool* era.

For the next nine years Leslie was to be in and out of Hollywood
regularly – in between plays in New York – only missing one year,
1932. In that time he completed twenty-two films, eighteen of them

in Hollywood. Four of them were adaptations of New York plays in which he had starred. However, at the outset of his film career in 1930, he seemed rather disenchanted with the idea of Hollywood – even though his part in *Outward Bound* was a step up.

Writing to his mother from the Lyceum Theatre, New York, on 11th April 1930, he confessed he would rather be 'outward bound for England,' describing himself as being 'particularly unhappy at being away from home, for I feel quite exiled here'. He went on: 'I miss England more than ever and find every trip here more of a trial. However, this is the most successful season I've ever had' – he was appearing in the John Balderstone play *Berkeley Square* – 'and that is the *only* consolation. I am going to close here 24th May and go straight to Hollywood to do a quick movie at *very high terms*. Again, much as I hate going, I feel I can't afford not to, as I will get enough money out of this film to buy our house . . . '

The house he was to buy at Dorking in Surrey was to be our family home for the next fifteen years. It cost, as I remember, £3,500, which was quite expensive in those days but surely not all he was to earn by this hateful journey at such *'very high terms'*.

However, it would not be fair to him to say that he took quite so jaundiced a view of America – and Hollywood – as at first appears from the letter to his mother for he added, almost as a postscript: 'I have been feeling rather rotten the last few weeks and have paid my annual visit to the doctor to be overhauled and find that I am in good condition – but bored – so now feel better.'

Of course, there was nothing surprising to us as a family in these lamentations and the talk of being an exile. He had, in fact, been a professional exile for years – since that decisive moment in 1920 when he first went to New York to appear in *Just Suppose* for Henry and Gilbert Miller. From that moment his career was to a large extent determined by what happened to him in America – in fact, until the day he boarded the *Aquitania* to come home, finally, in 1939.

His success in *Just Suppose* was the first strand that tied him to America and his subsequent successes in that country only increased the tethers. For him it was not only a professional but a physical divison. By becoming an Anglo-American actor he forced upon himself a nomadic existence which cut him off from his home and family for very long periods. Though he agreed with my mother that children should not be lugged around as so much theatrical impedimenta he did successfully uproot us quite often which, though we delighted in, my mother rightly disapproved of as being very bad for us.

I remember Leslie was always permanently gloomy about leaving home – or travelling at all which he hated – and he frequently referred to 'the awful annual exodus' to which he had to submit himself to earn a living. And he, equally, talked of being bored, as other actors did, with long runs. At the same time, he was quite well paid for his boredom. Certainly his first ten years as an actor had been a hard slog, and he was in and out of plays with, at times, sickening regularity, sometimes two or three a year. He then complained when they didn't run, and, later when they did, became bored with their constant repetition. That was where writers, he felt, had it all over actors: they didn't go on repeating the same lines, they wrote different ones. And directors preserved their sanity by directing different plays.

To his immense relief and delight, and as a brief distraction from acting, he was himself able to direct and stage a number of plays, in some of which he also appeared. One of these was *The Animal Kingdom* by Philip Barry and, in another letter to his mother (to whom over the years he was a remarkably good letter-writer) he described his feelings – and some of his difficulties. The letter headed Hotel Carlyle, New York and dated 1st February 1932 is, I think, a true working analysis of the problems involved in producing a new play as well as an insight into Leslie's constant dread of long runs. I quote the letter, apart from some personal matters, more or less in full. It begins:

Mother darling,

It seems – and is – ages since I wrote to you, but it has been, as usual, a hectic time since I arrived in this benighted country. We started our rehearsals almost immediately I landed and continued them without interruption for a month, and then went on tour for two weeks. During the whole of these six weeks we had interminable troubles with casting and rewriting of script. When I arrived I found that the cast they had chosen were, in most cases, pretty hopeless and several changes had to be made. We rehearsed for ten days with five different girls for the part of the mistress before hitting on one who could get near the part. And then, while we were at Pittsburgh, changed the other leading lady (wife) and two important men parts. Meanwhile I was very dissatisfied both with the play and my own part, and got the author, not always very willingly, to do considerable rewriting. During those two weeks we never played the same version twice running, and were constantly meeting new faces on the stage.

All this was a bit nerve-racking as you can imagine, and I was thankful when we finally hit New York in some kind of order. Gilbert [Gilbert Miller, his co-producer] was with us all this time, and behaved wonderfully, supporting my ideas continually, the author being a little difficult.

However, a little to my surprise, the thing turned out to be an enormous hit, about the biggest here this season. We opened on a Tuesday night, and on Wednesday morning there was a long queue at the box-office for the matinee, and we have sold out at every subsequent performance with large numbers standing. This in spite of the fact that we have one of the largest theatres in New York (which I am glad I insisted upon). Our prices are much lower than for *Berkeley Square*, but we are taking much more money, on account of the bigger theatre, and because of a lower running cost our profits will be doubled.

Gilbert is in his seventh heaven and so is the author who will make a fortune. Your eldest son is reputed to be marvellous, but for your private information I will tell you that it is nothing great either as play or acting. It is an easy job for me and does not come up to what I did in '*B.S.*' For that matter neither does the play. But it is an even greater success, so who am I to argue with them.

My great worry now is how long the wretched thing will persist. The bookings are terrific and far ahead. I ask the manager every night if he can hold out any hope of business falling off, and he shakes his head. He seems to be delighted for some reason or another. I don't know when we are going to get home, and I am already appalled at the prospect of being shut up interminably among these steel and concrete prisons.

I don't want to be indefinitely without either of the children, and think that Doodie ought to come out later. I miss her terribly, I miss them both, but have given up any hope of seeing Wink for ages. I can see this thing running well into the summer, and even then I may have to be ill to get away from it.

One gets from this letter a fairly clear picture of the aggravations and uncertainties of working in the theatre and of Leslie's reactions to it under difficult, though not uncommon conditions. First, the nerve-racking problems of rewriting and recasting, undertaken while already in performance, and the resultant despair sown in one's heart. Then the almost unbelievable surprise and relief of success – and, finally, the appalling realisation that the thing might go on forever! If one had said to Leslie that this was what putting on

38 *In Search of my Father*

plays was all about, he would have replied that such an idea was ridiculous and people must be mad to want to involve themselves in such haphazard undertakings. It was altogether too wearing and exhausting. He would always try to rationalise things even against his better judgement that entertainment was a chaotic business composed of frustration and heart-break. If this was a precedent, he would have said, it could not be tolerated by him or anyone else in their right mind!

I think a combination of things – sustaining disappointing roles, the constant, tiresome repetition, the desire to escape into direction or writing and the long absences from home and family – all served to increase Leslie's disenchantment with the role of actor. He often said in moments of infuriation, or even exasperated amusement at his predicament, that acting was a silly, futile, bogus sort of job and actors no more than clever performing seals, or, at worst, mere puppets jerked into life at another's bidding. In a more serious moment he would say they were too often at the mercy of unscrupulous, completely inartistic people who were simply in the business for the money – and it was they, the actors, who had to stand up and be counted when bad plays, put on by inept managements, got a critical pasting.

In such moments of depression, in the middle of a long run, even reasonably good plays lost their flavour and Leslie found it difficult to remain convinced, or convincing. In such a mood, he saw the whole business of acting as a sheer process of embarrassment, with its sheepish daubing on of grease-paint followed by a period of immodest prancing about in borrowed finery. It was supposedly sophisticated, yet somehow almost primitive and barbaric. What was this nightly spectacle of oneself but playing at pretences, the whole imitation of life as it was not – simply to take other people's minds off their problems? Though excusable in the very young it was, to say the least, lamentable in those approaching middle age. Now, Leslie realised this kind of provocation would probably be taken as a kind of wry Howard joke when perhaps he was a little under the weather, and people thought he was being sarcastically amusing and didn't believe a word of it. What most didn't realise was that his disenchantment with acting was, at heart, an instinctive reaction against the theatre, as it was then constituted, which he felt was a place of total unreality, a veritable cock-pit of contrivance.

Part of his exasperation was due to the appallingly poor quality of the popular theatre of the nineteen-twenties, plays which served as a mere extension of the life of the cocktail set and a lobby for the fashionable stars of the day to appear in the latest lingerie, looking like advertisements out of *Vogue* or *The New Yorker*. Having to appear in these inane products as a sort of clothes-horse to prop up a series of costume changes by the pet stars of the day must have been psychologically very debilitating. These bits of stage carpentry missed truth by miles and Leslie wondered if such truth might yet be found in films which could come closer to reality with audiences at some remove from the so-called sophisticated metropolitan centres.

More importantly, in Leslie's case, allied to his disenchantment with acting in these enervating circumstances, was a desire to create things, to initiate things and be a begetter rather than a performer. And this possibility of getting nearer to the truth and to a fuller creative function he began to feel lay in the film medium and the direction of films.

Let it not be thought that I have forgotten his instinctive genius for playing parts for which he was eminently suited, such as Peter Standish in *Berkeley Square* and Alan Squier in *The Petrified Forest*. But these were oases in a desert of trivia. His misfortune, along with many actors in the 1920s and early 30s, was to be associated with numerous pot-boilers and such banal pastiches, like the eminently successful *Her Cardboard Lover*, which were the popular money-spinners of the era.

As the thirties progressed, Leslie began to do less and less theatre work. The annual play became the bi-annual play and by 1936 his career as an actor in the theatre was over. Never a robust or emotionally powerful actor the arena of the stage was not really his battle place and he no longer felt any inclination to strut the boards. After *The Animal Kingdom* and *The Petrified Forest* there remained only *Hamlet* – and this was to be his swan-song.

Gradually he had been turning his attention more and more towards films. Here, he felt, was his true vocation, the real medium for his quieter technique, and over the next few years he made a large number of films both in Hollywood and Elstree, but as leading actor not director. Although, as I mentioned earlier, he had directed a number of plays he was still some way from directing a film. Yet this was always his ultimate aim. Film directing called for an entirely different technique, normally required a long apprentice-ship and was, in Hollywood, somewhat of a closed shop.

It was to be in England, in 1938, as a bargaining point, I suppose, for his services as principal actor, that he first had the opportunity to direct a film. This was to be the co-direction, with Anthony Asquith,

of the film *Pygmalion*. It was produced by Gabriel Pascal and it was to
Pascal that he owed his introduction to film directing. It was the
success of this film that opened the door to a new career.

By September 1939, as Hitler's Stukas and tanks stood mobilised
for the annihilation of Poland, the last phase of Leslie Howard's life
began. It was to be a most fertile and productive phase considering
the disruptive elements. Despite what Leslie was to say about the
'profound psychological deterrents' which affect 'artists of all kinds
in times of violence and destruction' he was yet to prove that film
entertainment – and propaganda – was not such 'a trivial occupation'
as he had at first envisaged.

*

Previously I have described Leslie's final departure from America
in 1939 and something of his earlier career. Professionally his life
had always been extremely well-ordered and well-balanced, little
left to chance and most of the important opportunities taken.
Looking back on his career there was an inevitability about it that
was almost predictable. It had proceeded on an even, rising
parabola from obscurity to stardom with no great surges or falls
indicating professional struggle. It went steadily, gently, predictably
upwards and by 1939 looked solidly established, built carefully,
brick by brick, with few being dropped on the way. Above all, there
was nothing emotional about it – no rows, no storms, no walkings-
out à la Hollywood. If he had disagreed with anyone he had quietly
done his own thing, taken his own way, written his own contract.
His career was a cool, highly technical achievement and, unlike
many theatrical careers, was supra-normal rather than in any way
abnormal or bizarre.

However, rather the reverse was true of Leslie's private life which
was not at all predictable. If he had a set of rules in his professional
life there was little evidence of them in his private life, which was full
of emotional inconsistencies, as if it was being conducted not so
much by an amateur as by a rather over-romantic schoolboy. In his
pursuit of notions about the fair sex he was frequently misguided –
or, perhaps, simply over-optimistic – for he put a number of
women on pedestals to which they were scarcely entitled. The
goddess-like statues he made of them too often had clay feet. In
most cases they fell, well short of expectation. Strange that such a
coolly detached man should have been such an impressionable
idealist about the opposite sex. Yet that was his mould.

Despite a lack of realism in these romantic adventures, mainly with actresses, Leslie conducted them with commendable discretion. If they were no more than the by-products, or side-effects, of more serious professional activities Leslie managed, in his careful, fastidious way, to keep the disparate elements apart – so far as the public was concerned – thereby drawing no undue attention to the odd shenanigans of the romantic idealist at loose inside the dedicated professional. They had a clandestine anonymity by which he cleverly concealed them from both public and press. He could fade into the colour of the background with the dexterity of a chameleon and some of his amours were almost invisible. How successful Leslie was in fostering this image of innocence, without a breath of scandal, may be measured by the fact that his many thousands of fans never doubted that he was the paragon of all that constituted the happily married man, whose background was one of undisturbed domestic bliss.

However, Leslie's public efforts of concealment were scarcely so well-concealed from my mother and, undoubtedly, in the early stages of their marriage, these theatrical liaisons, though short-lived, considerably bewildered and perplexed her. Ruth was essentially an earthier, simpler creature altogether than Leslie, a country girl who, on her first arrival in America, found the theatrical coterie in which Leslie circulated odd and unsympathetic. She felt herself something of an outsider in this sophisticated world of clever people and witnessed the temptations to which Leslie was exposed with some alarm. Yet over the years by forbearance, understanding and much swallowing of pride she preserved the outward image of an unruffled marriage.

Ideally, Leslie expected his domestic needs and extra-mural desires to be run together, as it were, in a double harness. The continental approach, perhaps, where once respectably married one strayed into affairs, yet carefully kept the marriage and the affairs separate, out of sight of one another and hermetically sealed by a kind of unwritten protocol. Equally ideally, in the English sense of the word, Leslie hoped not to be found out.

When I said earlier that Leslie was a man torn between opposites and that if he had looked into his heart he would have seen the face of Ashley mirrored there, I was not simply instancing a view of Leslie in cinematic terms. In his own private life he was subject to a Scarlett-Melanie syndrome of intense proportions. If he intensely needed his home and family at one moment, at another he equally intensely needed to escape from them. By such a process, Leslie

In Search of my Father

spent much of his life crossing and recrossing a kind of emotional
bridge of San Luis Rey. At any moment the ropes might snap
plunging everyone into an abyss of conflict and recrimination. With
many families, theatrical or otherwise, these peregrinations might
have led straight to the divorce court. Somehow, miraculously, in
Leslie's case, the strands seemed to hold, because the one enduring
strand, the life-line back to the family that never failed, was my –
usually forgiving – mother, Ruth.

But for Ruth's resilience, fortitude and patience the somewhat
rickety structure might well have collapsed years earlier. If she had
been hurt by the recurring romantic crises of Leslie's creation – and
she had often enough been hurt and jealous – she did her best not to
show it and, if she did, because she loved him, generally forgave
him. If I have referred to her as a strong strand in the bridgework
she was also – if I may mix my metaphors – the mortar that bonded
the brickwork of the family. Leslie was well aware of her unselfishness
and of his immense dependence on her, and Ruth, as the Melanie-
figure, was equally well aware of Leslie's Scarlett adventures. She
learned to gauge their rise and fall, if not with equanimity, at least to
a practical perspective. Following the birth of my sister in 1924
there were to be no more children and their relationship appeared
to reach a kind of undemanding quiescence, a plateau of acceptance.
They shared a home and family responsibilities – but occupied
separate rooms.

If Leslie played Russian roulette with his marriage he appeared to
have done so with an unloaded revolver. Whenever Ruth had
remonstrated with him over some amatory adventure, he had
reassured her there was nothing to worry about, no cause for alarm
or despondency. Whatever he was up to was extremely unserious,
their marriage was not, in any sense, threatened and he relied
implicitly on her good judgement not to mention or even think of
divorce. He needed his family desperately and, he assured her, he
would not give it up without a considerable struggle, particularly
over a gambol with some girl half his age.

Only once, in the mid-1930s, did the apparently quiescent
volcano threaten to erupt. Leslie, appearing at the time in a popular
play in New York, had got himself a bit deeper into a situation than,
perhaps, he intended. Not only that, he was actually living with the
lady in question in a somewhat luxurious hotel, while the family
occupied another, more modest one, only a few streets away.
Without formulating any specific plan, my mother decided to leave
for California to visit friends and, perhaps, seek advice. She may

have hoped it might have the effect of bringing Leslie to his senses. Whatever was in her mind, I travelled with her to Los Angeles and we stayed with an Irish Catholic family, great friends of both Ruth and Leslie. Mary was devoted to my mother and, I suppose, Ruth thought she might be at once a fountainhead of advice and source of consolation. However, at the precise moment of our arrival in Beverly Hills, these friends were in the middle of unexpected matrimonial problems. With trunks and bags packed for imminent departure in separate directions, they wavered between the ministrations of a priest and the advice of a lawyer. Eventually, before we departed for New York again, the priest won, the friends were reunited, and this may well have persuaded my mother that divorce proceedings were not, perhaps, germane to her problems.

In our absence, however, another factor had intervened. Leslie's idyll appeared to be in the doldrums. When we arrived back we found him, laid up in bed in the family hotel, incapacitated by a severe attack of boils. The poor man was literally covered with them, with one carbuncle, somewhat unromantically, on the end of his nose. He was being watched over by Doodie and Gargy, with a nurse in periodic attendance. If the boils had not entirely terminated the liaison they had, it seems, rendered it difficult, if not highly uncomfortable. He could honestly do no more than drag himself to the theatre – where the nurse went with him to dress his boils between scenes – and back again to bed at the family hotel. If this was a case of the biter bit, Ruth showed considerable restraint and, despite Leslie's squawks, rallied readily round to help deal with the boils. With some difficulty, Leslie completed the foreshortened run of the play and, then, perhaps with mingled mortification and gratitude, took us all on holiday to Bermuda. As we sailed from New York in *The Monarch* it seemed Leslie's infection of staphylococcus had conquered completely the other affection.

If this somewhat complicated romantic interlude had been more serious than others, it was not normally the case. As I said, Leslie's encounters with the opposite sex had, up to then, been basically ephemeral and short-lived. Though his needs and desires were constantly in conflict, his need for his family was greater – and always won in the end. He had once let it out that he did not 'drink, drug or divorce' which was, I suppose, his way of saying that he was a careful, well-balanced sort of fellow who did nothing to excess. And, certainly, this was partly true. The relationships with theatrical ladies had been evanescent – bright and beautiful, fast and furious – and, predictably, burnt their way out in a matter of months.

In an unseriously chauvinist way they were simply statements of his masculinity, a perfectly normal kind of vanity. If such liaisons were Leslie's expressions of the male prerogative – not to be questioned, of course – they need not really worry Ruth. There was no real threat in these Peter Pan escapades as they ran their predictable course. Onesided and selfish though they seemed, she had already begun to accept them, almost to condone them, as the calculated risks one simply had to take with an attractive husband who liked showing off. Like a bee visiting flowers, he always returned to the home-hive. In fact, despite the apparent seriousness of the last occasion, the attack of boils had helped put the whole thing in perspective. The somewhat pitiful developments, at times, almost made Ruth laugh.

But of course, with Leslie, once ended wasn't necessarily mended. Ruth had to accept that the situation could and, probably, would be repeated. Besides, there remained the distinct possibility that as the children grew up the old pull of home would grow less, the magnetic field of the family weaker. Not only that, as Leslie himself grew older the need for admiration and flattered vanity might increase. The engineer might be hoist with his own petard – and blown, unwittingly, at the moon.

A very few years later this is precisely what happened, and now the romantic adventure could not, so whimsically, be shrugged aside. It took a far deeper hold on him. Earlier, Leslie would have scoffed at such an unlikely eventuality, but in 1938, at the age of forty-five, he found himself drawn into a far more enduring relationship than he might have dreamed possible. It was not another peccadillo, another of Leslie's birds in a gilded cage – the hectic pursuit in the tight-rope world of the theatre, with a safety net for his fall. This time the girl was not an actress but a humbler, more modest sort of person altogether: a film company secretary. It was to develop into the most serious, the most compelling attachment Leslie had ever known.

He had met her during the production of *Pygmalion* at Pinewood studios in early 1938. Little did he know then that like the figure fashioned by Pygmalion she would become his image of perfect love and have a far more lasting hold over him than ever Eliza had over the intractable Higgins, a love that was to last five years to the end of her very short life. Her name was Violette Cunnington, a debonaire young Frenchwoman, striking rather than beautiful, who was working as personal assistant to Gabriel Pascal, the producer. By the end of the production, Leslie had persuaded

Violette to leave Pascal's services and enter his own, a fact which may or may not have annoyed Pascal, for good secretaries are not temporary or disposable items. However, as far as I know, Pascal yielded her up without a struggle and though she may have been invaluable to him as a secretary she was to become indispensable to Leslie. Just how indispensable was not calculated in the initial term of her employment. Somewhere in the course of the next five years that indispensability perceptibly changed from a business arrangement into something far deeper. A profounder link had been forged that was not even to be broken by her death at the early age of twenty-nine.

When I first met Violette in the spring of 1938 I naturally knew nothing of this, nor guessed it. She was simply Leslie's new secretary, a most attractive girl not much older than myself, with a serene expression, wide-set, almost smoke-tree blue eyes and freckles which bloomed perceptibly in sunlight. I must admit I was struck by other things about her which I suppose I shouldn't have been had I been more sensitive to the situation, and I thought Leslie terribly fortunate, at his advanced age, to have engaged such a stunning young secretary. Shortly after Leslie introduced her to me, I invited her to a May Week Ball in Cambridge and flirted with her in an entirely adolescent way which, had I known, my father wouldn't have approved of at all. Later, when I got to know Violette better and understood something more of the situation with Leslie, I realised she possessed other qualities more important than surface appearances to twenty-year olds – for the situation demanded an entirely new *modus vivendi*, far harder for Violette than Leslie, and involving a relationship which was expected to exist side by side with the status quo of his family life.

It asked of Violette considerable unselfishness and the most practical approach – for what Leslie wanted, though it was to go far deeper this time, was what he had always somewhat selfishly wanted – a kind of compromise involving neither divorce nor any severance of his family ties. This was a lot to ask of a young and attractive girl and there was much heart-searching on Violette's part and much guilt-ridden subterfuge on Leslie's. In France these relationships are conducted more openly and the parties involved generally reach a sort of rapprochement. I think this may have been what Leslie hoped for and I imagine Violette, realising it and not wanting to hurt him or cause a major disruption, decided to take a sensibly French view of the situation.

But this was not achieved without something of a struggle and

quite early on they decided to make a positive effort to see if they
could break the relationship. Of this Leslie later wrote:

> In fact, we tried to crush it all at birth . . . for not long after,
> doubting me, you went away to France. And I, from pride or
> stupidity – or perhaps from fear – let you go. And as you went I
> knew my life was in the aeroplane with you. So I went home and
> wrote you a letter. And you replied with two. And then they came
> in an avalanche, letters and cables, back and forth, each to the
> other.

Clearly, it could not be crushed, yet for its survival it demanded of
Violette far more than it demanded of Leslie – the role of mistress is
a dead end, with no guarantees, for the man can walk out when he
pleases, and there are generally no children. It is subject to
subterfuge, evasion and humiliation by its very nature. That
Violette accepted all this was due not only to the intensity of her
feelings for Leslie but to her sensitive understanding and unselfishness in playing the role she had decided for herself – and because
she would never have consciously upstaged anyone, least of all my
mother whom she not only admired but to whom she always
maintained what the French are schooled to observe in these
situations, a correct sense of protocol. She was a far more intelligent
and a far rarer bird than one normally encounters in the film world,
and Leslie was very lucky.

From the outset, Leslie was greatly concerned with the demands
that this relationship made on Violette and he conducted it with
great care and discretion – and I am sure this is the way Violette
wanted it. Certainly Leslie, with his fastidious regard for everyone's
feelings, used the maximum amount of concealment and subterfuge,
especially when anywhere in the vicinity of the family. Clearly,
Violette was initially very concerned about my mother and did not
want any unpleasantness, nor in any sense to appear as a femme
fatale. To maintain a kind of correct equilibrium Leslie behaved, to
begin with, as if he was dealing with gelignite.

In the early winter of 1938 Leslie was to travel to New York on his
way to Hollywood – ostensibly, and as far as Ruth was concerned,
on his own. The modus operandi was for Leslie to board the SS
Normandie off Southampton, Violette having joined the ship at
Cherbourg. To give the whole thing a totally unpremeditated aura
of innocence, my sister and I were invited to see him off and we
travelled with Leslie by car from Dorking to Southampton. As if to

assure us further that nothing exceptional was afoot we were invited to make the trip out in the tender to where the big ship, standing off, picked up her British passengers which along with Leslie included Noël Coward and Laurence Olivier. I, for one, knew nothing of the expected presence on board of a certain French passenger – nor, I think, was Leslie absolutely certain for when he got on board he could not find Violette and searched the ship high and low despairingly. Finally, disconsolate, he stood in his cabin, surrounded by his luggage, as the ship's siren boomed the *Normandie*'s imminent departure for America – and still no sign of Violette. What had happened to her – had she lost her nerve, changed her mind at the last minute, decided the whole thing was too ridiculous and meant not to come after all? Of this situation Leslie wrote: 'We are underway and something must have gone wrong with the rendez-vous. You have missed the boat train –mistaken the date – decided to have done with me. Something awful has happened!' Then, the cabin door opened. Violette was standing there.

They spent a fortnight in New York in mid-November where Leslie had discussions about *The Man Who Lost Himself* with Walter Futter (pronounced Footer), his co-producer, and RKO. Then, they travelled on to Hollywood together. Leslie wrote to his mother on 30th November from the Sunset Tower, Sunset Boulevard, telling her something of his plans.

> I was there [New York] about ten days and then came here by train in order to make a broadcast on the 28th for which we had to rehearse. The play we did was *Interference* which had such a long run at the St James's some years ago. Bart Marshall was in it with me and several old English friends . . . and came off most successfully. I have several other broadcasts to do and have been asked to remain and act in the film of *Gone With The Wind* which starts in a few weeks' time. I really don't want to stay here longer than I can help as I am fidgeting to get our English project started, but I feel I ought to earn as much money as possible while I'm here. We all feel this is such a stupid place (even Futter does) and miss England very much . . . I am expecting the family later on if I stay long enough to make it worthwhile . . .

Gone With The Wind had come up somewhat unexpectedly, but was to take much longer than Leslie envisaged. His attitude to the family coming out was clearly tinged with some uncertainty and, later, some misgivings. Obviously, it was not going to be easy and he used a number of delaying tactics in his communications with the family at Westcott.

Violette and he finally decided to rent a house in a quiet part of Beverly Drive which they shared with another English actor, also married, and his lady friend.

> The little house was, for a change, not Spanish style but English . . . They called it 'Tudor' even though it had bougainvillea growing all round the bedroom windows. The garden was a lovely seclusion where great lilies grew in the open side by side with gardenias . . .

It seemed idyllic and Leslie bought what he described as 'that embarrassingly smart red roadster' for them to travel about in. Violette's tastes in the matter of clothes seemed modest by comparison, and when they went shopping in Beverly Hills Leslie had difficulty in persuading her 'to replenish her wardrobe'. He admitted he had 'never ceased to be astonished at her incredible frugality in personal adornment'. However, he persuaded her to buy a dinner dress 'with squares in the palest pastel shades' and was amazed at 'how little it cost'. As for jewellery the furthest she would go was 'a necklet of leaves of gilded tin costing two and a half dollars!'

> Thus lavishly arrayed we sallied forth to one of Hollywood's grandest parties in one of Hollywood's renowned homes. There were two orchestras . . . strings of coloured lights . . . roses, orchids and gardenias in festoons from the ceilings – every kind of exotic food and drink – and dozens of stars.

This seemed something of a departure from Leslie's usual lack of interest in such affairs. Perhaps, he thought, among the many people at this vast function they might pass unnoticed – or was he braving it out, showing in his determinedly self-righteous way, that he didn't much care if they noticed or not? Whatever the case, he had little use for the sham prudishness of Hollywood and he was certainly not going to be bothered with the stratagems of secrecy and subterfuge that had cloaked his departure from Dorking and Southampton. Wherever they went now, if questions were asked, Leslie introduced Violette as his production assistant, and let those who enquired make what they wanted of that. If it was smiled aside as a mere euphemism by the more cynically-minded, it was just too

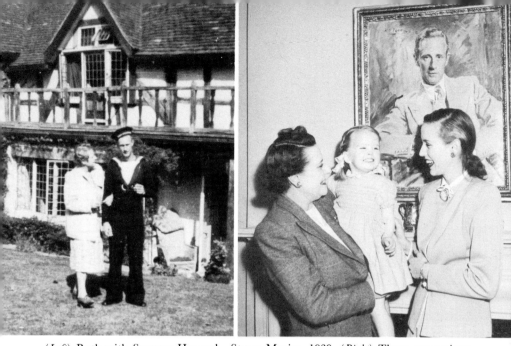

(*Left*) Ruth with Seaman Howard – Stowe Maries, 1939. (*Right*) Three generations –
Ruth, Doodie, Carolyn Dale-Harris.

Family gathering at Stowe Maries (*l to r* Leslie, his sister, Irene and fiancée, Jack
Jackson, Ruth, Trish and Wink).

Mother and son at Betchworth, Surrey (about 1963/4).

On set of *Pimpernel Smith* – Roland Pertwee, Leslie and Sub-Lieut Howard.

bad. The designation production assistant was a properly professional title and since it was the truth could scarcely fail to satisfy
the most avid seeker after respectability. He paid Violette a salary as
such and returned her with his income. It was quite legitimate.

Leslie was all too familiar with the bogus veneer of respectability
under which people in Hollywood lived while their private affairs
were conducted secretly out of town or, at least, out of sight, and he
refused to pay lip-service to these insincere moral codes. Hollywood's
married stars had always to appear to their fans as happily, almost
idyllically, married when frequently the reverse was the case. Their
contracts with the principal studios were well-laundered yet peppered
with legalistic moral clauses embodying the purest fidelity in
matrimonial matters. Having achieved this consensus the studio
bosses could sit back satisfied that they had done their utmost on
behalf of the League of Decency, Daughters of the American
Revolution and the Zionist organisations to all of whom marriage
laws were inviolate and, apparently, irreversible. Certainly, nobody
must live openly in sin in such a pious community for that was not
only bad for Hollywood's moral image but very bad for business as
well and could lead to instant termination of contract.

I suppose, in a way, these fatuous studio codes could have
applied to Leslie as much as anyone else if someone had been
small-minded or mean enough to take a closer look at his private
life. But Leslie did not normally reside in Hollywood nor had he
ever signed long-term contracts embodying these moral strictures
which the more permanent members of the British community,
such as Ronald Colman or Basil Rathbone were forced to put their
signatures to.

However, he was well aware that among less altruistic and,
perhaps, less savoury souls there was bound to be talk regarding his
precise relationship with Violette, and his agent sensibly reminded
him that he would have to face the possibility that columnists like
Louella Parsons and Hedda Hopper might inevitably nose it out.
Though this infuriated Leslie into one of his well-known, self-
righteous postures of defiance he did not, on cooler reflection, wish
either to scandalise or hurt anyone, particularly Ruth and Violette.
He just found it degrading and sickening that people should be so
unnaturally interested in his private life.

Of this situation he was later to write:

I know there were fears and sadnesses through that period of
happiness. We suffered from the barbarism of social-domestic

civilisation, from the materialism of the world where it impinged
on a delicate and profound relationship, from callousness and
misunderstanding and the gross coarseness of looks and words
and thoughts. There were times when we were not only in a
foreign country but in a foreign planet. Still, there was also
sympathy and encouragement – and comprehension . . .

His agent in Hollywood was certainly sympathetic – and compre-
hending – for he was in much the same situation himself, in love
with his secretary yet maintaining, for public consumption, the
semblances of a relationship with his wife and family. Indeed, I
think he brought this to Leslie's attention, suggesting that, for the
sake of appearances as well as to dispel any rumours then current,
Ruth's presence in Los Angeles might be more than beneficial,
outweighing any possible disadvantages. Of course, it would
involve a certain amount of inconvenience and juggling, but Leslie
was not inexpert in these matters, so that should not be too difficult.
It would also put a far better face on things, maintaining correct
protocol with the press, studio officials, publicists and so on. I do
not doubt that Leslie had all this at the back of his own mind and
needed little reminding of its somewhat tiresome good sense, and
so it was not surprising that, when my mother and sister arrived in
the film capital towards the middle of April, there was Leslie – in full
view of the public and press – a bunch of flowers in his hand,
waiting to meet them at the Los Angeles railway station. This was a
most persuasive argument for press pundits and other arbiters of
respectability that Leslie's long-publicised reputation for decency
and decorum were just as they had always said. And here was a
photograph of the happily married actor, greeting them, as if to
confirm it to the world. It certainly put a full-stop to any gossip-
mongering that had arisen and acted as a warning signal to Louella
Parsons and Hedda Hopper to re-sheathe their poisoned pens.

More than put a good countenance on things Leslie went further
and purchased an attractive house in Camden Drive, Beverly Hills,
as the official Howard residence, and here Ruth and Doodie settled
in for the duration of *Gone With The Wind* and set busily about
refurnishing and redecorating the place which had previously
belonged to Hedy Lamarr, whose tastes were somewhat less
conventional. If this was the price of peace and decorum it seemed
well worth it and Leslie, determined on being agreeable to
everyone, found dividing himself between his official residence at
Camden Drive and his hideaway in Beverly Drive not as irksome as

he had at first supposed. Though Ruth was no longer deceived she certainly took no action that might upset arrangements, and Leslie came and went making, for want of a better word, the best of both worlds. It was a case of Hobson's choice for all concerned.

As *Gone With The Wind* drew to its close and Leslie's involvement with it grew less, he was able to devote more time to his new project *The Man Who Lost Himself*, with which Violette was to be closely associated. The film was to go into production in England as soon as he got home, and Leslie continued to have meetings with his co-producer, Futter, as well as with the script-writer, George O'Neil. In fact, Leslie made tentative arrangements with O'Neil and Futter that they should all meet in the south of France where Leslie intended to go with Violette for a short holiday prior to production starting at Elstree on 1st October. There, presumably, at the Hotel du Cap, Antibes, the scenario would take its final shape.

These plans, which were never to be realised, involved a somewhat complicated domestic manoeuvre. Ruth and Doodie were to leave for New York by train while Leslie, under his agreement with Selznick, remained behind for possible retakes on *Gone With The Wind*. At the same time he would be able to see the finally edited version of *Intermezzo* with both Selznick and Ratoff. If all was well he would slip quietly out of Los Angeles by the night plane with Violette and join Ruth and Doodie at the hotel in New York immediately prior to embarking with them in the *Aquitania*. Violette would follow a week later in the *Ile de France*, disembarking at Le Havre. With her would travel 'the smart red roadster' in which she and Leslie would, they hoped, travel to the south of France.

These detailed and elaborate travel arrangements would meet all requirements: an uncontentious withdrawal from America that would raise no eyebrows, and Leslie's immediate production plans. As far as the press was concerned, Leslie would be seen both leaving New York and arriving in Southampton in the company of his family. It was a sensible and face-saving cover-plan calling for no explanations, no one would be hurt or embarrassed and it would meet all prevalent moral codes. Shortly after arrival in England Leslie would leave, by the back door as it were, for France, effect his rendezvous with Violette, travel south to complete the scenario with George O'Neil and Futter and finalise production arrangements while having a holiday at Antibes.

There was only one major snag: the war – and this was to alter everything. Leslie, Ruth and Doodie left New York on 22nd August. Less than a week later, Violette was on her way, with the car, in the

Ile de France, when she received a cable from Leslie which said simply, urgently: *Guerre inevitable. Descend Plymouth au lieu Havre. T'attends, t'adore.*

The whole thing had been something of a dream for there had always been, lurking in the background, the danger of war. Now that it seemed a reality not only were the plans for France abandoned but, eventually, the plans for the film. Other dreams had to be jettisoned, too, as Leslie wrote: ' . . . tantalising dreams of Hawaii, the Pacific Islands, Japan, the Orient. They remained dreams. We had touched our "farthest west" . . . ' Leslie was never to forget those few months in California and he described them in his letter of tribute to Violette after her death:

There were out of the eight months five at least of a joyous and rare perfection, of an awareness of the beauty of life that neither had known before. Long after, in a grey winter of war, you said wistfully: 'Those five months were the peak. We shall never have anything like that again.' And I argued – 'Of course, we will. One day we shall go back, we shall recapture them.' But you insisted: 'No, no – they are gone forever.'

To this Leslie added, as a footnote: 'Oh, my love, how did you know – how did you know?'

When Violette disembarked at Plymouth and drove that bright red, incongruous roadster to London, war was only a day away. The plans and hopes had been abruptly abandoned – and the dream – for as Leslie wrote: 'The dream was to drive the car together to the Mediterranean – through Normandy to Paris, through Paris to the Côte d'Or and Provence and on over the Alpes Maritimes, savouring the wines and the cooking, the inns and the villages, the sweet changing landscape.' And of that other dream, all that would remain of their 'farthest west' would be the memory of a bougainvillea -shrouded, neo-Tudor house on a Hollywood hill-top – and, perhaps, the still silence of the desert.

We shall see them, Violette and Leslie, two small figures standing close together against the dark immensity of the desert, standing silent in the still clear air; two faces upturned in wonder at the brilliant firmament: we shall hear their voices: . . . We are so small, so unimportant . . . What does the future mean for us . . . ? I am frightened – how can we hold together . . . ? What is the mystery of our coming together . . . ? We can never, never part – it was not just for nothing.

How curiously perceptive the questions must have seemed to Leslie as he recalled them a few short years later, sitting alone in a house at Stoke Poges – almost the psychic sublimation of their lives, as if they looked back upon their former selves from somewhere far off . . .

As eleven o'clock boomed out from Big Ben on 3rd September 1939, Leslie and Violette sat together in a flat in Chelsea Manor Street, and listened to a funny, dry, pedantic voice telling them that as no reply had been received from Herr Hitler a state of war now existed between Great Britain and Germany. No sooner had Mr Chamberlain finished his announcement when there came the first wail of the air-raid sirens. 'We were reunited,' Leslie wrote, 'just in time for the first air-raid warning.' He remembered how they spent the first hour of the war sitting in a Chelsea air-raid shelter – awaiting, perhaps, Hitler's devastation of London in response to Mr Chamberlain's rashness in declaring war!

It was a false alarm – but the war was not. To the two people, waiting the 'All Clear' in that Chelsea shelter, a new and unexpected adventure was about to begin that bore no resemblance to the somewhat golden dream that Leslie had envisaged. The war would be hard and exacting, and the adventure into the unknown would be one that neither could anticipate. Nor would they survive it, for their alloted span was to be three and a half years. But, perhaps, it might prove that the mystery of their coming together, their destiny, was 'not just for nothing' and they would, ultimately, never be parted.

CHAPTER THREE

The War of Inertia
September 1939-June 1940

While Leslie was in London listening to the declaration of war, the family heard it gathered round the radio at Stowe Maries. No sooner was the announcement over than the mini-siren, above the post-office in Westcott, shrilled out as had its larger brothers in London. As the first wail of its birth-cry reached us, someone, I think my sister, said: 'That was good timing. You don't suppose . . . ' – and we all looked at each other in some disbelief. Having, as yet, no shelter to go to, we trooped out into the garden, my mother and Gargy with us, to scan the skies for the possible approach of bombers. Why had Hitler decided to bomb Westcott, I suppose we thought? Was it the centre of some secret device we hadn't heard about. But no bombers came; only a cow bellowed comically at the strange sound of the siren, and a blackbird fluted nervously nearby.

When the 'All Clear' went everyone visibly relaxed. The imminence of war receded into something of an anti-climax. It was to remain an anti-climax for a long time – for this was the beginning of 'the phoney war', the gentleman's war, the war of inertia in which no one did anything but wait till someone struck the first blow. It was to last for over eight months, the war that wasn't a war, with all the disadvantages of total stalemate.

Later that day Leslie returned to Stowe Maries from London, his outlook clearly coloured by the declaration of war, his attitude in a state of suspended animation. He told us he had been having further discussions about *The Man Who Lost Himself*. Though a company, Major Pictures Ltd, had been set up for the production and distribution of the film and the finance arranged with RKO, he seemed less optimistic. He would have to be in town for several days, to see what progress could be made, so he would not be staying long at Stowe Maries.

My mother, after Hollywood, was attuned to his sudden arrivals and departures. No questions were asked, no answers expected. We had all accepted the facts of Leslie's divided life as a state of mind,

beyond question. It was the beginning of the time when his visits
would become less frequent – yet we all knew that, whatever else he
held dear, he dearly loved Stowe Maries, though for the next three
and a half years he would not be in it for more than brief week-ends.
But if that was the plan of his life it was the way he had arranged it –
in neat compartments.

Yet it was to Stowe Maries, I think, that he came as a man
returning *home* – to something permanent in a shifting, impermanent
world. Perhaps it gave him a perspective, put a distance between
himself and his too transient life. If houses can welcome one, then
this old house which had looked stoically out on the Surrey hills for
over three hundred years, welcomed him back in its own timeless,
unruffled way. One could stop in this house and be still, as quiet
and unhurried as the timbers and mortar that surrounded one. To a
man constantly on the move, living in suitcases, it was a place of
peace to come back to, even in war, to relax and be at home in, and it
certainly must have seemed to Leslie, after the evanescent excitements
of Hollywood, the touchstone of a less fevered and more real world.

Our conversation that night was confined to immediate generalities.
The declaration of war had come as a release from uncertainty; the
bogus air-raid, now explained as one of our own planes mistakenly
alerting the nation, seemed quite funny. But Leslie thought we
should be prepared: a proper air-raid shelter should be built in the
orchard opposite for the cellar was quite inadequate, and this was
shortly put in hand. Leslie took a supervisory interest in the general
lay-out, while the gardener and I did a lot of digging and filling
sand-bags. I remember there were tiers of bunks added and
furniture for sitting about. Funny, in a way, because I can't recall
one occasion when we ever used it; we always used the cellar of the
house when there were raiders overhead. Besides water seeped into
it and it became uncomfortably damp. Perhaps, Leslie thought
there was to be mass devastation.

Anyway, the work on this project of preservation kept us busy
during that warm, limpid month of September – without the
slightest interference from Hitler. He was busy, of course, with his
new allies dealing with the Poles. From all reports, Hitler was using
his Stukas to dive-bomb the towns and create terror, as if to remind
the Polish people how foolish they were not to come to an
agreement over the Corridor. Perhaps it was also to remind us that
we should get it later for being so foolhardy to declare war. As our
government departments were obviously aware, Hitler in his
present mood could attempt any monstrosity, and so we got our

civilian gas-masks in their little cardboard boxes, just in case. There is a photograph of us standing at the door of our shelter wearing these curious disguises. If it was taken for publicity purposes we were simply like other citizens preparing for the holocaust. It was obviously intended to show that even film-stars and their families were on a war footing, equipped not only for Hitler's bombs but his gas as well.

As far as Leslie's production plans were concerned this period proved to be not only frustrating but utterly negative. Such films as were already in production in British studios were rapidly concluded. But no further films were contemplated in the circumstances and all investment in commercial films suddenly stopped. Apart from *The Lion Has Wings* at Denham, it was to be well over a year before feature film production started again in its new guise of war-time propaganda. However, as Leslie's film *The Man Who Lost Himself* was to be financed direct from Hollywood, it was thought at first that this might go ahead and Leslie began to make tentative arrangements for studio facilities. He was soon disabused of that idea for only a few days after war was declared the financial backers got cold feet, and Leslie's co-producer cabled him that production in England was, regrettably, now out of the question. However, he was very optimistic that production could be switched to Hollywood and suggested Leslie hold himself ready to come back. But this Leslie was not prepared to do. In fact, his interest in the film had cooled considerably since war was declared and he was now, more than ever, determined to remain in England. Of this situation Leslie was later to write: 'The work I was to do in England had now been transferred to Hollywood and though all my plans, like everyone else's, were in chaos, I decided, contract or no contract, where my duty lay.'

His duty now, he felt, was to offer himself, in any capacity, where he might serve the interests of his country. A little old for soldiering – at least in these early stages of 'call up', though they might want him later 'to plug a gap', he put in good-humouredly – he thought it best to offer himself for some sort of propaganda work. Shortly after arriving home he had got hold of the recently published *British White Paper on the Outbreak of Hostilities* and read it with enthusiasm. He considered Sir Nevile Henderson's efforts to avert, or, at least, postpone, the catastrophe of war in themselves remarkable feats of diplomacy. He also felt this whole period with its tense negotiations, the sudden, hastily improvised meetings into which the excitable Hitler would erupt violently – 'up to the point where,' as Leslie put it, 'Henderson, his bags packed, was still prepared to fight for peace – and try to talk sense into the megalomaniac' – all this, Leslie felt, would make an exciting and dramatic documentary. 'And it ought to be filmed as a record of why we declared war and clear the air of misapprehensions.'

But the document was dull. It needed to be dramatised 'for people to be visually aware of what was going on all those months before the final break-down and collapse into war.' Leslie incorporated these thoughts into his *Notes on American Propaganda* in which he urged government consideration for documentary films and speakers so that 'our message' could be 'carried direct to the American people'. He was very specific that 'the first of these films should concern itself with placing the war-guilt irrefutably upon the Nazis.'

Ian Colvin, in *Flight 777*, described Leslie going to see 'a Whitehall official' – somebody in the Films Division of the newly formed Ministry of Information. This official politely poured cold water on his project. He drew Leslie's attention to 'the obstacles' to making films in war-time, quoting rationing, manpower, materials, petrol etc.

'We are trying to get organised to fight a war. We've never been awfully successful at making films in peacetime and to start now in war-time seems crazy to me.' As to Leslie's suggestion of a documentary on the basis of the British White Paper the official was far from sanguine. Anyway, the Foreign Secretary, Lord Halifax, would have to be consulted and his permission obtained, let alone the other 'obstacles'. He suggested Leslie might apply for a liaison job such as Noël Coward had in Paris, countering enemy propaganda. 'I don't think I would be very good at that sort of job', Leslie told him. 'The only business I know is making films.' The official shrugged as if to imply that Leslie's business should be fitting in with the country's business.

However, not entirely despairing that something might be done, Leslie went home and wrote to Lord Halifax urging his official approval of a film, based on the Blue Book, and enclosing his *Notes on American Propaganda*. Leslie had stressed in his *Notes* that our declaration of war over Poland was a matter of principle: 'With nothing to gain we have voluntarily undertaken the obligation of fighting for a remote state for no other reason than that we cannot stand by and see an ever increasing area of the civilised world dominated by a bully and subjected to gangster force.' Leslie pointed out that in our American propaganda there should be no mention of Americans 'fighting at our side, lending us money, sending us food or blood being thicker than water.'

Of course, Leslie was well aware of the immense difficulties and stumbling blocks that lay in the way of Anglo-American cooperation. From the outset there was the very real difficulty of persuading Americans that we would ever survive Hitler. Many felt he would bury us, along with the relics of the British Empire, and that we had been foolhardy to declare war over far-off Poland as a matter of principle. It was going to be a supreme task to persuade them to support us on the basis of conscience rather than logistics –for they had no particular conscience about Europe: they simply looked at it on its merits. In this respect, Britain's cause to the bulk of Americans was a lost cause already. Knowing Americans as intimately as he did, Leslie understood their suspicion of us. The larger part of them came, with unhappy memories, from middle Europe and many from Irish stock – and memories died hard. Only the New England element was basically pro-British and even that would not necessarily be on our side.

Later, the following year, when Leslie began the broadcasts that were net-worked across the United States and Canada, he did so with some trepidation realising the immense gap that lay between us as people and our belief in the cause for which we were so desperately fighting. There was no cosy polarity because we spoke the same language: the American language was a blend, as it were, of all the European languages. The resultant mixture was the composite *homo Americanus*, a proud and independent being who, having extricated himself from Europe, had naturally no desire to be closely involved with it again. Nor were the Americans keen to fight for a British political ideology. They were neither in favour of socialism nor the preservation, or possible extension, of the British Empire. They knew we were fighting to survive, but for what sort of post-war set-up?

If Leslie had the advantage of being able to talk to Americans as almost one of themselves, he was still, though Americanised, an Englishman. All his life he had never been quite able to vault the hurdle to American citizenship. He knew the bulk of Americans, of whatever ethnic source, always coalesced into a very strong American identity. And, at heart, they had the somewhat naive belief that to become an American citizen was about the highest of human endeavours. Indeed, they would have thought it foolish of Leslie, not to say churlish and ungrateful, not to want to become a one hundred per cent American. Leslie was prepared to admit, in his broadcasts, his immense debt to America, and that he had been, perhaps, a little foolhardy renouncing his American way of life to get embroiled in a European war. But he gently reminded them of their common heritages in Europe by confessing that he was, after all, a bit of a hybrid himself!

I think the fact that his loyalties were divided gave him added persuasive strength when he began those broadcasts. I imagine his *Notes on American Propaganda* must have had a force of immediacy and value to the departments of our propaganda and information services that were interested in getting, and keeping, the initially isolationist and extremely sceptical 'All-American Ear'.

Unfortunately, at the moment, no one seemed to be listening for there was, at this early stage of the war, no official propaganda policy towards America. Government departments felt that they had to be very careful that they did not either anticipate, or unduly influence, American reactions, or cause offence to the many shades of opinion in that homogeneous country of polyglot origin. And so, at first, they did nothing – believing that benign inanition was preferable to possibly provocative action. Apart from welcoming his advice and suggestions no official approval was given to Leslie's project. Eventually it was vetoed.

While all these matters were still in the boiling pot of the general uncertainty, Leslie was working busily with Anthony Asquith preparing a Memorandum for the Ministry of Information entitled *The Film Industry in Time of War*, with which Michael Powell and other leading members of the industry associated themselves as signatories. I well remember 'Puffin' and Leslie hammering out the details of this manifesto of intent seated in the garden of Stowe Maries during that first week of war. It embraced many of Leslie's ideas in his *Notes* but was more detailed and technical, covering both home and overseas propaganda, training and instructional films, quota legislation and labour relations.

When Leslie was not engaged in somewhat unprogressively badgering 'officials' or preparing manifestoes that fell on deaf ears, he was to be found in the company of Jonah Barrington, the radio correspondent of the *Daily Express*, who was a near neighbour. It was Jonah who took him to listen to the desperate and pathetic broadcasts coming from Poland as the German panzer armies rumbled across that country towards their eastern allies. Lord Beaverbrook had at Cherkley, his estate near Leatherhead, a short-wave receiving station able to pick up broadcasts from much of Europe and the Balkans. It was specially tuned at this time to news bulletins coming from Poland. Round the receivers, each on the wave-lengths of Polish transmitters, clustered a number of interpreters, busily scribbling the translations as the news came in.

This 'source' was the last means of contact with Poland and not only kept the *Express* readership up to date but also our own Foreign Office, now that their sources were silent and their legations occupied in extricating themselves. Cherkley 'Short Wave' listened in to Poland until the last 'free' transmitter was silenced. In fact, it was as they heard the German announcers, speaking in Polish, that the interpreters knew that, for them, the war was over. Hearing the news happening like that must have been upsetting for Jonah and Leslie, but to hear it happening to your own people and, possibly, families must have been heart-rending to those writing it down knowing there was nothing they could do.

Despite Leslie's efforts to involve himself in the war the difficulties of getting anything done, or of persuading anyone to do anything positive, dismally persisted through the months of October and November. The war of inertia seemed to have got them all by the throat. Leslie realised, after his encounter with the 'official' from the Ministry of Information, that the blank wall of apparent uninterest was not so much indifference to new ideas as inability to know which way to turn in unplanned for situations. The civil service mind tended to fall back on a certain built-in resistance when faced by the sophisticated requirements of film producers and others engaged in non-essential occupations.

'Why don't you take your problems to ENSA,' one man told Leslie, eager to be rid of him. 'They understand these things.'

J.B. Priestley had had experience of the official mentality at work. He described a confrontation with a mind of such polarity (*Postscript*, 21st July 1940).

'I hadn't been in his room more than two minutes when this official and I were looking at each other as a cat looks at a dog. We just weren't getting on at all . . . He saw me as an impatient, slap-dash, dangerous sort of fellow, wanting everything done at once, bringing out all manner of half-digested notions . . . and I saw him as a coldly conceited, ungenerous, sterile kind of chap, never throwing himself into anything . . . He made those little movements that politely suggest to a caller that it's time to go. He said: "We might be able to form a sub-committee; then, perhaps, you'd like to send in some kind of report, just a short memo, embodying . . . "And I said: "No, I don't think so. Good morning," and went. And he said to himself: "Well, thank goodness I've got rid of that fellow, barging in here as if he owned the place. He can't begin to understand our difficulties." and I said to myself: "Stuffed shirts and Mandarins, oh dear, oh dear . . . " Two entirely different and opposed types of mind, you see, the warmly imaginative against the coldly rational . . . the creative against the administrative. Clearly, we must have both types of mind working now at full pressure and it's absolutely essential that each should have its own sphere of activity. It's in the relation of eager, imaginative, creative minds and cool, punctilious, administrative minds that we tended to go wrong.'

Well, the relationship wasn't right then and Leslie seriously doubted if it ever would be. At least, in the present climate, it seemed clear that if one wished to make films which embraced wider topics than, say, how to operate a stirrup-pump or make black-out curtains, one would have to go elsewhere than government departments for support and encouragement. One would have to set things up oneself, raising the necessary money privately. In peace-time, of course, there would have been no problem. Leslie's name and reputation would have guaranteed it. Unfortunately, with the war barely two months old, the wells of British film finance, never noticeably liquid, had now dried up altogether. It seemed British cinema moguls had for the time being decided to go to earth. They took the view, quite understandably, that the expected enemy air-raids in the metropolitan areas which had forced them to close their cinemas in the first fortnight of war might force them to close them again, perhaps indefinitely. What was the point of further investment in films if their box-office returns were to be non-existent or negligible? As a result a total stalemate of film enterprise ensued which was to last for over a year – in fact, until well after the Battle of Britain and the subsequent invasion scare (Sea-Lion) had passed into history. Something like sixteen months was to elapse before the first commercially financed main feature film, with a propaganda theme, finally went into production at Denham film-studios. It was January 1941 – and the film was Leslie's *Pimpernel Smith*, the first British war-film to be made.

*

Looking back on this long period of total inaction one realises what a dilemma people in the entertainment profession were really in. They were told to carry on with their work until called up for the services or be retrained for industry. But many had no work to do.

There was no television to speak of and the film studios were rapidly closing or being taken over as depots by the services. Only the theatres continued, with gay abandon, to function until the Blitz made them untenable – and only one, the Windmill, 'never closed'. However, there was one other major outlet and source of employment that 'never closed', the BBC, which, though later bombed, continued to be the Voice of Britain, disseminating information and propaganda to the world throughout the war without a break. And it was from the BBC, later in 1940, that Leslie received his first wartime job, as a broadcaster, introduced by J.B. Priestley, with whom he became firm friends and established a lasting rapport.

However, this was all still nine months away. For Leslie now, in the ensuing months of the 'phoney war', the prospects were scarcely promising. His contract with Major Pictures for the production of *The Man Who Lost Himself* had been broken because he had decided 'where his duty lay'. But this was the problem: where, in fact, did it lie?

'I feel rather like Stacpoole's hero – but lost in a more than fictional sense,' he was to write to me in November, 'and I am beginning to wonder why I am here and what I am doing here. Certainly, a lot less than you . . . ' At that time I was serving as a sailor in one of His Majesty's yachts off the coast of Anglesey. Leslie was to visit me in early December, in company with my mother, to see how I had 'shaken down' in my rather unwarlike ship. (The yacht's main gun was made of wood and all it could have fired, even in anger, was sawdust.) Despite its aggressive limitations, I escorted him over the vessel and introduced him to my mess-mates. When he left to go back to London he remarked, not without a touch of salty humour: 'Well, at least, one of us seems well-found!'

I suppose it must have felt strange to him standing in the wings, as it were, marking time, when he had been so much in the limelight, so much in demand. Strange, suddenly, not to be wanted, a man whose personality had become so fashionable that it was almost embarrassing, not to say irking, to be out of the tide of things, inappropriately high and dry. Distressing, too, to have come rushing back from America full of hopes and ideas, and wanting desperately to be of use, only to find himself in a cul-de-sac of inactivity. His decision, he knew, had perplexed his friends in Hollywood: now it perplexed him that the only service he could offer, apart from awaiting a distant call-up of reservists, was to carry a stirrup-pump in the village Air Raid warden's detachment – to put out fires due to air-raids which had so far not materialised.

'I'm doing an awful lot of planning and thinking,' he wrote, 'and I'm meeting a lot of people in much the same boat as myself – and we're doing a lot of talking. At the moment, it's all so much hot air!' One of the things he talked about was a holiday trip he'd made to Austria just before the Anschluss in January 1938.

He had taken my mother and sister on a skiing holiday to Kitzbuhl in company with Gabriel Pascal and 'Puffin' Asquith. Leslie didn't do much skiing but the holiday gave him the opportunity to have discussions with Gabby and Puffin about their forthcoming film of *Pygmalion*. It went into production at Pinewood Studios at just about the moment Hitler's storm-troopers entered and annexed Austria. I gather a curious feeling of apprehension pervaded the otherwise bracing air of Kitzbuhl, and both Leslie and Gabby noticed how the normally affable Austrians grew gradually more constrained and uncommunicative.

One man that Leslie was introduced to, a painter by the name of Alfons Walde, was less constrained and told Leslie disquieting stories of friends liquidated by the Nazis. Walde who came from Oberndorf, near Kitzbuhl, went to the Vienna Academy, and later made quite a name for himself as a painter and architect. He had a house, high on the Hannenkamme, and he invited Leslie to visit him there. In the privacy of his studio he told Leslie that Austria was finished as an independent country, would shortly be annexed by Germany and become a strait-jacketed *Lebensraum* for German thinking and *Diktats*. With a shrug he indicated his pictures, sketches, murals and so on. Far too free and expressionist in conception, Leslie realised at once they would be anathema to the Nazis. Undoubtedly they would be condemned as decadent by the Nazi clique – the Führer preferring the art of the tinted photograph and his Minister for Enlightenment, Josef Goebbels, those over-life-size, mechanical reproductions of burly, square-jawed peasants and strapping *Hausfrau* women typical of the 'approved school'. There was no hint of this 'safe' fashion of painting in Walde's studio. Like all other works of this nature they would certainly be condemned as Jewish bait.

The fate of Walde and many like him worried Leslie. He knew already of the great number of professors, doctors, teachers and pastors who had been discharged from their posts for intellectual 'aberrations', racial impurity or simply refusing the prayers of the enforced *Deutsche Christen*. They had disappeared – or been murdered – and he wondered about Walde. 'I have many good friends here,' Walde told him, 'but within weeks we'll have new masters – and, then . . . ' he smiled and added, 'it will be a little unstable. I may have to get out, or go into the cage with the other wild beasts.'

Though this chance encounter led to no further contacts between them, and Austria was annexed six weeks later by National Socialist Germany, Leslie was not to forget his meeting with Alfons Walde. In fact, it was to become the germ of the idea for the film *Pimpernel Smith*. As my sister was to write in her biography of Leslie (*A Quite Remarkable Father*) ' . . . the setting should be Austria in 1938; a famous painter, who was also a violent anti-Nazi, is arrested by Hitler's thugs. He must be saved somehow . . . ' Leslie made a plan, a treatment, for this 'escape story' sometime in the early part of 1940, but feeling the need to get an authentic background he looked around for someone more familiar with the contemporary Austrian scene. Introduced by chance at a party to a writer called Wolfgang Wilhelm – who, in fact, had escaped himself – Leslie mentioned the idea and Wilhelm, on the spur of the moment, made some suggestions which Leslie thought excellent. Later, he had several meetings with this German expatriate and together they worked on what was to be the first treatment of *Pimpernel Smith*, but, of course, at this stage the character of a modern Pimpernel had not emerged. It was simply an escape story.

When they had roughed it out Leslie got in touch with a friend of his – the novelist, Archie MacDonnell – and asked him if he would be interested in fleshing out the bare bones of the treatment so that a proper basis could be laid for a scenario. This MacDonnell agreed to do and, thus, became the second, not counting Leslie, of five various writers engaged on the project.

Looking back it seems no less than incredible that it required this number of professional experts to cobble the film together. However, one should not be too surprised as it was common practice both in Hollywood and Elstree in the 1930s, and by the time a film reached production several of the earlier combinations of writers had vanished from the film altogether, their contributions not even mentioned in the subsequent credit titles. They had had their work written over, or simply written out. In the case of *Pimpernel Smith* all five writers did have the satisfaction of seeing their names in the credit titles. Nevertheless, this was far from a guarantee that the film would ever be made and many such costly experiments were abandoned without a foot of film being shot.

In the best of times it would be a platitude to say that films are not easy to finance. In war-time it was almost an improper joke to mention the subject of money. Film-financing was extremely tight

(*Left*) Leslie's first film at Bushey, 1918. (*Right*) Successful Hollywood actor in full regalia (circa 1935).

Oblique angle proposal – or staircase syndrome – Leslie and Olivia de Havilland about 1935.

Leslie as Peter Standish in *Berkeley Square* with Jean Forbes-Robertson.

and banks were even more wary of entertainers than usual. For nearly a year Leslie hawked the escape story about, trying to sell his 'brain-child', as it were, in circumstances which, for a man in his position, might be thought humiliating. Naturally, not knowing which way Hitler was going to jump, no one seemed too interested. They made polite noises, but that was about it. Leslie admitted it was all too like being a travelling-salesman – even when you had a foot in the door the sale could slip up. One could always get prospective backers to read the story but they inevitably hedged or demanded costly rewrites before they dreamed of putting a penny in the kitty. They might – or might not – want to invest in it depending on how the 'rewrite' came out. Leslie coined a phrase that stories were not written, they were simply rewritten to order. And he had to pay a lot of writers. He began to realise that before one even reached the threshold of the creative part of film-making there were deep disadvantages to the whole business, financial pitfalls of the simplest kind. One had not only to placate the person who might eventually put up the money but many other people, en route – 'would-be-angels' who indicated interest by polite approval and, then, began telling one how the script could be improved by doing this, that or the other – and, finally, when one had attempted to meet their objections, declined further interest.

'I spend weeks getting people interested – rewriting and so on. And they're absolutely charming, showing burning enthusiasm. Then, they back out!' He said this very pointedly about *Pimpernel Smith*. Suffice to say that the final version of the film, the shooting script of January 1941, bore little or no resemblance to the simple escape story involving the rescue of an Austrian painter unpopular with the Nazis. It had burgeoned into a Scarlet Pimpernel story of considerable elaboration, with a deeply satirical theme, and a sub-plot involving a romantic interlude with a Polish-American girl as make-weight for the box-office. It had become a compilation of ideas from many sources, knit together by the burning of much midnight oil. Leslie referred to this process as 'Long hours of going from place to place, from person to person – long discussions, often tiring, more often discouraging.' He well knew the laboured methods of putting films together were simply the hard graft of getting agreement, of satisfying differing elements, with but one aim in view – raising the necessary money to begin. Once that was achieved the rest was comparatively plain sailing; one had got the creative latitude one needed to give the film one's own particular hallmark and, once it reached the studio floor, one's expertise in direction and acting – generally without interference. He was, however, to learn that it was vitally important to appear to give way – even over major points – in the early stages of negotiation and seem prepared to make changes of a radical nature, without the slightest intention of abiding by them, if only to save argument and delay. But it still remained an exhausting process.

*

In January 1940, Leslie found other uses for his time-consuming, unfulfilled sense of purpose – and other avenues to explore in the more immediate interests of propaganda. One of these was a trip to Paris and to British GHQ at Arras.

In Paris, in May 1939, there had been formed, due to the efforts of Sir Campbell Stuart, a joint Anglo-French Propaganda Council, ready to function if war came. Later, in September, on the very day the Germans invaded Poland, Sir Campbell had an appointment with Jean Giraudoux, the French playwright, recently appointed Minister of Information in Monsieur Daladier's government. Of this meeting with Giraudoux, Sir Campbell wrote:

Giraudoux was, and remained until he almost imperceptibly vanished from the political scene, an unknown quantity. He had a peculiarly sensitive mouth and a pleasant though on this occasion somewhat nervous smile. One could see in him the author of *Amphytrion 38*, of *Bella* and of *Siegfried* which so successfully struck the note of the middle twenties in France. I told him briefly of my department. I had made it my business to know a great deal about him and I had learned that he had a great admiration for the English stage and in particular for Noël Coward. He expressed great satisfaction when I told him that I had arranged to send Noël Coward to Paris as my representative on the Anglo-French Propaganda Council. It was agreed that André Maurois should represent the Minister on this Council . . . I returned to the Crillon where I was staying. M. Maurois came to luncheon . . . In that brief period I told him all I could and that Noël Coward would shortly arrive to confer further with him . . .
    Noël Coward left for France in the second week of the war. It had originally been suggested to him that he would serve the cause best by entertaining the troops with his unquestioned gifts but when I asked him to help me in France he assented. I chose him not as a playwright, which had appealed to M. Giraudoux,

but as a man with great ability who wished to serve his country in her time of trouble quite properly in some other way than as an actor. One of the disadvantages of a 'secret' department is that any well-known personality working in it is bound to serve as a magnet for comment, questioning and criticism, and Coward's was an appointment for which I was much criticised, as he knows.*

When Leslie went to Paris in January, he did not go, as far as I am aware, in any 'official' capacity. Quite apart from any feelings he had that he would not have made a good official appointee, I think he suspected that entertainment people were not well-suited, by temperament or disposition, to official appointments. Indeed, he would, I think, have agreed entirely with Sir Campbell Stuart that well-known entertainment people could have drawn a lot of undesirable attention to themselves and become more of a liability than an asset. Of course, Leslie was a far less extrovert personality than Noël Coward and would not have wanted to sustain that sort of appointment. If he was to do anything in that capacity it would have to be by, perhaps, less obtrusive characteristics – not drawing attention to himself and remaining a free agent, completely independent of any departmental framework. He also realised it would have been quite impossible to produce the sort of films he wanted in a government harness.

His trip to Paris was undertaken at the invitation of the joint Propaganda Council to give advice and to discuss with the French the possible setting-up of a Film Entente for the pooling of ideas, production facilities, finance and so on. And for that purpose he had meetings with Giraudoux, Maurois and Noël Coward. On the other hand, the trip to British GHQ, Arras, must have appealed more strongly. Not only had it the charm of being unofficial but was more interesting as the invitation had come to him personally from the Director of Military Intelligence, Major-General Mason-MacFarlane. At the same time, Leslie would have the opportunity of meeting once again his old friend, Reginald Eves, RA (now an official War Artist with the BEF) who had painted several portraits of Leslie in the years just prior to the war. Eves was now engaged in doing 'heads' of some of the BEF's 'top brass' – among them General Gort and 'Mason-Mac'. Leslie had met Mason-Mac at Reggie Eves' studio before the war and was strongly attracted by

* Sir Campbell Stuart; *Opportunity Knocks Once*, Collins, 1952.

his sympathetic and arresting personality. They very readily saw eye-to-eye about the Nazis. Mason-MacFarlane was a man who spoke out, with an edge of sarcasm, if he disagreed about things – and he had frequently been in conflict with authorised views on Germany. In this Leslie found much to sympathise with.

Mason-Mac had been Military Attaché in both Vienna and Berlin (1937/39) and had witnessed the German Army's entry into both Austria and Czecho-Slovakia. Of this earlier phase in Mason-MacFarlane's career the *Dictionary of National Biography* has this to say:

> Concluding that Hitler's word was not to be trusted and that Germany was bent on unlimited expansion by military aggression, Mason-MacFarlane believed that to attempt to negotiate with the Nazis was futile and dangerous. Since war appeared to him inevitable he argued further that Hitler should not be allowed to choose his own time but should be driven into aggression when circumstances were unfavourable to him. These views brought Mason-MacFarlane into conflict with authority.
>
> To his staff he was a most inspiring leader. He had the panache and idiosyncrasy which focus, but also the common touch which retains, the loyalty of troops. He was impetuous to espouse causes which were lost or nearly so. Less well-liked by contemporaries and those under whom he served, he was too often right and there was a sarcastic edge to his tongue.

Precisely what was discussed in these two days that Leslie spent at British GHQ one will never know. It would seem that as Leslie had, as yet, no particular niche for his activities and with no formulated plans was feeling at rather a loose end, it may reasonably have occurred to him that he might serve his country in some other capacity, possibly of an 'intelligence' nature, without drawing undue attention to himself. Perhaps, after talking to Leslie, this may have occurred to Mason-MacFarlane as well. Indeed, it may have lain behind the invitation. I, for one, have never dismissed the idea that Leslie may, at about this time, have slipped into that category of person which the Germans referred to as V-Personen – and as such become a part-time intelligence agent. (*Vertrauens-Personen*: Confidence Persons, working occasionally, paid or unpaid, for a secret service.) Anybody, even as well-known as Leslie, could have entered this category quite casually and the world would have been none the wiser. This remained – and will remain since it is unlikely to be proved – a theory of many people I spoke to regarding the 'non-public' side of Leslie's activities in the war years. Much later, even the Germans themselves began to believe it.

In this respect, it is interesting to note that at the time Leslie was in Spain in 1943, on a lecture tour, Mason-Mac was Governor and GOC, Gilbraltar, and a man I met after the war, who served on the 'Rock' in the RAF, swore that he had met and spoken to Leslie there in May 1943. He imagined Leslie had come down to entertain the troops as a member of ENSA. Whether Leslie took time off from his visit to Madrid to go to Gibraltar I have no idea, but certainly not as a member of ENSA. Perhaps it was a case of mistaken identity, perhaps not. Nevertheless, the German Abwehr attributed all kinds of secret activities to the travels of British lecturers – many of whose journeys were innocent of anything more contentious than cultural propaganda. But at that time in Spain even a talking-parrot was suspected of being a British agent, preferably of communist persuasion. Whatever the truth of the story, Leslie could certainly have got down to Gilbraltar as the British Minister in Madrid, Arthur Yencken, had his own private plane.

Leslie was to go to Paris again in late April 1940, in company with Kenneth Clark, then Director of the Films Division, MOI. Here, it seemed was some opportunity to implement the earlier proposals of the Anglo-French Propaganda Council. Talks took place to finalise arrangements for a joint propaganda film starring Leslie and Danielle Darrieux. It was to be directed by René Clair. Though everything appeared to be settled the film was never produced. It was the last time Leslie was ever to see Paris. A fortnight later the Germans broke into Belgium and Holland and began the advance which was to culminate in not only the occupation of Paris but the complete French surrender.

Referring to these visits, the penultimate and the final one, Leslie wrote:

> But in spite of all, in spite of the cessation of normal travel, in spite of restrictions, red-tape and regulations, I was to see Paris again *twice* in the months that France slumbered behind her Maginot line. Again, there were forces at work, forces more omniscient that had planned it. The first was in the winter, the coldest for forty years, when we lunched and dined in a blaze of non-rationing. The last time was a lovely and early Spring . . .
> Almost as soon as we were out of the aeroplane, we walked slowly up the Champs Elysées from the Rond Point to the Arc de Triomphe – and marvelled at the setting sun, the soft warm

air . . . *L'ambiance inoubliable*. We marvelled at the traffic, at the
lovers shuffling along the gravel sidewalks and, like most other
people on this Spring evening, were drugged into a complacent
ignoring of the greatest crisis in human history. But every
moment of that visit was precious beyond the imagining of the
moment – because it *was* the last time, the last ever. . . .

The lovers were, indeed, shuffling along the Champs Elysées in a
state of torpor, unaware, if not quite as Leslie said – 'of the greatest
crisis in human history' – at least of the greatest crisis in French
history. Leslie as a great Francophile may be forgiven for seeing
history in French terms, but 'drugged' seems an apt word to
describe the dream-like unreality in which we all lived at this time.
We had all been slumbering, even as the French behind their
supposedly impregnable Maginot line, or, perhaps, we had been
blithely sleep-walking towards disaster. For most of us 'the phoney
war' had become 'the bore war'.

But a fortnight after Leslie's 'last ever' visit to Paris the twilit lull
that had comfortably encased us burst like a soap-bubble. In the
early hours of 10th May we were unpleasantly awakened by the
news that German panzers had crossed the eastern frontiers of
Belgium, Holland and Luxembourg, preceded as in Poland by an
onslaught of Stukas. Untouched by conflict we seemed scarcely able
to comprehend it. Apart from our activities in the Norwegian
campaign eight months had elapsed with little to indicate, save the
odd air-raid on the Orkney Islands, that the country was at war at
all. During this period the Chamberlain government had carried
on its bland and bloodless administration quite undisturbed by
Herr Hitler. He had in no way seriously incommoded us. It was
almost as if he was giving us a chance to think again, to change our
collective minds and opt out of a war which he might reasonably
have considered an error of judgement, hastily arrived at.

But on 10th May Hitler decided to temporise no more, thinking
he would soon bring us to our senses. At this precise moment our
administration changed hands. Mr Churchill took the place of Mr
Chamberlain and headed the coalition government that conducted
our affairs until the war's end, five years later.

The French High Command seemed not to have learnt the
lessons of panzer war. The German methods of *blitzkrieg*, perfected
in Spain and Poland, tore holes in the static lines of defence. The
lightly armoured infantry armies were swiftly penetrated and swept
aside by the mechanic masses of the tanks following the saturation

bombing of the Stukas. As the French armies fell back in disarray, Mr Churchill made a number of determined sorties to France – their object being to exhort Monsieur Reynaud, the French Premier, to hold on. Mr Churchill expatiated at length on much that could not be substantiated, and in which the French General Staff no longer believed. The principal cornerstone of this appeal to French honour and integrity was the well-intentioned but over-optimistic belief in American aid and participation. Even that strong and high-minded President, Franklin Roosevelt, could not guarantee to buttress the French Republic. His hands were tied by his own Congress, a Congress which would weigh its considerations of military aid very carefully in view of the French collapse. Besides, Congressmen had to consider their own security and the 'America First' principles on which their Constitution was founded.

Though Winston Churchill may have seen 'light at the end of the tunnel' that light was not even faintly visible to the bewildered Reynaud surrounded by his own defeatists. The faith of that little man who had, incredibly, said, 'I believe in France because I believe in miracles', was not to be rewarded by the survival of his beloved country, by miraculous or other means. And the promise of a Franco-British Union, with common and equal citizenship, must have seemed at this stage no better than a hastily improvised and tardily administered anodyne to a dying man. There only remained the Generals and the aged Marshal – and, finally, the table in the railway carriage at Compiègne round which they would sit faced by their conquerors, bargaining for small concessions, while France was systematically dismembered.

Within a few weeks the lowest point in the war had been reached. Incredible to think that in April the United States had believed in Allied victory: by June it was convinced of our defeat. The tragedy of the rapid and unexpected collapse of France shocked the world. To us, in Britain, the shock was to realise that we were now entirely alone. Round us the recriminations rose. The French General Staff, as a salve to military defeat, accused us of entirely letting them down, holding our contribution to their defence as pitiful. They predicted that within three weeks Britain would have its 'neck wrung like a chicken'. Haughtily, the aged Marshal Pétain referred to Mr Churchill's offer of union – so little faith had he in our ability to survive – as 'fusion with a corpse'.

The Battle of France was over and the Battle of Britain seemed about to begin. But at this moment, following his victory jig at Compiègne, Hitler was feeling magnanimous. On 19th July in his speech to the Reichstag he made us a peace offer. He appealed 'once more to reason and common sense in Great Britain as much as elsewhere' and he added: 'I can see no reason why this war need go on . . . I am grieved to think of the sacrifices it must claim . . . Possibly Mr Churchill will brush it aside by saying it is merely born of fear and doubt of final victory. In that case I shall have relieved my conscience in regard to the things to come.'

Various representations were made through the Vatican, Sweden and the United States where the German Chargé d'Affaires communicated on the subject with our Ambassador. It was decided, however, to dismiss Hitler's gesture and in a broadcast our Foreign Secretary 'brushed aside' Hitler's 'summons to capitulate to his will' with the words, 'We shall not stop fighting until Freedom is secure.' Within a few days of this rejection, Hitler put into effect his invasion plan, 'Operation Sea-Lion'.

Our relations with the United States, though cordial, were not such as to give us great confidence in our conduct of the war. Though certain supplies of ammunition and old rifles had been forthcoming in a quiet way the primary request for 'the loan of forty or fifty of your older destroyers', which Mr Churchill had initiated on becoming Prime Minister, was to be the subject of much delay and procrastination. During these critical times it was a subject to which Mr Churchill repeatedly returned and many overtures were made for its implementation in what appear to be blunter though less hopeful terms. Much of it was involved with the future of the British Fleet and the guarantee of its arrival in the Western hemisphere should Britain be defeated. Over this the Prime Minister could only give his word and much depended on American interpretation of it.

This was the crux of the matter. How far could America go, and how far would she go, in view of our precarious position? In the end the matter of the destroyers took four months to resolve in our favour, by which time we had won the Battle of Britain, Sea Lion was indefinitely postponed and American opinion had been coaxed into the belief that we were not a nation of 'quitters'. We had to reassure Americans of our faith in ourselves and this was the duty of not only the Prime Minister but of everyone concerned, and by every means of human communication.

Our principal information services, the Ministry of Information and the BBC, issued daily reminders of the facts that we were 'alive and well' – and even beginning to win the battle. The world, and particularly the United States, must know not only how we fought but what we were fighting for – and that we were determined, as Mr Churchill said, 'never to give in'. It was a most difficult and vexatious task persuading Americans to commit themselves. We were asking them to gamble on us while the issue was in doubt. Nor were they at all keen, at this stage, to participate actively.

As Sir John Wheeler-Bennett expressed it in *Special Relationships:* *

The predominant desire of every American I talked to was an unqualified determination to keep out of the war by all possible means and woe betide those who might be foolhardly enough to try to make her do otherwise. Their attitude to England varied . . . On the whole, the inherent isolationism of the Middle West made for anti-British feeling – partly because they distrusted the anglophile Eastern seaboard and partly because of an unpleasant nagging impression that the British were 'too clever by half'. The climate of ideas which I found in the Middle West were prevalent throughout the country. The American people as a whole were determined to keep out of the war at all costs. They were united in condemnation of Hitler and his policies, but they were wary of the British.

* Macmillan, 1975.

CHAPTER FOUR

The Various Voices of Britain
July-October 1940

At this low ebb in our affairs, as Hitler prepared his strategy for Operation Sea-Lion, the overture to which was the Battle of Britain, the BBC faced a new and daunting task of presenting Britain with its back very much to the wall. But it was a different Britain – very much in the crucible of events and fired by a new determination. There was to be no hint of our past in this new approach, no looking back on what we may have been. We were simply a small island, geographically far from impregnable, fighting for its life. As did the country so did the BBC marshal the most up to date and least perfidious ammunition for the battle ahead.

One of principal spokesmen for the impending battle on the home ground was J.B. Priestley, who had been coming regularly to the microphone to present our case. He was to become, as much as Mr Churchill, the 'Voice of Britain'. His *Postscripts*, after each Sunday's main news bulletin, were eagerly listened to by the nation as a whole even if, in some sectarian quarters, their 'messages' were considered a little too provocative for comfort. But Priestley spoke from the collective heart of the country rather than its head. He spoke for the small man suddenly afflicted by the political sickness of Europe. Once this 'Fascist' sickness was purged, Priestley felt, we could begin the reconstruction, if not of Europe, at least of our own country – and on very different lines, with no back-sliding to the past. He saw new political verities emerging and a new Britain rising from the ashes of the blinkered, profiteering, happy-go-lucky bad old days when we were the victims of the illogicalities of the balance of power.

Of course, not all people were as public-spirited as he and saw in some of his broadcasts statements of intent that discomforted them. They felt our business was to win the war – not devise panaceas for the future. Besides, many of them were fighting for the preservation of ideas and beliefs dear to them. They did not want them swept away. Priestley saw such people as diehards who wanted to get back to the old status quo once the war was out of the way. In his gruff, North Country manner he castigated them for what he considered to be partisan positions of self interest, and drew their attention to the more harmonious, Beveridge-type Britain he envisaged after the battle was over. In the main Priestley was to be proved right. Britain was never to be the same again and many of the diehards were swept away in the war never to return. The swing of the 1945 election seemed conclusive. It may only be remarked that at this stage in the war his somewhat polemical approach was not guaranteed to win him entire favour here nor, for that matter, in the United States where the system was diametrically opposed to the 'brave new world' he anticipated.

By mid-July Hitler's air force had begun the softening-up process, the prelude to Operation Sea-Lion, and the battle was daily visible in the skies over Sussex and Kent. At this moment, the BBC was looking round for new spokesmen for its North American 'beam'. It was particularly seeking speakers with knowledge of America and persuasion with its people. Perhaps a copy of Leslie Howard's *Notes on American Propaganda* had found its way to the BBC for an approach was now made to him with a view to his broadcasting in the recently inaugurated *Britain Speaks* series. There is some correspondence on this though most of the negotiations seem to have been done by telephone. Mr Anthony Weymouth, a senior Talks Producer, was mainly responsible for the initial arrangements, as he was for the editing and general supervision of the series. Leslie was, in fact, to broadcast in several other programmes during July.

His voice was first heard in the United States and Canada at about 7.30 pm (EST) on 16th July 1940. It was broadcast from London in the early hours of 17th July to coincide with evening news bulletins in North America. He came to the microphone under the aegis of J.B. Priestley – 'under his wing' as he was later to say. It was as a fledgling broadcaster that Priestley introduced him in the second half of his programme. I do not think that either Leslie or the BBC had entered into any firm commitment, at this stage, as to the number of broadcasts he would make in the *Britain Speaks* series. They simply 'played it by ear', but a fortnight later he was back again at the microphone, this time on his own, and from then on became a regular contributor to the series until January 1941, when he relinquished them owing to starting production of *Pimpernel Smith*. In the end he made twenty-seven broadcasts in the series (with repeats going out till April 1941) besides making many appearances

in the *Brains Trust*, *Britain to America* and *Answering You* series. He also
acted in BBC productions of *The Petrified Forest*, *Nelson* and readings
from *Hamlet*.

In the company of such experienced broadcasters as C.E.M.
Joad, Arthur Newell (President of the American Outpost in Great
Britain), L.W. Brockington, Stanley Maxted, Christopher Morley,
Gerald Bullett and J.B. Priestley, Leslie must have seemed something
of an amateur. Most of them were professional writers and
broadcasters with a gift for phrasing and able to conjure words from
the air, even when unscripted, and certainly never lost for them.
Leslie had spent most of his life learning lines written by others and
though he had written witty stories, of theatrical inspiration, for *The
New Yorker* and *Vanity Fair* in the twenties and thirties, they were
more the effusions of an actor with a literary turn than precise
products of a practising writer.

However, Leslie tackled his broadcasts with his usual immense
enthusiasm, writing and presenting them all himself and, if they
started uncertainly, they soon developed a depth and range and an
individuality of style very much his own. In fact, the BBC seriously
considered him to take over the *Postscript* slot when Priestley gave it
up towards the end of October. Though Leslie only did one
Postscript programme on the 10th November, *Picture Post*, in its issue
of 30th November, under the title 'Is He Priestley's Successor'
began an article on Leslie with the words:

> So the downright, take-it-or-leave-it, North Country Postscript of
> Priestley may be replaced by the indolent but elegant diction of
> Leslie Howard. If the BBC makes this switch-over then it will
> certainly achieve a triumph of contrast.

I doubt very much if Leslie would seriously have considered the
job had even the BBC offered it to him. Not only was he modest
enough to realise his limitations as a broadcaster, particularly in
such a 'cat-bird-seat' as *Postscript*, but he found, with his film plans,
one broadcast a week was enough – and sometimes more than
enough – to cope with. Besides, he rightly felt that whatever assets
he had as broadcaster would be better deployed on the American,
rather than the home, front. He had considerable persuasion with
Americans, was almost a household word and frequently made a
point of bringing Americans in by discussing American themes,
Jefferson, the Constitution, the Presidential Election and so on.
This gave him an intimacy with American families sitting round

their own firesides, thereby completely avoiding that somewhat intimidating BBC description 'of a personality commenting on topics of the hour' from a too strictly British point of view.

Certainly with Leslie there was no danger of a sectarian viewpoint which might upset Americans. In this respect he was quite different to Priestley, being basically apolitical. Though there was always the fighting element of Britain at bay in Jack Priestley's broadcasts, the political undertones were inescapable. If they crept into his American broadcasts they could only have been misunderstood by the bulk of Americans who had little faith in even the mildest extension of socialism. Though Leslie and Jack Priestley were great friends – and there was much for common cause in the general humanities of their war-aims – there was a gulf between their ideologies. Leslie's attitude towards politics was freer, less schematic, at times almost non-existent. If he had any leanings at all they were liberal and laissez-faire. He always admitted he would have made 'a rotten planner' as he suspected planners were doctrinaire sort of people, lacking humanity, who once they got power put pressure on – and this led to political enforcement. There were enough enforcers in the world in the persons of Stalin, Hitler and Mussolini. No doubt these men were great planners; they were also mechanically inhuman. Leslie was politically naive, believing in a sort of ultimate human goodness whose only guidelines were Christian ethics, and these were certainly not enforceable. If this was a fault it was perhaps a good one when we needed unity in our efforts to overcome evil and a politically uncluttered approach to our problem of survival.

While Leslie persevered with his broadcasts through the height of the Battle of Britain and the subsequent Blitz on London he, at the same time, pushed on with his plans for the 'escape story'. He had begun to realise that the story as it stood, involving the rescue of an Austrian painter whose face didn't fit with the Nazis, was too limited for the central theme of a film. It would have to be a lot bigger and broader, involving a number of rescues conceived and carried out by the central character as well as a number of confrontations with the Nazis. This central character would be played by Leslie – but who and what was he to be?

One day, talking it over with Archie MacDonnell, they hit upon the idea of a professor who would initiate these rescue operations and be the principal figure in the story. Archie confessed he had in mind the prototype for this character, a former professor of archaeology at Oxford, a scholarly though absent-minded man who had had the habit of taking his students for 'digs' in various countries during many a long vacation. They agreed, however, that though aesthetically right, their professor would have to be bolder and more adventurous than Archie's archetype, and have a bit more style about him, a sort of composite of Shaw's 'Higgins' and Stamford Raffles.

'Why not a modern Pimpernel?' Archie suggested.

'Well – not exactly,' said Leslie, a little averse to the idea of cashing in on *The Scarlet Pimpernel* in which he had been successful some years before. (In fact, Leslie never cared much for the finally selected title *Pimpernel Smith*, finding it catchpenny and trivial. The story of the rescue from the guillotine of persecuted aristocrats and Huguenots in the 1790s seemed to Leslie to have little to do with Hitler's racial proscriptions terminating in the gas-chambers of the 1940s.)

'Let's just call him Smith,' said Leslie. And Smith he became, Archie only venturing the Christian name Horatio which added a dash of adventure to humility. Still, it was clear – despite Leslie's misgivings – that a kind of modern Pimpernel had emerged. Professor Horatio Smith would have, under a learned and suitably vague exterior, an unsuspected panache and vitality. Beneath the spectacles, behind the short-sighted, studious eyes loomed the man of action who would organise the rescue of artists, professors, scientists and pastors who were, at this moment, under close scrutiny by the Nazis for failure to cooperate. Smith's job would be to get them out of Germany before Hitler's SS, experts in truth-twisting and distortion, manufactured those charges of crimes against the State which would land them in concentration-camps, or worse, gas-chambers.

For the purpose of the film a story line was now hammered out in which the Professor's archaeology students would assist in the rescue operations. An early German community of cave-dwellers had come to the Professor's attention, and needed closer investigation. This interesting stone-age dwelling, successfully dug by his student earth-removers and filled with suitable discoveries, became Professor Smith's head-quarters and the eventual hiding place of his emigrés. The actual site of the film 'dig' was an elaborately constructed subterranean affair in the Denham studios. Such was the relation of fact to fiction.

Quite apart from the mechanics of the scenario, Leslie realised the story had to be relevant to the issues at stake and the deep divisions between ourselves and the Nazis. If it didn't face these facts and exploit them then, indeed, as Leslie had earlier said, film entertainment would never succeed in being more 'than a trivial occupation where there remained such tremendous and historic tasks to be done'. The film must mirror faithfully the 'tremendous and historic' times through which we were living, otherwise it would not only be insincere and trivial but useless as encouragement and propaganda.

By the time Leslie had reached this stage in the scenario he badly needed an experienced screen-writer, which Archie admittedly wasn't, to forge all their thoughts into a screen-play. It was while filming *Pygmalion* with Gabriel Pascal in 1938 that Leslie had first met a young writer called Anatole de Grunwald, Russian by birth though brought up and educated in England. Among the screen-writers engaged on *Pygmalion* his name appears alongside those of W.P. Lipscomb, Cecil Lewis, Ian Dalrymple and last, but not least among this camaraderie of screen-credits, George Bernard Shaw. Two years had elapsed since that first meeting and 'Tolly' (as he was always known) was now writing screen-plays for Filippo del Giudice, head of Two Cities' Films. He already had several good credits to his name, including the scenario of Terence Rattigan's *French Without Tears*.

One of Leslie's associates at this time was P.C. Samuel, a production manager of considerable experience who was to work on the majority of Leslie's war-films, and it was he who unreservedly recommended 'Tolly' as 'one of the cleverest young writers in the business – and probably the fastest'. Needless to say, 'Phil' Samuel had heard a lot about the 'escape story' from Leslie himself, and being an experienced film-maker realised that as it stood the story, though interesting, was scarcely a commercial proposition.

This clever and fast writer de Grunwald was a tonic to Leslie and he found his own ideas stimulated and revived by the freshness of Tolly's imagination and inventiveness. However, at this precise moment, though the story line was now clear and the screen-play well advanced, *Pimpernel Smith* as a film remained, stubbornly, financially insolvent. This was scarcely surprising for the Battle of Britain still raged overhead and the threatened invasion awaited its cue from Hitler.

While no doubt wondering about the outcome of these momentous events Leslie, in company with MacDonnell, Tolly and a cameraman, went down to Oxford to decide on a location for Professor Smith's college. For this purpose they stayed at the Randolph Hotel for several days discussing and planning the University sequence and writing this important prelude to the Professor's adventures. His college rooms would, of course, have to be duplicated in the studio but they would be based, as nearly as possible, on the actual professor's rooms, with all the necessary archaeological properties, pottery, stone-implements and so on, retrieved from various digs. Also by close observation and contact with the real thing Leslie would be able to think his way into the skin of the Professor.

Though it was important to get the background clearly established in all their minds and to get the feel of a university town aesthetically and visually, it has always struck me as an extraordinary example of undiluted optimism that such elaborate preparations could be made when, first, they still had no money to finance the film and, second, more importantly perhaps, German paratroops might shortly be dropping all over Britain. In the best of times film people are inclined to live in a fantasy world – but at a time like this their faith in themselves must surely have struck them as more than a little mad. Such, anyway, at that time was the relation of fiction to fact. It may only be said that Leslie's theories about 'the inertia which strikes artists of all kinds in times of violence and destruction' seemed not to apply to himself, and his optimism, in the circumstances, was remarkable.

From Oxford Leslie returned to London in time for another *Britain Speaks* broadcast. He still continued to lead his bisected existence quite happily – his weekend foot, as it were, planted at Stowe Maries and the other pied-à-terre, with Violette in London. They had now moved from Manor Street to a new, rented, flat in Flood Street – Swan Court. It was on the top floor, a sort of penthouse apartment, a little exposed in air-raids, with a tiny balcony running round it.

Leslie had decided to visit Portsmouth to get material for a broadcast on Civil Defence and as Seaman Howard was stationed quite nearby at Fareham he had got in touch with me. Leslie was to be taken on a tour of inspection round the badly bomb-damaged old sea-port town by a Mr Thompson, the chief air raid warden – and would I meet him later? As he said in his broadcast 'A Day by the Sea':

'I finally parted reluctantly from the inimitable Mr Thompson and was glad to find my son waiting for me, looking bright, cheerful and ship-shape in his uniform of a Royal Naval rating. I had not seen him for some time and we went to have a cup of tea and discuss life – and forget air-raids . . . '

Professor Smith and shop assistant – Leslie with Violette in her first and only film role – *Pimpernel Smith*.

Professor Smith and romantic interest – Leslie and Mary Morris in *Pimpernel Smith*.

A mixed gathering at the British Embassy – *Pimpernel Smith* – Leslie, Roland Pertwee, Raymond Huntley, A. E. Matthews and Jean Compton (Mrs Arthur Howard).

Noel Coward discussing with Leslie his 'voice only' appearence in *In Which We Serve*.

When we reached the little side-street cafe we sat down, ordered some tea and exchanged the usual civilities – I don't think we 'discussed life' – congratulating ourselves on having so far survived the war. After a long moment, during which Leslie studied me reflectively, he confessed he was thinking of doing another broadcast with a serviceman. He had recently done one with an American who had come over and joined up as a soldier in the British Army, winning a Military Medal at Dunkirk.

'I should like to do one with the Senior Service this time,' he said.

'Good idea,' I replied innocently.

'Why don't I interview you?' he shot at me quickly, disarmingly. I think I may have looked a bit startled, suspecting, unfairly perhaps, an element of nepotism.

'Nonsense. Why not you instead of any old sailor? We could work on it together, a joint father and son composition.' He shrugged. 'I don't think the BBC will object.'

'My Admiral might, though,' I said.

'Oh, don't worry about that, old boy. I'll fix it and you'll get some leave.'

'I doubt if he'll release me,' I replied. Leslie looked very surprised.

'I see. Forgive me, Wink, I never realised you were that important to the war-effort.'

Shrugging aside his leg-pull, I lowered my voice.

'The fact is – I'm on an alert.'

Leslie glanced quickly round the café as if I was about to indulge in some careless talk. He leaned forward, close to me.

'Alert?' he whispered. 'What sort of . . . ?'

'Invasion,' I said quietly between my teeth.

'Good God!' He looked at me as if uncertain whether I'd made a joke in poor taste.

'Are you serious?'

'Never more so. I've been sleeping in a cow-shed and standing-to at 5 a.m. every morning to repel Germans.'

'Incredible!' he replied. 'They don't tell us anything in London. How long has this been going on?'

'About a week. Mind you, I think we'll be stood down tonight. They say the tides won't be right for another month.'

'Well, well . . . ' was all he could muster. At that moment the air-raid sirens went. Nobody in the cafe stirred, just looked up a little sadly.

'Have another cup of tea?' I asked him.

'Yes, good idea,' he replied absently. I had just got to the counter to ask for two more cups of tea when the naval 'four-sevens' opened up. A moment later an ARP Warden appeared and told everyone they would have to take cover. Leslie and I walked round the corner to the nearest shelter. There were quite a lot of people in it already. The ARP Warden stood near the door, looking up. He didn't have to wait long. There came a whistle and, then, a closer, rattling sound like pebbles cascading onto a tin roof. We all crowded back. The bomb thudded down not far away, shaking the shelter.

'Bastards!' somebody said. 'Penny Street getting it again.' The guns took up the barrage – followed by more 'crumps'. When it quietened down a bit, Leslie went forward and spoke to the Air Raid Warden. They chatted for quite a long time. I was impressed by Leslie's coolness under fire.

The All Clear went about half an hour later and Leslie and I walked up to the station. Apparently, there had been an attack on the dockyard by Stukas, but the barrage-balloons had proved quite effective. Two Stukas had been shot down.

'A pleasant day by the sea, I must say,' Leslie said. 'Quite bracing!' He patted my collar, as one did with sailors.

'Lucky!' he remarked.

As we waited for the London train he asked: 'Now what about this interview with a sailor? Are you keen?'

'If it would get me out of Portsmouth for a day or two I would be,' I replied.

'Sorry about that,' he said, as if the raid was, in some way, his fault. 'I'll ask the BBC to get in touch with your Admiral – to see if he can spare you!'

'The CO at the Training Establishment would do,' I told him, as the train drew in. As he got in he turned back, leaning from the window.

'We're living dangerously. Take care!'

'Aye, aye, Sir.' I came to attention and gave him a salute as the train drew away.

Leslie was right. We *were* living dangerously. Whenever we happened to be together we drew bombs like iron filings to a magnet. It seemed the German air force was determined to liquidate us. Perhaps there was some sort of jinx on us. Twice at Stowe Maries we had been bombed *in situ*. One evening seated in Leslie's room with tankards of beer and tobacco smoke curling from our pipes, we had been rudely shaken by a tip and run bomber caught by flak and searchlights. He started ditching his bombs about half a mile from the house, each one seemingly closer. I remember shouting, 'On your face!' and we fell on the floor in a cloud of tobacco smoke. The bombs rumbled round us, shaking down ceiling plaster and pictures from the walls.

On another occasion we were standing outside the front door riveted by a German bomber held like a silver toy in the searchlights when, suddenly, we heard the stick of bombs coming towards us like successive express trains leaving a tunnel. At that precise moment the front door slammed and I fell face down on the stone steps putting my hands rather futilely over my head. I remember my body actually bouncing up as the bombs fell in the neighbouring woods. Through half-closed eyes I saw bright orange flashes as they detonated. It was all over in a matter of seconds. Then, the front door was cautiously opened and a shadowy head appeared.

'Are you all right, old boy?' asked a shocked voice. 'I thought, at first, you'd come in with me – then, realised, to my horror, I'd shut you out among the bombs! They must have been close. You're not hurt?'

I got up, dusting myself off. 'Not a scratch,' I replied. 'Mind you, if they'd been any closer, you wouldn't be asking questions. We'd have all gone up with the house around us!'

A few days after Leslie's visit to Portsmouth I was summoned before the Captain among a group of requestmen.

'Off cap! Quick march!' said the Master-at-Arms. 'Request to broadcast, Sir.' There was an unpleasant edge of sarcasm to his voice.

'To what?' said the Captain. The request was repeated. The Captain, a lantern-jawed, slightly perplexed-looking man shuffled the application paper on his desk, studying it bleakly. This was something out of his experience altogether – one of his ratings being asked to broadcast. Security might be involved, to say nothing of King's Regulations, Admiralty Instructions and the Naval Discipline Act. The blue eyes under the bushy-eyebrows shifted to study me.

'What, precisely, Howard, are you going to talk about?' he asked with a gleam of baleful humour.

'They haven't told me yet, Sir.'

'Haven't told you!'

'No, Sir.'

'But this broadcast, Howard, what part d'you play in it?'

'I believe I'm interviewed, Sir, by the BBC.'

'It says here *Britain Speaks*. Is that you?'

'I shouldn't think so, Sir.'

'I see. Have they sent you a questionnaire?'

'No, Sir.'

The Captain shrugged helplessly as if faced by something totally impractical and irrelevant, the sort of thing dreamed-up by unservice-minded people. When he spoke it was in an aside, as if half to himself and half for the benefit of the Master-at-Arms.

'It really is most irregular. Trouble is they're not a service department. Don't work to KR's like we do. Rather long-haired.' He stretched out his enunciation of 'long-haired' in an indefinite, though disapproving, way. But there was nothing indefinite in the electric-blue look his eyes gave me a second later.

'Just remember, Howard, you're under the Official Secrets Act – and the Naval Discipline Act. No loose talk about activities down here and so on.' He waved his hand. 'And get your hair cut!'

'Yes, Sir.'

'Very well, Master-at-Arms. Approved.'

The Master-at-Arms stiffened like a ram-rod and barked: 'Approved! On cap! About turn! Quick march!'

When I got home I found Richard Green, the actor, staying at Stowe Maries for a few days. He had just come from Hollywood to join up and looked very sun-tanned among our white English faces. He seemed to me different from the rather prettified youth who still loomed on hoardings at railway stations advertising a hair-cream product. I pulled his leg about it.

'Oh, come on, Wink. That was my pre-war face!' he said, dismissing the raillery. Over the next couple of days I worked with Leslie on the broadcast 'Interview with a Sailor'. My part in it struck me as rather bogus and embarrassing. For some reason Leslie would insist on including excerpts from a poem of mine – a somewhat melancholy one about the submarine *Thetis* which had sunk, tragically, on its trials in Liverpool Bay. I warned him about my Captain being a bit of a tartar and what he had had to say about the Official Secrets Act.

'Anyway, I bet the BBC cut it,' I told him. 'It's a rotten poem – and doesn't do justice.'

'You're always too modest, Wink,' was Leslie's rejoinder. 'Besides, as far as the Official Secrets Act is concerned, the *Thetis* sank before the war – not in action. Naturally, it's a rather sad poem but none the worse for that, and it fills out a nice spot in the programme.

Remember, we were running short.' So, on that basis, the poem stayed in.

The following morning Leslie, Richard and I set off to drive to London. Driving in a car it was difficult to know if a raid was in progress. Alerts varied from sector to sector and with the engine running it was impossible to hear anything. Somewhere along the Kingston By-pass we were flagged down by an irate ARP Warden who told us to get out immediately and take cover as there were raiders overhead. He directed us to his post, a sand-bagged affair in the middle of the road where a few other motorists were already crouching. Bombs had apparently been falling in the fields and woods nearby. After about half-an-hour of this we obtained the Warden's permission to push on and arrived without further incident at Leslie's Flood Street flat.

That afternoon at Flood Street seemed part of a diabolical pattern. As far as Leslie and I were concerned it always seemed connected with tea or beer-drinking. We were all sitting down to tea in the penthouse flat at Swan Court when we heard what sounded like gun-fire some distance away. Putting down our cups, we adjourned to the terraced walk outside to see what was happening. From this roof-top position one not only got a splendid view over a large part of London but of the river Thames stretched out far below. There seemed to be a dog-fight in progress somewhere in the direction of Bermondsey. We could actually see the fighters wheeling about like specks in the sky and hear the periodic crackle of their machine-guns. To begin with we could not see any bombers. Richard Green was tremendously impressed – as if the whole thing had been staged for his benefit – and was enjoying his first grand-stand view of the Battle of Britain. I suppose at a safe distance it must all have looked rather unreal, like a mock air-fight from *Hell's Angels*.

After a few minutes I began to feel the fight was moving in our direction, the gunfire growing sharper and louder. We could now see the bombers round which the fighters were angrily weaving. One of the bombers fell away over South London, smoke pouring from its tail. The air battle was now crossing the Thames, approaching us in a north-westerly direction. I remarked on this to Leslie.

'I disagree, old boy,' he replied airily but with utter conviction. 'They're making for the City.' I was quite happy to be convinced of that and as I was rather proud of my ability to identify enemy aircraft. I indicated to the others that I could now see three Heinkel 3s quite clearly.

'No, no, Wink – Dorniers,' Leslie corrected me as he watched, fascinated, the approach of the bombers. At this stage the whole thing began to look to Richard a lot less like an old Hollywood film.

'Much as I hate to disagree with you, Leslie, I think they *are* coming this way. Oughtn't we to take cover?' And Leslie, aiming at utter sang-froid as an old London resident, replied there was nothing really to worry about, except that the tea was certainly getting a little cold. No further encouragement being necessary we gladly went back inside but before anyone had so much as got a tea-cup to his lips there came the rushing sound – with which Leslie and I were altogether too familiar – of a bomb descending. As it landed with a violent crash only a street or two away no further time was wasted discussing in which direction the Heinkels – or Dorniers – were headed. We were out of that room in a flash and running down the stairs to what we hoped was terra firma. The next bomb, in fact, struck the building and detonated at the bottom of the lift-shaft with a diabolical explosion.

As Leslie described it in a broadcast, 'First Fortnight of the Battle of Britain': 'A great gaping hole had been blown in the building and the iron window frames had been torn out like so much paper and lay twisted in the courtyard. The rest of that raid we spent in the shelter attached to some tenements down the street. The tenement dwellers were our hosts and very good they were to us.' Later that night, crawling in a taxi through the blitz and black-out we reached the BBC just in time for our broadcast to America.

Two days afterwards I returned to Portsmouth – rather relieved to be out of London – to resume my duties as an ordinary seaman, and it was to be several months before I saw Leslie again. In fact, we did not meet again until the production of *Pimpernel Smith* had become a reality. We were not, however, to be entirely out of touch for a month or two later he wrote me a somewhat cautionary letter couched in strong, though paternal, terms. The circumstances were these. After I got back to Portsmouth I found myself among a group of candidates selected for possible commissions in the RNVR. In due course, we were sent along to the King Alfred training base at Hove and, after being put through a rigorous course in signals, navigation and gunnery, were turned into temporary officers and gentlemen of the 'hostilities only' variety. I, thus, became a Probationary, Temporary, Acting Sub-Lieutenant of the Royal Naval Volunteer Reserve. Leslie was delighted at my promotion – though thinking my title a trifle insecure – and decided, there and then, to bolster my somewhat meagre sub-lieutenant's pay by giving me an allowance of £3 a week. This would not only enable me to purchase extra kit and other small sundries but allow me a bit more latitude to live in a style more becoming a temporary officer.

However, the extra money appeared to have gone to my head. I decided to become engaged, announcing shortly thereafter to all and sundry my intentions of getting married. This was not exactly what Leslie intended when he made me the allowance and, when my mother informed him of the dire course I was set upon, he wrote me the long, serious and cautionary letter to which I have referred. It was the most sensible, intelligent and wise letter I ever received from him, yet, hot-headed and impulsive as I was, I paid scant attention to it, and rushed, even faster, into the ill-advised marriage. I will only add here that his prognostications of disaster attendant upon my 'impulsive decision' were entirely justified – and he was proved right. My hastily hurried-into wartime marriage was not to last. In fact, it proved as Temporary and Probationary as my 'hostilities only' commission.

*

Leslie and Violette did not return to Swan Court except to collect their personal belongings as the building was without services and, owing to extensive bomb-damage and another unexploded bomb nearby, was considered unsafe. Only one trunk had been lost in a cellar store-room – yet we had all had a fortunate escape. As Leslie said: 'One bomb had fallen on the street where we had stood the day before. I looked at the wreckage fascinated, for the bomb had hit the exact spot where we had taken refuge. Seven of the humble, friendly people we had been with lost their lives . . . '

Violette and Leslie moved temporarily to one of those West End hotels where no one during the Blitz went to bed above basement level.

One arrived at the hotel with a suitcase, booked into a room, went out about one's business and, finally, on returning simply went back to the bedroom to change into pyjamas. One then descended to a subterranean area where a large number of people were sleeping, or preparing to sleep, side by side, on mattresses and camp-beds in dormitory style. It was divided into three areas of occupation – men, women and married couples – by discreetly drawn curtains. Here, one was almost as safe from bombs as Londoners sleeping in the deep Underground Stations. It was said of this hotel that one could go to sleep beside a Cabinet Minister and wake up beside a theatrical impresario – the Cabinet Minister having departed, while one slept, for a late night debate at the House of Commons and the impresario having arrived from a theatre after the evening performance. In fact, Leslie himself returned to this bomb-proof dormitory after appearing in a radio show with Sarah Churchill and Vic Oliver which was presented at the old Criterion Theatre forty feet below street level. Here people worked, ate and slept while air-raids thundered overhead.

By the beginning of October, Leslie decided he had had enough of living in London under Blitz conditions and sleeping on mattresses in hotel basements. 'After some days of day and night bombardment, including a direct hit on my apartment building, I decided to heed the exhortation of the popular song and "get out of town". In fact, I got out of town with a quite undignified haste, arguing to myself that one can prepare a film for production just as well in the country.'

Leslie's decision to leave London was probably hastened by an invitation from Anthony Havelock-Allan, with whom he was shortly to work on a documentary film involving three Dominion servicemen. Havelock-Allan and his wife, Valerie Hobson, were then living in a house known as The Cottage, Purton Lane, Farnham Royal, and I imagine Leslie and Violette moved in with them on a sharing arrangement. The Cottage appears to have been more commodious than its name implies, almost of concertina-like proportions, for in addition to Leslie and Violette and the Havelock-Allans it served as a sort of 'shooting box', in the filmic sense, for quite a number of people connected with Leslie's film plans including Harold Huth, Irene Howard, his sister, and finally Mary Morris. In fact, for the next six months, it became the virtual hotel of a complete film community and people came and went according to work schedule.

Another person who joined the community at the Cottage was Roland Pertwee. As I described earlier he was an old friend of Leslie's from the Hollywood scene of the thirties. He was also an extremely versatile dialogue writer. One evening Leslie showed him a script of *Pimpernel Smith* and asked him whether he would mind doing some work on it, pointing-up and reshaping scenes, writing additional dialogue and so on – to which Roland agreed. This, of course, happened some weeks before production started. But it was not always Leslie's method of working which could be infuriatingly fluid and often went on during production. One of Leslie's besetting sins was a weakness for re-writing scenes shortly before they were put on film, sometimes improvising dialogues minutes before a scene was shot. Roland was frequently obliged to do this, re-writing rapidly before the bell went for a take.

To some, this was almost a sine qua non of film production and they were far from surprised. They were old hands at the game and sat round sipping cups of tea till the revisions were ready. To others, particularly actors, who had come prepared to work according to the shooting script only to find the scene they had learnt gone and three new pages of dialogue being concocted on the side of the set it could be an upsetting modus operandi.

In an affectionate letter of reminiscence written some years later Roland recalled this period of re-writing and Leslie's methods of improvisation.

I spent the mornings writing and in the evening read what I had written to Leslie. It was difficult to know what he thought of the stuff for it was his practice to sit in a low armchair with a copy of *The Tatler* or some other illustrated glossy on the floor between his feet. While I read he would idly turn the pages and sometimes would chuckle softly, but whether at some witticism of mine or some predicament of 'Briggs', the butler, is anybody's guess. At the end he would hold out his hand and go upstairs with the typescript to mull it over in seclusion.

It was rare for him to play a scene as written and in the final analysis what appeared on the screen was an amalgam of my stuff and his own improvisations. His mind did not work quickly and as he refused to hurry it, he was a great squanderer of time. On many occasions he did not appear on the set until noon. This characteristic cost the studio a hell of a lot of money and was, indeed, the despair of producers; for while he ruminated upon this or that the clock ticked away thousands of pounds and played havoc with the shooting schedule. When this obvious fact was pointed out to him Leslie was quite unmoved and would smilingly argue that the only thing that mattered was to get the best out of the scene. If the best was not available before eleven or twelve in the morning it was a pity but could not be helped. The answer is, of course, that he was a perfectionist and what to the business mind suggested idleness and a lack of discipline was, in fact, an example of incorruptible conscience.

During this pre-production period, Leslie continued to lead his usual divided life as far as domestic arrangements were concerned.

For the purpose of BBC recordings, script and business conferences, he spent the working week in London or Farnham Royal and Saturdays and Sundays in Westcott – a little like Persephone dividing her time between the dark, hot world of Pluto and the harvest-fields of Mother Ceres. Leslie accepted this as quite normal – it was a factor common to many people in the entertainment world – and managed quite happily to reconcile one with the other. Anyway, his ideas about home and family life were never particularly conventional – and he lived by the conditions of the moment. Every week-end he dutifully arrived at Stowe Maries and turned himself into the father-figure, the family man, for a couple of days. He had convinced himself that there was nothing odd about living in two worlds, in separate compartments, so long as one kept them watertight. If my mother had found this a strain to begin with, she gradually accustomed herself to its inevitability, and Leslie, dividing himself into neat halves and hurrying between the poles of his affection, played his dual roles with conditioned skill.

If this really satisfied nobody but Leslie, it was the dilemma he had to live with, the way he had stacked his cards. He had no intention of sacrificing one way of life for the other. In fact, he felt nothing could be so cruel or so unnecessary as having to make decisions that would hurt others. And so he went on trying to satisfy, and accommodate, everyone and, perhaps, in the end only succeeded in satisfying his own conscience.

CHAPTER FIVE

Into Production
November 1940-May 1941

The move to The Cottage considerably facilitated Leslie's production plans for *Pimpernel Smith*, and it was not far from the Denham studios. Much to everyone's relief the very protracted period of gestation attendant on Leslie's plans appeared to be over. After the many vicissitudes of its creative labour *Pimpernel Smith* now really seemed about to make its entrance into the cinematic world.

An 'angel' had been found in the shape of Lewis Jackson whose company, British National Films, was prepared to advance the production finance and a contract was duly signed on 31st October 1940. Studio and office space could now be firmly booked and Phil Samuel, Leslie's production manager, set busily about its implementation. It was, perhaps, a good omen that Leslie was returning to the Denham studios, owned and built by Sir Alexander Korda, where in 1935 he had made the highly successful *Scarlet Pimpernel*. The only other change that was to be made now – a purely academic one which would not affect production – was that Professor Smith's university became Cambridge instead of Oxford. An exploratory trip to Cambridge was undertaken at about this time by Leslie and Tolly, who had been at Caius College. This shift to the lighter blue also fitted in with Leslie's idea to use quotations from the poem 'Grantchester' by Rupert Brooke.

Before Leslie became too deeply immersed in the production which was due to start, it was hoped, the first week in January, Anthony Havelock-Allan asked him if he would appear as himself in a short film Allan was preparing for the Ministry of Information. The principal characters were the three Dominion servicemen I mentioned earlier – a Canadian, an Australian and a New Zealander – and since it was called *From the Four Corners (Henry V)* it seems probable and logical that Leslie represented the fourth corner. For the purpose of the film he was to act as cicerone, escorting the servicemen round the ancient landmarks of London. In one of Leslie's programmes for *Britain Speaks*, entitled 'Three Soldiers', he describes to his three new friends something of the motive of the war – a more profound motive than, perhaps, they realise.

'To show them this I do rather a strange thing. I take them to the top of St Paul's Cathedral and show them, from that great height, the city that Hitler had been trying for three months to destroy.' It was clear that this was something of a revelation to them – for Hitler had, signally, failed.

'I felt that never, not in years and years of diabolical attack, could it ever be destroyed . . . I turned and looked into the faces of the lads from Canada, Australia and New Zealand. Were there tears in their eyes – or was it just the effect of the winter wind blowing over the pinnacle of St Paul's?'

His participation in *From the Four Corners* completed, Leslie returned to Denham and began to form a production team round himself. The make-up of the film's technical credit list was impressive. He had already got Phil Samuel; now he added Mutz Greenbaum, as lighting cameraman and technical supervisor (an interesting combination of superb camera craftsman and useful advisor in matters German) Jack Hildyard (now the doyen of cameramen and, then, the best English camera operator) Sidney Cole (today a distinguished producer) as supervising editor and, as film editor, Doug Myers. Both Cole and Myers were to work again with Leslie on *The First of the Few*.

The casting was no less carefully sought and balanced. By this time Leslie had brought in his younger sister, Irene Howard (later for many years chief casting director at MGM) as casting director. Through her familiarity with repertory, she was able to advise on many new actors and actresses with whom Leslie was unfamiliar.

But once Leslie had seen Francis L. Sullivan he knew he had found his General von Graum, the satirical simulacrum of Hermann Göring. Though scarcely resembling the Number Two German, save in size, Sullivan's screen performance was disturbingly unpleasant yet had, at the same time, something of the eerie geniality of the much-bemedalled, over-perfumed Reichs Marshall. However grim the struggle there was a healthy tendency in the British to see the funny side of their enemies. To Leslie there was a Grand Guignol character about the Nazi hierarchy which he found decidely comical. Yet Sullivan's performance was far from a caricature, even if to British beholders he looked an elephantine figure of fun, for, despite the white suit and medals, he took the idea of world conquest with dead-pan Teutonic seriousness.

Another excellent performance was that of Raymond Huntley as the drily polite, sneeringly deferential Gestapo chief. In supporting roles, equally well-played, were Dennis Arundell, Allan Jeayes, Hugh McDermott, David Tomlinson – and Joan Kemp-Welch. Leslie tested most of the leading actors himself having them read their lines in front of camera to get an idea how they would look and play their various roles.

One part proved exceedingly difficult to cast – that of Ludmilla Cole (or Koslowski as she was originally known) the daughter of the left-wing Polish newspaper editor, imprisoned by the Nazis, who was to be used by them in their efforts to trap Professor Smith. It was the female lead and for it Leslie had tested a number of talented young actresses without getting near the girl he wanted. (The number of girls tested has been put as high as thirty-two!) Production had already started when someone mentioned a girl's name at random. It was Mary Morris. Those who heard the name looked round in surprise. Few had heard of her – and Leslie certainly hadn't. He had neither seen *Prison Without Bars*, in which she had played a hard-bitten little reprobate in a girls' reformatory, *The Thief of Baghdad* in which she had figured briefly nor *Major Barbara* in which she had spoken one line. But undaunted, though a little desperate, in his search to fill this important role he asked if she would come down to Denham for an interview.

Mary Morris, though comparatively unknown in England, had, in fact, been invited to Hollywood the year before after being discovered by a talent scout. She had been given a six months' contract and her passage money. But, after four months, nothing came of it. She might, indeed, be a potential star but what could they do with a girl who kept her hair close-cropped, wore no make-up and dressed in slacks all the time? It wasn't the way Hollywood worked on the distaff side. Didn't she realise that ladies in Hollywood movies had to look feminine and glamorous? 'I looked like Clark Gable, anyway,' Mary said, 'and when they plucked my eyebrows I looked just like a boiled egg!' In desperation, they gave her the balance of two months salary and told her to go home.

Mary described to me the sort of life she had been leading in 1940 before she met Leslie – and how things turned out afterwards.

'After the 1940 raids my sister, who was attached to the Air Ministry, was evacuated taking my mother with her. I eventually went to live in a railway carriage on the coast at Felpham. There was no money, no work. Two of us lived on thirty shillings a week, mainly on leeks and cabbages, and the weather was terribly cold. I must have had enough money to come to London just before the

New Year and went to my mother's house where there was a letter waiting for me from my agent (we had no phone in the house). Leslie Howard wanted to see me and I was to telephone Denham Studios.'

Mary described how her friends rallied round and got her looking 'fairly respectable' and put her on a train to Denham. 'Leslie was kind, said he'd like to make a test and gave me a script. I was to be there early – 8 a.m. for make-up and hair-do – on 1st January.' But there was to be a slight hitch – which might have cost her the film.

On New Year's Eve she was invited by her friends Lucia Parry and Michael Wilding to a party at Elisabeth Welch's flat. 'Lucia who had been so good to me during those difficult days decided I should not be alone for New Year's Eve. I wasn't used to anything to drink ('Tizer' had been my last fling!) I think the excitement, wishing me well, being warm for the first time in two months – and, obviously, whatever it was we drank the New Year in with was all too much . . . At 9.30 on New Year's morning I woke with the horror of the time staring at me. I was already an hour and a half late and realised it was too much to expect Leslie to even think of employing me on this sort of recommendation.' Almost in tears, she rushed to find Michael Wilding who was sleeping on a sofa in the drawing room.

'What on earth am I to do? Look at the time!' And Michael, getting somewhat unsteadily to his feet, advised, 'Extreme calm – and a clear head which I haven't got!'

' "What time were you supposed to be there?" he asked.

' "Eight o'clock for make-up," I said. Michael made a wry face and, replied: "Well, Leslie – fortunately – is one of the most sympathetic men in the business. He is, also, not one of the fastest people out of bed in the morning himself. Maybe he was celebrating, too. Let me ring the studios and sound things out." '

'Michael was wonderful. I heard him on the telephone – "We have all only just come to . . . Yes, I'm afraid so . . . What should she do?" And the awful silence as I sat waiting the sentence. Michael turned to me: "Mr Howard thinks it would be better to make the test tomorrow". Someone waiting to be hanged has the door thrown open and told they are free – I would imagine they would feel as I did – the trap had opened and I had fallen through death into life.

'It was dark when I arrived at the studios the following morning. The make-up was slapped on and too much chatter. They will talk and all I wanted to think of was the lines. Then Leslie came. He was smiling and relaxed, not a word about "What happened to you, yesterday?" It was all going to be fine, he said, we'll just do this and that. The cameras were set up – lots of the usual fuss. Leslie stood by the camera feeding lines to me so that I played the scene with him, several set-ups. It was all over before I knew it. Shaking and soaked with sweat, I was led back to have my make-up off. There was a man being made-up. Very surly, not a word did he utter. He was now in check-shirt or lumber-jacket. He had a moustache . . . Heavens, it was Laurence Olivier. What was it – *49th Parallel* perhaps?' (It was – the Michael Powell film in which Leslie was also to appear.)

Later that morning her agent arrived and told Mary she had got the part. They were going to pay her £250. 'What a lot of money!' her agent remarked. But what part was she going to play?

'I didn't know. I had no idea that I was being tested for Leslie's girl in the film. Then the room was full of people – and Leslie congratulating me. There was a large man – Samuel, I think – Harold Huth, Tolly de Grunwald and others. I was told I was to take lunch with them. But, first, to Leslie's suite – offices, dressing room all combined. I was warmly congratulated by Violette who looked after Leslie and was playing the tiny part of the girl (in the perfume shop) who suggests he buy a box of powder for me.'

Both Leslie and Tolly sensed that Mary had to be protected. Tolly thought the money they were paying her ridiculous. 'We cannot pay your leading lady £250 for the whole film. She must have at least £500.'

(Leslie agreed and so it was arranged. In those days actresses playing opposite Leslie got £500 and the American stars £1,000.)

'But did it matter?' Mary said. 'I was to be playing opposite him.' Describing her faith in her own ability to give as good as she was given and not be outmatched by the stars of the day, she said: 'I had felt cheated for I always knew what I could do. From childhood I never questioned or had any doubts about acting; therefore, I was never ambitious. That, of course, didn't help my career. I was also a little ungrown-up and afraid of the sophisticated people one met in the entertainment world. I should have been on a cloud – there was every opportunity – and Leslie was ready to make me into a big star.'

Mary was going to have to live near the studios, London was too far and the journey too precarious in war-time. But where? Uxbridge was full up. 'Violette got the last bed in the house made up in Leslie's dressing room. I had to be at the studio long before anyone else. I remember those cold, dark mornings when I crept through Leslie's bedroom scarcely daring to breathe. Leslie's car was waiting and wrapped in a rug I was driven away . . . One morning there was a full moon, everything seemed to be stationary and I wished it would never end . . . '

Describing their work in the studio Mary said: 'Leslie did everything – direct, act, the lot. He knew exactly what he was doing while on the surface he appeared to be the vague, eccentric professor. He never seemed to lose his temper – though once he was angry with me. A journalist was getting people to sign something to do with Michael Redgrave who had the BBC down on him for his political views. I am not a political animal and felt no actor should be. At the same time I felt no one should stop you working for your beliefs. Though I was a bit muddled I felt certain both Leslie and I should sign this petition saying we thought it disgraceful that Michael Redgrave was not going to be allowed to work. I caught Leslie unawares – he was fussed over a scene – and in the end he said 'yes' and signed it. The next day, in the papers, there it was. He didn't want to be dragged into it and accused me of pushing him (which, indeed, I had). I got angry with him. I said: "You know you did what you wanted to do, and that it was the right thing. We're surrounded here by a whole lot of people who wouldn't mind if Hitler walked in tomorrow . . . " The day was terrible. We both growled – but it broke the tentativeness and we worked better after that.'

Mary told me of the difficult, and at times somewhat hectic, conditions while she was living in the over-crowded Cottage at Farnham Royal.

'The house was full of people. Dinner was torture. I sat on Leslie's right, Violette on his left. I can only remember Valerie Hobson and her husband, Harold Huth and Leslie's sister, whom I liked but didn't know she was Leslie's sister for ages. Behind where Leslie was sitting were rows of pills on the window ledge. A great silence – and he'd take a pill. Then, the clatter of knives and forks, and someone would start to talk. The talk always seemed jerky – a rush of words, then, silence. I find words difficult to learn so mostly I only heard a noise. I was more concerned about those pills – different colours being consumed. One day I told him how silly I thought he was being. He was rather amazed that I should stun the table into silence like this. Did I think him a hypochondriac, he asked? Yes, I did. "Hum . . . " – he often paused and then made this funny little sound. It was like a word which could mean anything you took it to mean, a useful sound.'

Mary admitted how totally inexperienced she was at coping with people, in a worldly sense, and how she thought it would have done Leslie good to be teased a little more. 'I think I could have had a lot of fun with him. I did tease him a bit but I didn't really have either the know-how or the courage.' In the end, she confessed: 'I got nervous living like that and they tried to get me billeted. Eventually I was given a camp-bed in one of the make-up people's room. I only slept there and we both had some transport at the same time each morning to Denham. At night I'd eat at the pub. My diet was one baked potato so well done there was scarcely anything inside it – and milk. I had to lose weight as I was a buxom little thing. For the first few weeks at the studio it was only cabbage. It would have been just as well if I'd swallowed Leslie's pills and forgotten about eating altogether. I didn't like my clothes but wasn't brave enough to make a scene. Why couldn't I be free and wear a loose evening dress with a wide belt that made me look a bit feminine? Instead I was trussed into pale blue, accentuating my no bosom and enormous diaphragm, which gave me the matronly look as though a large bosom had settled around my stomach. And my hair-do made me look like the hairdresser, like every hairdresser, with a strange roll at the neck and quiff on top. But Leslie didn't notice. Maybe it was what he wanted.

'Come the end of the film, I had lost heart. I remember that day so well. Leslie seemed far away, preoccupied. The scene wasn't jelling. There was this empty set, all dusky, with light filtering through. [The station waiting room at the German frontier.] It was the scene where the Nazis make me believe he'd abandoned me and I told them all I knew. Suddenly he appeared, had come back for me. There were very few words. The rehearsal and the studio was deathly quiet as Leslie said, "Come," putting on my coat. I said, "Leslie, you should kiss me now" – and he looked a little surprised and said, "Do you think so?" "Yes," I said. He turned me slowly round and gave me a gentle loving little peck.

'There was a long, silent pause and, suddenly, everyone in the studio was clapping. The men in the gantries started it. Leslie looked up and sideways from a slightly bent head which he didn't move. It was his sudden awareness I sensed and, without moving, he said simply – "Yes . . . " The camera settled down – silence – "Action . . . " He put the coat round me, the same turn, pause, the little kiss, another pause and, then, "Yes . . . " He kept the word in with its different meaning. One take. From then on I wished we could be doing the film all over again.

'Two or three more days – the lovely train scene and it was all over. I'd found myself a little flat in Uxbridge by then.'

To Mary's surprise Leslie turned up, unexpectedly, one day after lunch. Perhaps he had come to say goodbye. Or was there something more to it than that?

'I was a little surprised. You see, Leslie wasn't in love with me, but, somehow, he thought he ought to be. Hence, the visit, out of the blue. It was all right. I convinced him it was just a lovely romantic idea, so we sat and talked and had tea. I think I shed a tear when he left for I had a feeling we would never meet again – and we didn't.'

I think there is something infinitely sad about the brief, precarious relationship of actors – however professionally one looks at it, for it can become so intensely emotional for the short period they work together that even the actors may be deceived into believing it more real than it is. Acting is the most self-deceiving of all professions and actors become so deeply involved with each other that it is easy to lose sight of the fact that their elaborate passions are just so many feet of celluloid to be cut up by a film editor's scissors. Even Shakespeare, who was familiar with the behaviour of actors, tells us through the mouth of Hamlet of a player who 'in a fiction, in a dream of passion, could force his soul so to his own conceit that from her working all his visage wann'd, tears in his eyes, distraction in's aspect, a broken voice, and his whole function suiting with forms to his conceit: and all for nothing!' (Conceit – i.e. his imagination.)

Perhaps this is the saddest thing about acting: it really is all for nothing, and yet so intensely believed at the time. I think what Mary Morris said of Leslie – not being in love with her but thinking he ought to be – is the sort of misconception into which actors fall, who so lose themselves in their roles that they become them in their imaginations. And in this situation they fall in love with shadow not substance. It was said of Humphrey Bogart that he fell in love with the part that Lauren Bacall played in their first film together and, I suppose, it was a little unethical of him, shortly afterwards, to have married the substance after falling in love with the shadow. Perhaps, in Leslie's case, it was simply a bit of male vanity coupled to a powerful imagination for, though he fell in love with several leading ladies I doubt very much if he would have advocated it as an essential to acting. In fact Leslie once said: 'On the contrary, I think that in most instances it would be a decided handicap for an actor to be in love with his leading lady. They would be swayed by their personal feelings and emotions rather than by the feelings and emotions of the characters they were attempting to portray. It is the job of the actor or the actress to make the audience *feel* and if they do all of the feeling themselves the audience is very likely to be left cold and unmoved.'

Acting apart, looking back on *Pimpernel Smith* forty years from its birth, it seems as an example of film craftsmanship to have had more wit and style and satirical point than most other war films made in the heat of the moment. Though produced in the early months of 1941, it wasn't really a war film at all for its action took place on the edge of war. It dealt not with blows or blood – yet it remains, with its subtle investigation into states of mind, probably the most virulently anti-Nazi film the war produced. It was not only a comparative study of mental attitudes but a kind of metaphysical essay in gamesmanship: the rigid-minded Nazi professional against the sporting English amateur, the bludgeon versus the butterfly. It was certainly very true of the English – and something of a paradox to the efficient German mind – that a professor and his amateur troop of undergraduate assistants should be foolhardy enough to attempt to take on, and even out-wit, the much-vaunted Nazi machine. I think it may have been the first and, perhaps, the only British war film to have explored the possibility that such rigid efficiency might have weaknesses to an agile and imaginative opponent. Certainly, the inelasticity of Nazi thinking and their somewhat baleful sense of humour was made much of in the film.

To the Nazis, of course, it could not have been more provocative. Quite naturally they took themselves very seriously, almost like characters out of Grand Opera and if Leslie saw them as Grand Guignol that was, to say the least, impertinent. To them the fun of the film was perverted, not to say, hostile. (In fact, in Sweden it had to be withdrawn from even private showing on orders of the Swedish Foreign Office because of pressure by Dr Goebbels.) I do not doubt that the Minister for Enlightenment and Propaganda in Berlin managed to get hold of a copy of the film and found it a very unfunny and grossly insulting caricature of important Nazis. And the insult would, probably, not be forgotten when an occasion arose to mete out punishment.

There is an interesting reference to *Pimpernel Smith* under the chapter heading 'Myth, Magic and Politics' in the book *Politics and Film* (Furhammar and Isaksson*). In it the authors suggest not only a mythical element in the film but a religious one.

* Studio Vista, 1971.

Leslie Howard's *Pimpernel Smith*, one of the most successful films of World War II, illustrates how well propaganda may be served by mythological elements from various sources. Smith is a latter day version of the quick-thinking folk hero who confounds . . . expectations by outsmarting evil. The villain is as gross, stupid and evil as any fairy-tale giant. The beautiful, fragile heroine is held captive by the giant – in this case, blackmailed into running the villain's errands. Characters who have been spellbound or led astray are very common, in both folk-lore and film propaganda: they are forced to serve an evil master but are forgiven when the spell has been broken . . . *Pimpernel Smith* may also be examined from a religious standpoint. This satire of Nazism does not have any explicit religious references, but it is not surprising that Western propaganda fiction should reflect Christian mythology or . . . that the Leslie Howard character should show striking parallels with Christ . . .

Pimpernel Smith is a saviour in the literal sense, who has arrived in an evil world where his origins seem very mysterious and the authorities go all out to destroy him. No one has his ability to pass from this evil world to the ideal one. He is a teacher, surrounded by a small group of disciples who at first do not understand his greatness and his mission . . . They are not convinced of his identity until, at a later stage, they see his 'pierced' hands. These wounds have been explained, with perfect consistency, in a scene in which Smith, disguised as a scarecrow erected in a concentration camp, is on a cross, hanging with arms outstretched and head falling forward as if in a Passion painting. His hands is gorily pierced by a guard. The film ends with Smith announcing that he will soon be back.'

Sidney Cole, Leslie's supervising editor, had some interesting things to tell me about the production and those who worked on it.

'As to writers I am clear that the script that was shot was principally the work of Tolly de Grunwald. Leslie had Tolly with him on the floor . . . in order that dialogue could be modified by him as Leslie needed. Harold Huth was also there throughout. What it meant was that after Leslie had decided the set-up and run the action through with his stand-in, Harold would be in charge behind the camera during the actual takes.

'Leslie was always ready to listen to suggestions while remaining charmingly, but definitely, in control. He insisted that I should also be on the floor throughout the shooting so that he might consult me from an editing point of view. It was a most enjoyable and creative professional experience. We had only one real disagreement. For a scene he played with Mary Morris, he covered the whole action in a two-shot of himself and Mary, then took a single of Mary and said, 'That's it.' I objected asking for a single (close-up) on him, too. For a moment Leslie lost his temper and said: 'Why do we have to cut the picture before we've shot it?' I stood, huffily, on my dignity, saying: 'Oh, very well, I won't make any more suggestions.' A moment later, Leslie came over to me and asked what lines of the scene did I wish him to cover on the close-up. I told him, explaining I needed them to balance Mary's close-up. He appreciated this and took the shot. I relate this, not to show I was right – it was a standard requisite in such a scene – but because it was so characteristic of Leslie that one tiny clash should have been over my request for a single on himself.

'So, in fact, the improvisations on the floor, far from making things difficult for editing, were a considerable help. Leslie's sense of style, and the timing of his performance and direction, consequently informed the whole of my editing approach and dictated its rhythm, often down to the smallest detail. It was the most stylish movie I had edited up till then and, with but few exceptions, ever since.'

*

At the beginning of February, while Leslie was still in production on *Pimpernel Smith*, the Michael Powell production *49th Parallel* went onto the floor at Denham. This was the film for which Laurence Oliver was doing costume and make-up tests when Mary Morris saw him earlier in January. Emeric Pressburger, with whom Powell was to be continuously associated, had written the story and screenplay. The film was an Ortus Production; 'Ortus' is the palindrome of John Sutro, the company's managing director. The film, involving a U-Boat crew's adventures in Canada following the scuttling of their U-Boat in the St Lawrence, had a very strong cast, including Laurence Olivier, Raymond Masscy, Eric Portman and Leslie. Its supporting players featured Finlay Currie, Raymond Lovell, Glynis Johns and Niall McGinnis. Glynis, who was then only fourteen, was a replacement casting for Elisabeth Bergner. She, fearing the Nazis, had given up the part and gone to live in America.

Eric Portman had the real star part in the film as the First Lieutenant of the U-Boat who leads the escapers across Canada. As the dedicated Nazi and constant quoter of *Mein Kampf* he is brought into conflict with the other four principal characters in the story. During these several encounters the 'Master Race' philosophy of the Nazis is shown in conflict with the simple lives and faiths of the inhabitants, including a religious community of Hutterites led by Anton Walbrook.

One of the characters, an author preferring solitude while he researches aboriginal Canada, lives in a tepee at the side of a lake high in the Rockies, befriended solely by Indians. It was John Sutro, I believe, who suggested Leslie for this part and Powell and Pressburger agreed. The fact that Leslie was in production himself on the next stage made it physically a simple matter and Leslie's participation in *49th Parallel* involved no more than a few days, perhaps a week at most. Despite its brevity – the part involved one dialogue scene – there was contained in it the whole argument between ourselves and the Nazis, the ethics of an elected government, freely chosen, against the Nazi caucus who mocked such a philosophy.

This scene between the author and the U-Boat men was the crux of why we were fighting the war, and in a long speech of considerable passion, directed principally at Josef Goebbels, Leslie attacked the half-truths and distortions on which the Nazi system was founded. Again, I suppose, a scene that Goebbels would not easily forget when the occasion arose for punishment as the film, like *Pimpernel Smith*, was later distributed in neutral countries like Sweden, Spain and Portugal. Such studied attacks would not be forgiven and, by 1943, Leslie had promoted himself to 'star-billing' on the German Black List. In fact, William Joyce was to announce that 'this sarcastic British actor' would be liquidated 'along with the Churchill clique'.

Some time towards the end of March, Leslie moved to a house in Denham village, 'The Pantiles,' so as to be nearer the studios. *Pimpernel Smith* was now in the tenth week of production and the end, if not quite in sight, was within measurable distance. Leslie always worked carefully, though scarcely quickly, and was not known as 'Leisurely' without reason. He took his time to get things right so that production was inclined to drift on beyond what is known as 'the guarantee' – which meant the amount of money advanced before certain penalties were imposed regarding completion. Leslie, seeking his own kind of perfection, generally went over budget, but I do not think impositions or penalty clauses would have had much effect. He would not have mended his ways or 'Spoiled the ship', as he would have put it, 'for a ha'porth of tar', even if that ha'porth amounted to several thousands of pounds.

Through the month of May he was busy cutting and editing *Pimpernel Smith*, so that the film could be released by late June or early July. Though he had his company, Leslie Howard Productions Ltd, to handle routine matters at the studios, Leslie formed another company in June to deal with financial arrangements involving his services as producer, director and actor. The directors of this company were Frederic Burgis, his solicitor, John Sutro of Ortus Films and Alfred T. Chenhalls, a well-known and respected West End accountant, whose company acted as financial advisors to a host of film and theatre personalities.

Of the three, Alfred Chenhalls was perhaps to grow closest to Leslie. A sort of spontaneous combustion took place between them due to their entirely different mental and physical chemistry – Alfred, large and gregarious, Leslie, slight and solitary – so that one acted as catalyst to the other. It was the kind of relationship to which Leslie readily responded – a contrast of types – for he had always sought an outward-going and cheerful friend. Bill Gargan, the American actor, had just those qualities in relation to Leslie, pulling his leg outrageously and making him laugh at himself.

There was this side to Alfred's and Leslie's relationship and there was the other – Alfred's hard-nosed business-sense and acumen in film affairs on which Leslie came to rely for advice and guidance. Later, they were to travel to Spain and Portugal together, and, finally, they were to die together, side by side, in the same plane returning from Lisbon on 1st June 1943. If one believed in fate or destiny perhaps this was part of a more elaborate design or mosaic, a kind of ultimate connection.

Alfred was a man of considerable charm, talent and persuasion, sometimes in his powerful enthusiasm a little over-persuasive. Robust of frame and rumbustious of humour, with his perennial cigar, Alfred was popular at theatrical parties not only for his gregarious nature and sense of fun but also for his skill as a pianist. Wherever there was a piano he was frequently found behind it with a deft pair of hands for a keyboard ranging freely from the classics to Cole Porter. Alfred appeared to take life lightly, with a ready twinkle in his eye for a pretty actress, yet as a film-negotiator he was second to none and was himself director of no less than nine film and distribution companies. From now on he was to exert an increasingly strong influence over Leslie both as friend and associate.

CHAPTER SIX

Spitfire Prelude
June 1941-December 1941

As production of *Pimpernel Smith* was now over and most of the editing completed, Leslie began looking round for another filmable subject. They were not all that easy to find. Obviously it would have to be a story with a strong theme linked to the war, a document and yet an adventure story.

In the quiet backrooms where writers work such a theme had been explored, and it came to Leslie in a somewhat roundabout way. The theme was the Battle of Britain and the man behind that battle, the designer of the famous Spitfire fighter, Reginald J. Mitchell of Vickers-Supermarine. Mitchell, born in 1895, was dead 'by 1937, of cancer, and so never lived to see the final glory of his plane in the air-battles of 1940 and the vindication of his designs.

The nurturing of Mitchell's particular genius began in 1916 at the Supermarine Aviation Works and his talent as an engineer and designer was soon recognised by Scott-Paine, the managing director of the company. His promotion was rapid. By 1920 he was chief engineer and designer. Mitchell had no formal training and was a largely self-taught genius. In 1922 the company entered its first sea-planes for the Schneider Trophy contests at Naples and thereafter Mitchell was responsible for the S4,5 and 6 and the 6B of 1931, the most remarkable of the series which could fly at 500 feet per second.

In 1930 the Air Ministry had announced a specification for a new fighter aircraft but the S series was not a practical design for the tough work of aerial combat. Then in 1933 Mitchell came up with an advanced design, smaller and combining a retractable under-carriage. In that year, however, Mitchell became ill and underwent a colostomy. He was, in fact, now working against time – the time he had left – to complete the prototype of the fighter version. This was the Spitfire K 5054 built in 1935 and first flown in March 1936 – the year before Mitchell died. On June 3rd 1936 the Air Ministry placed an order for 310 of these machines, the Spitfire Mark I, and the first deliveries began in June 1938, two years to a month after Mitchell's death and just over a year before war started.

This, then, was the background of the man and the plane on which an Australian writer, Henry C. James, began work in the closing months of 1940. He had approached Mitchell's widow to get her assent to a story of his life and he showed her his outline plan. When the story was completed, Mrs Mitchell gave it her approval. This story went from hand to hand till it came to the attention of George King, a film producer, who thought it worthwhile to take an option on it and get a film treatment done.

In the early months of 1941, James's story found its way via George King to a talented writer and dramatist called Miles Malleson, who was also an actor of some note and had been connected with films since 1930. Malleson set to work to write a scenario and while he was engaged on it showed it to an old friend, the actor Robert Donat, who lived at Wendover not far from Malleson. Donat was very excited by the idea and wanted to play Mitchell. He would have been very suitable casting for in stature and appearance he was not unlike Mitchell – in fact, more like Mitchell physically, to my mind, than Leslie who ultimately played the part. Donat was under contract to MGM and he approached them about it. But Metro wouldn't do it unless they had sole rights and King wasn't prepared to part with them. In any case, Metro had no production facilities in England and the subject would have been totally unrealistic in Hollywood which had neither the technical resources nor the experience of war, neither the Spitfires nor the pilots who had flown them in battle.

George King obviously realised the subject had to be made in England. But King, being a comparatively small name in films, had neither the facilities nor the organisation for such a large and technically difficult subject; nor had he a star of first dimension, for the role of Mitchell. In effect, the company King formed, British Aviation Pictures, served as little more than a holding company for the rights to the Mitchell story.

How Miles Malleson's scenario reached Leslie I do not know. It may be Miles brought it to him at Denham when he realised Donat couldn't do it – or he may have shown it to Tolly de Grunwald, a close friend, who saw the immense potential of getting Leslie interested. Or possibly an energetic and imaginative young woman, Moie Charles, a film writer herself, had come across the script in the office of David Henley, who was Leslie's as well as Bob Donat's agent. Anyway, once it reached Leslie and he had read it, he said he would be very interested in producing it. He would also play

Mitchell now that Donat was not available. George King was naturally delighted that his foresight in investing in the Mitchell script might now reap the reward of Leslie's participation.

To Leslie it seemed there was only one man in the film industry who could successfully underwrite such a project and that was Arthur Rank of GFD. Leslie knew Rank personally and had been a guest at his house near Reigate on several occasions. He spoke to Arthur Rank on the phone, explained his interest and said he would like to produce the film if GFD was prepared to back him. Rank invited Leslie to come over and discuss it with him and Leslie went, taking with him his much-esteemed production manager, Phil Samuel, to help him thrash out the details. Rank received the idea with enthusiasm and, subject to final approval of script, was prepared to furnish the entire production costs. It also gave Rank considerable confidence knowing Phil Samuel was to be Leslie's second-in-command, for he had great faith in Samuel's judgement and production ability.

To Leslie it seemed nothing short of a miracle. Never in his experience had the raising of a large sum of money in war-time for such an elaborate, ultimately protracted and costly film seemed so simple. For over a year he had struggled to wheedle and conjure money out of people to make *Pimpernel Smith*, which was to cost nothing by comparison. Now, suddenly, he had done it in a matter of hours by simply going to Arthur Rank and asking for his help. Of course, it was easy to understand why this subject had such tremendous appeal. Not because of the struggles of an ailing man to get an aeroplane off the ground that might one day win a battle, but because that plane, and others like it, piloted by a handful of young men, had gone into the air hopelessly outnumbered, and miraculously and gloriously won that battle, snatching victory when all seemed lost. Indeed, we were a nation who had grown accustomed to defeat. We had lived defeated and seemed about to die defeated. Now these young men of the RAF had given us a miraculous delivery, a breathing space and something wonderful to shout about. So it was not really Mitchell that the philanthropic Arthur Rank and the majority of the people of Britain wished to thank and remember with gratitude – the majority hardly knew his name – but the young dare-devils who had flown his plane and won the battle.

Leslie, of course, knew the film had to be about Mitchell. Twenty years of a life had to be encompassed, with all its struggles and disappointments, not simply twenty days of victory rolls in the skies over Kent. The Battle of Britain was the pay-off, the final tribute to

'Mitch' for what he had done. It must be seen within that context. Leslie was determined that the public, both here and abroad, should learn something of this unassuming man and all those whom he had worked quietly in the background, with little credit or congratulation, during the twenties and particularly the thirties when Britain drifted blindly through the twilit years of appeasement. Nobody had listened much to Mitch, then, who had seen what was happening in Germany with his own eyes on several visits, and who knew how the Nazi state was massively behind their aircraft industry while our government dawdled and drifted. All this must be in the film, not just the Battle of Britain.

Once the decision with GFD had been reached, things began to move and production plans went ahead rapidly. A new scenario was put in hand by a marriage of writers' talents when Leslie brought in Tolly de Grunwald to work with Miles Malleson. Assistance and cooperation on all sides was tremendous. Churchill himself wrote a To Whom It May Concern letter from Downing Street requesting that all possible facilities be accorded the production, and Sholto Douglas, C-in-C Fighter Command, was rung up personally by Winston to see that such assistance became effective. As a result shooting was allowed to take place at a number of frontline Battle of Britain fighter stations. A Mark II Spitfire, unserviceable for operational purposes, was obtained from Northolt and brought to Denham studios. Phil Samuel told me later that he had Churchill's letter copied as a kind of *laissez passer* in the event of difficulties with officials and that it got him into a lot of otherwise inaccessible places.

Leslie was lucky to get hold of Georges Perinal as lighting cameraman. Perinal had been principal cameraman on famous French films like *Le Million* and *Sous les toits de Paris*. In 1933 he had been brought over from Paris by Alexander Korda, and his credit list of Korda films included *The Private Life of Henry VIII*, *Catherine the Great* and *Rembrandt*. It seems that Perinal had heard or read somewhere that Leslie was interested in making a film of *Hamlet*. The idea of lighting *Hamlet* took possession of him. Here was a photographic canvas for the brush of a master cameraman. Perinal went to see Leslie in high hopes. His Gallic spirits were, however, terribly cast down when Leslie confessed it wasn't *Hamlet* he wished him to photograph – but aeroplanes. Though Leslie was keen to have Perinal he was even keener to have Jack Hildyard, with whom he had a close rapport, as his operator and perhaps this choice persuaded Perinal to overcome some of his disappointment.

As to casting there were the usual problems of suitability and availability. For Mitchell's chief test pilot Leslie decided on a composite figure, a combination of Captain J. 'Mutt' Summers, Mitchell's principal test pilot and his fellow pilots Quill and Pickering, plus the various RAF men, Boothman, Stainforth and others, who had flown in the Schneider Trophy races. The composite character was to be called Crisp. Leslie knew there was one very good young actor with the necessary panache for the part, an Englishman who had been making quite a name for himself in Hollywood just before the war – and whom Leslie knew well. This was David Niven. He had come home at about the same time as Leslie, but being on the reserve of officers was not exactly non-combatant and had rejoined his old regiment, the Rifle Brigade. Would he do it – and could he be got out of uniform for the duration of the film?

Leslie approached David direct, told him about the part of Crisp and wondered, if David was interested, could the War Office be persuaded to release him? Fortunately the War Office assented and David temporarily laid aside his army uniform to become Mitchell's right-hand man, later Wing Commander Crisp of the RAF. Other well-known actors and actresses soon to join the cast in principal roles were Roland Culver (as Scott-Paine), Anne Firth, David Horne, Rosalyn Boulter, Derrick de Marney and, finally, Filippo del Giudice, Head of Two Cities Films, who, because Italian actors were scarcely two-a-penny in wartime England, agreed to play an Italian air force chief, and gave his fee to charity.

But once again Leslie was having trouble casting his leading lady, in this case Mrs Mitchell. He had tested a number of actresses, none of whom seemed quite suitable. It was, then, that Moie Charles, David Henley's assistant, who had an office at Denham, suggested a young actress called Rosamund John. Miss John, after a season at the Old Vic, had recently been at Harrogate Rep and was staying at Wendover.

'When I was summoned for my interview I was up a cherry-tree, picking fruit, and wearing old slacks. Since one seldom got a chance to meet an actor of such calibre I dropped everything and went along.' Rosamund had no idea what part she was being interviewed for and imagined it must be one of the smaller roles still uncast.

'When I got to the studio Leslie, I well remember, said: "She doesn't look in the least like an actress. I think she should do a test for the wife".' When Leslie saw Rosamund's test he was not only confirmed in his opinion that she didn't look like an actress, she didn't act like one either. There was no conscious striving for effect. She became the character in a convincing and completely natural way – she lived it not acted it – and Leslie unhesitatingly offered Rosamund the role of Mrs Mitchell. It was to be the beginning of a long association.

Of course, there are always major difficulties impersonating real people instead of the fictions of an author's imagination. An actor invariably alters a character to suit his own style and personality and in the case of Mitchell, still very much in living memory, Leslie's personality had little in common with the chief architect of the Spitfire. With Professor Horatio Smith, Leslie had had considerable latitude for invention, with Reginald Mitchell comparatively little. In such a case how far may the actor depart from the original in his search for a convincing interpretation?

Rosamund faced similar problems – perhaps more so than Leslie for Mitchell was dead – as hers were somewhat compounded by the fact that Mrs Mitchell was not only very much alive but very much in evidence when the film later went into production. She attended the studios regularly as, I suppose, a sort of technical adviser in matters involving the Mitchells' domestic life and spent much time, seated in a chair on the set, watching the scenes between herself and her husband as they unrolled before her, perhaps, astonished eyes. It must have been difficult for her to put her seal of approval on this sort of make-believe. The fact that neither Leslie nor Rosamund looked much like the originals, and seemed, indeed, rather romanticised versions of her late husband and herself, must have been something of a disappointment and a strain to Mrs Mitchell with a keen eye for accuracy and precision of portraiture.

It was equally a strain for the artistes performing in front of her their necessarily fictionalised versions of reality. Whether Mrs Mitchell actually protested that 'Reggie wouldn't have behaved like this' or 'I wouldn't have made a face like that' I cannot tell, nor I suppose did it bother Leslie unduly who must have realised he could never match up to Mrs Mitchell's memory of her husband, or, for that matter, even vaguely resemble the chief designer of Vickers-Supermarine. For Rosamund the problem was magnified by the fact that Mrs Mitchell sat, not two feet behind the camera, her eyes glued to Rosamund's every movement.

Undoubtedly in the film certain liberties were taken to humanise the characters and make them more attractive. Certainly the facts of Mitchell's mortal illness were scarcely underlined and, though Mitchell knew he was in the grip of cancer, in the film it was an unmentionable word. The film stressed that Mitchell refusing to take a holiday – or rest at all – simply worked himself to death. In the final analysis Mrs Mitchell and, to an extent, her son Gordon who frequently accompanied her to the studios, had reservations about the way the film depicted Mitchell. Perhaps Leslie had carried the humanising process too far. Of these differences, Rosamund said: 'Mrs Mitchell and her son were determined at all costs to preserve the image of the great hero untarnished and could not see that it made him so much more attractive to be a human being.'

While still at work on the scenario for the Mitchell story, so far still untitled, and having 'story conferences in the sunny garden of the house called Pantiles', Leslie and Violette decided on a move. Anyway, the lease was due for renewal and Violette had found another house – Monkseaton – at Stoke Poges. It was small but, as she said, 'just big enough for two.'

'If you like it,' Leslie answered, 'let's have it.' It had, as Leslie described it, 'two toy white gables hiding shyly under the roof . . . We stood and looked at it and I glanced at you and found your eyes smiling hopefully at me. I laughed. "It's all right," I said, "I like it." '
It had elms, poplars, pines, a rowan tree in the garden. When a little later they moved to Monkseaton Leslie could not visualise the future, the brief year that lay ahead. 'I could not see the destiny hanging over the low roof, could not know that "like" would soon be changed to desperate affection and that I must have the little house, buy it, keep it . . . for your perpetual home. *La maison de Violette.*'

But now they saw no shadow of destiny under the 'toy white gables'. Now, in September 1941, all their thoughts and energies were concentrated on the film ahead.

By mid-September Tolly de Grunwald and Miles Malleson had completed the scenario and Leslie had come up with a title, *The First of the Few*, which put Mitchell at the head of the 'few' to whom Churchill had paid his now famous tribute. With the weather forecasts good into October it was decided to get as much location work done as possible, taking advantage of the long, sunny days.

Of paramount importance to Leslie was the image of the gull, and this he saw as Mitchell's inspiration, the bird image which on the drawing board was to become the Spitfire. Yet to Leslie there was another connection, more than sheer technical wonderment – a spiritual value he wished to establish at the outset, a sort of psychic link between man and bird which is repeated at the end of the film when the gull hovers over the dying Mitchell in the garden, and Leslie saw as the final metempsychosis of man-spirit into bird-spirit. This relationship was only to be hinted at in the opening sequence of the film when Mitchell, stretched out on the cliff head-land, watched through binoculars the wind-tossed parabolas of the gulls. It was to be another point of divergence between Leslie and the Mitchell family. Mitchell was too practical a man for such a romantic view and had never been known to visit sea-swept headlands to get his aero-dynamics right from observations of bird-flight. The stresses and strains of rigid machines were quite different and such inspiration as he found was found indoors, bent over a drawing board at the Supermarine Aviation Works, his head crammed with mathematical notations rather than the airy images of gulls. Leslie was, however, determined that there was to be this other, imaginative, side to Mitch – and, when, towards the end of September, the film unit set off from Denham for Cornwall, Leslie had this very much in mind.

'We started filming in Polperro,' Rosamund told me 'We had to go that far to find a bit of coast-line that wasn't festooned with barbed wire at that stage in the war.'

Whether technically true to Mitchell or not, Leslie's gull-watching scene was pictorially most effective and opened the film up with its sweeping views of sea and cliffs. It must also have cheered up Georges Perinal – that there were other things in the film besides photographing Spitfires. This sequence not only introduced Rosamund to the film, in a romantic interlude with her husband, but it also introduced her to that other side of Mitch, his intense dedication.

While the fine autumn weather lasted a number of fighter station sequences were included in the location work, at Iddesleigh in Devon, Warmwell, Dorset and at an air-field near Christchurch. In fact, while the building of sets was going on at Denham, frequent opportunities were taken to film exteriors and, even while Leslie was shooting interior scenes at the studio, Phil Samuel would be in charge of a second unit directing location work. Even production weekends were worked to get the RAF material which was to be included in the special Spitfire montage sequence.

Another addition to the production team of *The First of the Few* was the director Adrian Brunel. Adrian was a long-standing friend of Leslie's, dating back to 1918, when he was working at the old Bushey Studios in the fairly early days of British films. Leslie, at that time, was making his first appearance in the West End theatre, as the juvenile, in a comedy by Arnold Bennett called *The Title*, and he rented a cottage at Bushey where he, my mother and I – a few months old – stayed for the summer. Already Leslie's interest in films was emerging and, not only did he see a lot of Adrian, but they decided, with the intrepid optimism of youth, to form a film company together, Minerva Films. Its creative directors, a company of four, consisted of Leslie and Aubrey Smith, as actors, A.A. Milne, as writer, and Adrian Brunel as producer/director. They made, according to the company's prospectus, three comedies, *Bookworms*, *The Bump* and *Five Pounds Reward* – and then went, quietly, into liquidation.

When Adrian joined forces with Leslie again twenty-three years had elapsed – and their situations were a little altered. Leslie was now the producer and director and Adrian became, what was designated, his production consultant. The job involved a number of functions, nothing too specific, and I think Leslie offered it to Adrian as much from a sense of loyalty and affection as a realisation that Adrian was going through a bad patch. Adrian had recently helped to launch the MOI's film department, but that job had come to an end. In his autobiography (*Nice Work*)* Adrian described this new relationship with Leslie.

Initially I was to be a technical guide for Leslie but in view of our old association and the extraordinary similarity of our artistic and spiritual approach, it became much more than what was originally designed . . . We were together from early morning – no, not quite so early, since Leslie was never the first on the floor – until late at night. We were in constant and most confidential contact, and he was too generous in his appreciation of my contribution. I certainly gave everything I could, for not only did I love him, but he and his job were worth what I could give . . .

Of Leslie himself, and his general approach to both direction and acting, Adrian went on to say:

Leslie had a first-class brain and, in spite of his inclination to roam, he had great concentrative ability. Before he began to direct a scene, we would usually discuss its shape; he would outline his plan, using me as a sounding board and getting my technical reactions . . . Then, he would either go from his

* Forbes Robertson 1949.

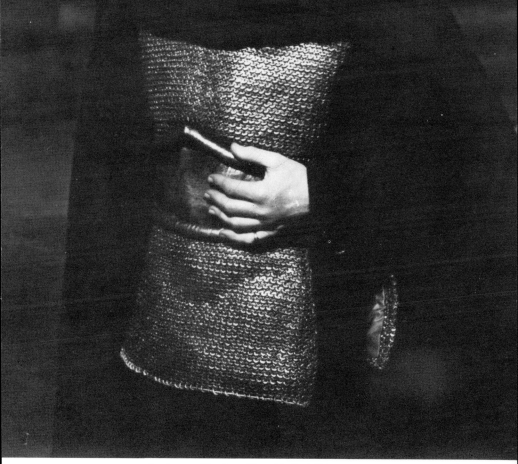

Leslie as Hamlet, New York 1936.

Gallic courtesy – Georg[e] Perinal with Rosamund John on location for *The First of the Few*.

Going over the words on location near Polperro – Adrian Brunel, David Niven, RAF Officer(?), [Les]lie and Hazel Wilkinson (continuity girl).

dressing room, where our discussions often took place, or he would break away from our huddle in the corner of the studio, and take charge on the floor.

Finally, he would go over his own lines – if it was a scene in which he appeared – and by a tremendous power of concentration, would speak the lines without fault. When we came to photograph a scene the lines came from him with such apparent naturalness and effortlessness, with such clarity, sincerity and mastery of meaning, that it was a revelation. He was a really great artist.

One of Adrian's functions, besides acting as a technical guide and sounding board, was to devise a montage sequence for use with William Walton's 'Spitfire Fugue', the music specially composed for the film. This involved taking a film unit to several aircraft factories producing Spitfires and filming material to be edited into a sort of ballet mechanique. Unfortunately, to Adrian's dismay, a lot of this material was lost in the final editing and cutting of the film.

One of the very large sets to be built at Denham involved the Schneider Cup race at Venice in 1927. For this a tank had to be constructed, with a slip-way for the S5 sea-plane, and special stands for the officials and guests witnessing the race. For this race sequence between the Italian and the British machines an S6 had to be mocked up to look like an S5. The technical difficulties were immense considering all this had taken place sixteen years before the film was made and much of the technical equipment was no longer obtainable. Perhaps, as Dr Gordon Mitchell was to admit later, 'the film company had gone to all this trouble to give Mussolini a kick in the pants!'

Most of the RAF location shooting had been completed by November when principal photography began in the studio. One of the interior sequences concerned the stratagems that Mitchell and the managing director of Supermarine were forced to resort to raise money for the design and construction of the Spitfire prototype. As the government of the day dare not dabble in rearmament and was set on a course of appeasement such finance had to be raised privately. Their principal benefactress was, in fact, a very rich woman, Lady Houston*, who strongly disapproved of the government policy of inaction. Like Mitchell she saw what the Nazis were up to, secretly rearming while Britain did nothing – yet

* Lady Houston, an eccentric and wealthy character, earned the thanks of a nation for the £100,000 she gave Mitchell.

to help Mitchell she must use secret methods, too, that would not attract world publicity.

To effect this she employed the services of a go-between, an obscure, unobtrusive character who would be well-paid to keep his mouth shut. The part for this individual though extremely small, involving one day's filming, called for an actor of some skill and invention – and the actor finally sent down to be interviewed was Bernard Miles. Lord Miles told me the story as he remembered it.

'At the time I was a tiny part actor at the very beginning of my career. My agent told me there was a part in a new film *The First of the Few*, a role of very special interest, only one day's work, but they wanted for it a very inventive actor. They handed me a script and said would I read it. Later I was called to the studios where I met Tolly de Grunwald and Miles Malleson who had written the screenplay from a story by a chap named Henry James, and they asked me how I would propose to play the part. While I was describing how I would dress myself as a shabby down-at-heel picked up by Lady Houston, as it were, off the streets, the door opened and Leslie walked in and joined the conference. After being introduced I said: "And I think I would wear a pair of strange spectacles, perhaps with magnifying lenses", and Leslie laughed and said: "Good. I think you are our man." The contract was duly sealed for eight guineas a day, no miserable pounds in those days – solid guineas.

'On the day I was called for work I duly arrived at 8.30 a.m. for make-up and was ready by 9 a.m. and the shot was all set up – at least as far as the camera was concerned – by 9.30 a.m. But so far as I remember it was approaching 11 a.m. before the great man appeared in dressing gown and carpet slippers and smoking a pipe, as if he had only recently got up. And so far as I know that was indeed the fact. He was living at the studios in modest comfort and the financial pressures so ruthless today were not then operating. Indeed, I don't think they ever could have made it operate with him; he was in my brief experience so easy, relaxed and effortlessly charming that no tough organisational method would have worked with him. On my great day of work – only two shots so far as I remember – I was given a canvas chair next to his, with my name printed on it for the first time in my life, and we exchanged easy talk about acting and, I have an idea though this may be pure fantasy, that I was one of the people who said he should attempt Hamlet one day. I suppose he had in him a harder core than he allowed to appear, but my single experience of him was of a person of unutterable charm, ease, courtesy and relaxation – the ease and relaxation being of course the sine qua non of great film acting.'

As I mentioned earlier the subject of Mitchell's fatal illness, cancer, was never discussed in the film and his death was attributed to 'actual exhaustion in the face of medical warnings that only rest could save him'. *Time* magazine said this, in its review of the film in June 1942, adding: 'Mitchell had a year to live, doctors assured him, unless he quit working.'

Leslie, by nature, wished to avoid any unpleasant reminders of human frailty and so had no difficulty avoiding the subject of cancer. In fact, he made Mitch's death no more unpleasant than a rather tired man dropping into a deep sleep. If that was squeamish, he felt he was right: there was already too much pain and suffering in the war. When he came to film Mitchell's death scene he did it peacefully, stretched out in a reclining chair in the garden, remarking to Phil Samuel that 'death must be a beautiful thing'. The spiritual value of the scene was emphasised by the hovering gull which seemed to Leslie to be the visible destiny of Mitchell's spirit. Referring to this scene and her part in it, Rosamund John said:

'Leslie hated death scenes and refused to have one, hence the stratagem of leaving him smiling in the garden – and, then, the sudden realisation of his death dawning on my face. It was very difficult to do. After heaven knows how many rehearsals, Leslie's stand-in, anxiously seeing me getting progressively more over-wrought, said helpfully, 'Don't let it get you upset!' And to cap that, Perinal said: "She does not look pretty when she cries!" ' Of her relationship with Perinal, Rosamund remarked: 'I think he liked me because I could talk to him in French, but his ideal of a film star was Merle Oberon so he was fairly miserable!'

Rosamund was to learn much from Leslie, appearing in his last three films, and her affection for him deepened. 'I owed him a great deal. He taught me most of what I knew about film-making. I think he despised the razzmatazz that went with it, but had a very professional attitude and deep instinct for what really counted with the public. He once said to me, "Nothing else matters in filming but your eyes. If you're thinking about your appearance – or something equally irrelevant – that is what's going to come over. Leave all that to the technicians. Just concentrate on your feelings." And yet he could direct the other actors and put over that sincerity at the same time. Always the dual control: intensity of feeling and critical objectivity.'

In December 1941, beyond the small world of the Denham

studios where Leslie led his actors through their scenes, greater events were taking place. He had gone briefly to London to record his part in a *Brains Trust* programme when the news of Pearl Harbour came, followed swiftly by that of the sinking off Malaya of the battleships *Prince of Wales* and *Repulse* by Japanese dive-bombers. Within a matter of days the United States was at war with both Japan and Germany. Just prior to these events I had gone up to Scotland to join a ship at Dalmuir on the Clyde. After refitting for the tropics she had proceeded downstream to Greenock, preparatory to sailing for the Far East. I managed to get some embarkation leave and came down to Westcott. Leslie drove over from Stoke Poges and we spent my last week-end in England together at Stowe Maries.

I remember all of us – Leslie and Ruth, my wife, Trish, and myself, my sister and her fiancée Bob Dale Harris – going for a walk on the Sunday afternoon in the Deerleap Woods. Nothing spectacular was discussed on that walk – not even the pros and cons of war-time marriages, though the long separation ahead was to put paid to mine – and when we turned for home the orange, winter sunlight cast long shadows before us. Shortly after tea Leslie prepared to leave for Stoke Poges again and we said goodbye standing out in the drive by his car. He knew it would be a long time before we met again for my foreign commission was to last two and a half years.

'Unless I'm sunk, of course, by the Japs,' I reminded him, 'in which case I'll get survivors' leave.'

'Oh, you'll survive, Wink,' he said in his dry way. He put his hands on my shoulders and gave me a quick hug.

'I'm hopeless at separations – but cheer up, old boy, it won't be too long before we're all together again. Keep your pecker up – and keep us posted.' And with a cheery wave he got into his car and disappeared into the gathering dusk.

Long after, recalling those funny words about keeping one's pecker up – they made us all laugh a bit at the time for that was the last thing, in that context, I would do – I was surprised to remember they were the last words he ever spoke to me. I never saw him again.

CHAPTER SEVEN

Swedish Invitation
January 1942-October 1942

In the new year the Ministry of Information, in conjunction with the British Council, began preparing a list of lecturers to visit Sweden in which Leslie's name figured. Though Sweden leant culturally in a western direction, the bulk of her iron ore and heavy industrial produce was moving eastwards into Hitler's Germany. As Winston Churchill wrote: 'For Sweden the choice was a profitable neutrality – or subjugation.' And as if to underline the delicate position of her neutrality he further said: 'Our relations with Sweden require careful consideration. Germany acts upon Sweden by threats.'

Despite our acceptance of what was an inevitable situation for Sweden with Germany its powerful close neighbour, we were nevertheless eager to maintain our old friendship with this democratic kingdom and prevent her neutrality becoming too German-oriented. To draw Sweden and ourselves closer together and promote cultural exchange a number of speakers had been discussed by the British Council and the MOI. The MOI list of 19th February contained the names of Sir Kenneth Clark (due to leave for Stockholm immediately), Miss Ellen Wilkinson, MP (for the middle of March), Dr Parsons for May, Mr T.S. Eliot for April and Professor Julian Huxley and Mr Leslie Howard for June. To these were now added the names of Dr Malcolm Sargent, Miss Eileen Joyce, Mr John Gielgud – and several bishops. Mr J. Somers Cocks of the Northern Department Foreign Office, not without a touch of dry humour, attached a Minute to these lecturers' names: 'The MOI list is a pretty good one, provided the stars don't fall out and leave only the less distinguished luminaries!'

At the time these invitations were sent out Leslie's film *Pimpernel Smith* was being shown in Stockholm, not publicly because that would not have been allowed under the stiff Censorship rules applicable to neutral countries, but in the private Press cinema attached to the British Legation. This method seemed, perhaps, a covert way of getting round the censorship for though it had been shown privately it had, over a period of time through repeated showings, been seen by thousands of people. The Swedish Foreign Office thought this constituted an infringement of the censorship rules – and to put a fine, though German, point on it had made the showings public not private. They, therefore, demanded that further exhibitions of the film be discontinued.

When the reasons for this suppression were asked, the Swedish Cultural Minister replied that he had just arrived home from Germany, where he had been discussing the confiscation of American films destined for Sweden, when he had learned of the further private showings of *Pimpernel Smith*. His reasons for asking the Legation to refrain from further showing were these: the Swedish law relating to private entertainments was for one or, at most, two entertainments intended for personal friends of the host or bona fide members of a society. If these entertainments became too frequent the guests would include many not known to the host, and the Germans would retaliate by taking several theatres and showing quantities of unsuitable films likely to cause trouble. He added that the Swedish press had been silent as regards *Pimpernel Smith* from which we could draw our own conclusions.

I think the conclusion one can reasonably draw from all this is that the Swedish Cultural Minister, when in Berlin, had been invited to call on the German Minister for Propaganda, Dr Goebbels, and been told point blank that the film was offensive to Germans and must be suppressed. It seems to me the Swedes, frightened of the Germans, over-reacted to their demands and that legally, within the privacy of our own Legation, we were entitled to as many showings as we wished. Nonetheless, the film was taken off and never shown again. A further Minute to the Swedish injunction was added by Mr Cocks of the Foreign Office. It read:

> I imagine the Stockholm Legation was right in withdrawing *Pimpernel Smith*. It is about as provocative as a film can possibly be and if the Legation hadn't given way about it they might have had their style seriously cramped *in the future*.

If this was the official view of the provocative nature of the film then, from the fuss made about it, it had clearly succeeded, even in its limited showings, in being quite potent propaganda.

As far as Leslie's lecturing invitation to Sweden in June was concerned, it simply never happened. He became one of the stars who 'fell out'. This was entirely due to the fact that *The First of the Few* exceeded by many weeks its, perhaps, optimistic schedule. Referring to the film's longevity and cost, Adrian Brunel wrote:

And so I worked on and on – the longest picture with which I had been associated. When I became anxious about the time and money involved, Leslie shook his head. 'Money is the *least* important thing in life,' he said, and then launched into his theories about the first essential – a good picture – and the fallacy of convention economics in war-time.

But, of course, *The First of the Few* was the most complex and technical film Leslie had ever worked on. Every detail had to be checked thoroughly with both Supermarine and the RAF. Besides, there were other factors in war-time – not only connected with air-fields and fighter-stations – that caused problems and delays. Studio staff and technicians were constantly being called up and replacements were hard to find. Not only camera crews but cameras and camera parts were in short supply – and the same went for sound equipment. Essential studio requirements were not being manufactured. If cameras broke down they had to be repaired with old parts cannibalised from others. Since the war came first – and particularly the war in the air – days were lost waiting at air-fields for pilots and planes away on operations.

It was not surprising, therefore, that it was already June before principal photography in the studio and second-unit work at fighter-stations and factories had been completed. Only now could cutting and editing of the material begin. During this period of selection and assemblage Leslie and Sidney Cole, began to piece the film together into what is called a rough cut. In this process a large percentage of film shot ends on the cutting-room floor – and with the lost footage may be sacrificed some cherished scenes, snipped out by the editor's scissors. Thus, much of an actor's work may be lost and his arduous preparation and performance become no more, in cinematic terms, than 'the face on the cutting room floor' to be swept up and burnt. It is simply the price of continuity and story-telling.

Once Leslie and Sidney had assembled their rough cut this became the basis of the finished film. Leslie would then leave his editor in charge to synchronise the special effects and add the musical accompaniment.

Earlier Leslie had discussed with William Walton the sort of theme music the film needed. Sidney arranged a run-through of the film so that Walton could plan his musical approach.

'Leslie gave me very full instructions to pass on to Willie Walton about his feelings regarding the music. These, after the showing, I dutifully relayed to Walton. He listened carefully, then, observed drily: "I see. Leslie wants a lot of notes!" The result was the famous Spitfire Prelude and Fugue.'

While Leslie rested at home, he began to consider future plans. For some time a subject had been nagging at the back of his mind and he looked out some notes on it, which set him wondering how feasible it was in the present circumstances. It was, in fact, the very subject that Perinal, the cameraman, had mistakenly, imagined he had been engaged by Leslie to film: it was *Hamlet*. In 1936 Leslie had produced the play in New York in a Danish ninth century setting. Now, looking at the play again, he began to see it afresh, realising that his approach to it could be contemporary with the war. It intrigued him to think that without altering or transposing a line of the original text he could bring it from the ninth to the twentieth century simply by setting it in present day Denmark. It would be an allegory, the ninth century historical allusions fitting the present war-situation like a glove. It would scarcely please the purists or neo-Elizabethans and generations of Shakespearian scholars would revolve in their graves. But it was, Leslie felt, a risk well worth taking for the origins of the play had considerable contemporary political relevance.

To some of his friends with whom he had discussed it this original treatment of the subject appealed strongly, to others it seemed an ingenious innovation too out of context for serious consideration. Leslie, disagreeing with such reservations, did not think *Hamlet* in any way remote from the present conflict. He argued that *Hamlet*'s Denmark was on a war-footing as much as England and the Danes preparing to resist Fortinbras as much as we to resist Hitler. Leslie quoted Marcellus's lines from Act One, Scene One to confirm this point of resemblance:

Good now, sit down, and tell me, he that knows,
Why this same strict and most observant watch
So nightly toils the subject of the land;
And why such daily cast of brazen cannon,
And foreign mart for implements of war;
Why such impress of shipwrights, whose sore task
Does not divide the Sunday from the week;
What might be toward that this sweaty haste

Doth make the night joint-labourer with the day:
Who is't that can inform me?

Leslie explained, in the words of Horatio, that these warlike
preparations were entirely due to the threats of Fortinbras of
Norway, whom Leslie saw as the prototype of Hitler. This Fortinbras
had 'sharked up a list of lawless resolutes for food and diet to some
enterprise that hath a stomach in it.' For this enterprise, an attack on
Denmark, Fortinbras was employing the same softening-up process
of outrageous demands and threats Hitler had used when preparing
to invade Czechoslovakia. The ambassadors Voltimand and
Cornelius had been dispatched to buy Fortinbras off and 'suppress
his further gait herein' in much the same way that Nevile Henderson
had been dispatched to placate the unreasonable Hitler. And what
did Hitler do, Leslie asked, but tell Henderson he had no further
territorial ambition and certainly no quarrel with England – even as
Fortinbras vowed never to attack Denmark – then, having swallowed
Czechoslovakia, promptly attacked Danzig and invaded Poland.
Fortinbras did much the same, pretending no quarrel with Denmark
in order to gain 'quiet pass' across it to attack Poland. In the end,
much stronger, he re-entered Denmark as indisputable conqueror.
In fact, Fortinbras was no more to be trusted than the obtuse Hitler.
As for Claudius who had seized the state in Hamlet's absence at
Wittenberg – 'popped in between the election and his hopes' – here,
indeed, Leslie pointed out, was the archetypal Quisling-Gauleiter
surrounded by his court of Nazi sycophants and yes-men.

Of course, in his enthusiasm for a contemporary setting, Leslie
had not forgotten that the play was about more things than politics
and war. Above all it was a reflection of the workings of Hamlet's
mind – and here was the kernel of Leslie's thinking, the point he
wished to drive home. In Hamlet's mind was the inner within the
outer war, the inner battle of attrition between a man's heart and
head, between softness and hardness, to decide a course of action.
Indecision is only overthrown by an extreme exertion of will. And
this was to be the final parallel. To Leslie Hamlet represented the
embodiment of national resistance driven into irrevocable action to
rid his country of the forces of evil and bring down the Quisling-
usurper Claudius. Hamlet symbolised for Leslie the Resistance
leader of a contemporary Denmark.

It would certainly have made an original and daring film and
from what I remember Leslie telling me about the project he had
every intention of using the war-time background, with the

modernised historical allusions as framework. The setting, as distinct from his 1936 production, would have been quite contemporary – the actors dressed in modern clothes as courtiers and diplomats surrounded by their lackeys in their equivalent military uniforms. In fact, the leading characters would have vaguely resembled the political heroes and villains of the day: even Fortinbras's army would have driven tanks and carried machine-guns.

Leslie's desire to realise this film was very intense and nagged at him to the end of his life, and I am sure that but for his sudden and unexpected death he would have produced and acted in it. But, of course, it required an immense amount of preparation – and time – which at the moment with the editing and preparation for release of *The First of the Few* he could scarcely spare. But that he was laying plans to film *Hamlet* was never in doubt and this was borne out by his friend and collaborator, Roland Pertwee, in a letter of reminiscence he wrote some years later.

> A few days before that disastrous visit to Spain which ended in his death, Leslie had agreed to make a film version of Hamlet and had asked me to work with him on the script. That he did not live to make it is, I have always felt, a great screen tragedy, for I know that he would have given a performance of extraordinary sensitivity and intelligence. On his last night in England we sat up until the small hours planning his approach to this most challenging of all films and even trying out subtle inflections for this line or for that.

In the last paragraph of this letter Roland paid a personal tribute to Leslie coupled with an appreciation from another distinguished man of theatre and film world who had known and admired him.

> I shall ever cherish the memory of his friendship for, as an artist, I shall not look upon his like again. After the preview of his film *The First of the Few*, Noël Coward said to me that his performance was acting that transcended acting.

*

Another factor which may have contributed to a change in Leslie's plans and certainly to a postponement of *Hamlet* came about in an unexpected way. Nearing the end of filming on *The First of the Few*

Leslie's production consultant, Adrian Brunel, came to him and asked if he might be released as he had just been offered a directing job. Leslie, delighted for Adrian's sake, agreed and asked him what film it was. Adrian told him it was a recruiting film for the ATS, based on a story by Moie Charles, which the Ministry of Information was keen on.

He admitted to Leslie he had turned it down initially because he had some reservations about the script, but Derrick de Marney, the producer, having got del Giudice of Two Cities to finance it, had persuaded him to overcome his scruples. Leslie, wishing Adrian good luck with the project, thought no more about it.

Adrian had a bit of a shock, however, when he heard it was to be made at the small Highbury Studios.

The shock came when I went to the studios two or three days before we were due to start, only to find that we were not to make the film on their small ground-floor stage but on the minute upstairs stage. It was the smallest studio I had ever seen – it was not, of course, built as a studio but was a converted room. However, I was in for it and determined to do my best.

But after four days of production in this 'match-box' with 'insufficient space and lamps, together with old cameras that didn't work' Adrian became a little desperate. 'Another complication during the four distressing days there was the fact that the studio projector was not working properly – we could only just see our daily rushes but could not hear them.' As a result of these many difficulties production was suspended.

Undoubtedly Adrian's problems were very real yet he expressed the conviction that 'with a new camera and the four days experience in the tiny studio all would be well.' But there are always two sides to every film story – as there was to this one. That Derrick de Marney, the producer, had 'only a limited technical knowledge and no technical experience' was probably true – but it was not de Marney who made the final decision to discontinue production: it was Filippo del Giudice. He had been advised to take this action by Phil Samuel, Leslie's production manager on *The First of the Few*. Phil expressed the circumstances of the suspension in these words:

'Filippo called me in to see the first week's rushes – which were rubbish – and he asked my advice. I, then, read the script and advised him to stop production which seemed to have little to do with the script. Eventually Filippo got Leslie to start again as director.'

Leslie had, of course, at this stage no inkling of his involvement with the film and it came as a complete surprise when Filippo rang to ask if he would take over the direction. Busy editing his own film he was far from keen on stepping into what amounted to a rescue operation, particularly as it was Adrian's project, and he delayed making any decision until he talked it over thoroughly with everyone concerned. One of the people concerned was Jack Beddington, of the MOI, who did not want to see such a useful propaganda film permanently immobilised. He urged Leslie to give it serious consideration for, quite apart from its recruiting value, with Leslie's name attached to it the film would have greater appeal.

Leslie, after an initial meeting with Derrick de Marney, realised the problems he and Adrian had had at the Highbury Studios and that if the film was to be produced at all it would have to be at Denham with proper facilities. If these conditions were met he would direct with the proviso that Adrian come in again as his production consultant. As far as casting was concerned he was entirely in agreement with the original arrangements Moie Charles had made. The seven girls chosen for the film – Lilli Palmer, Joan Greenwood, Rosamund John, Joyce Howard, Joan Gates, Barbara Waring and Jean Gillie – could not, Leslie felt, be bettered. He was, naturally, delighted that Rosamund was among them. Though Leslie agreed to start the film again at short notice he was far from happy with the script or the way the girls had been presented, thrown together without any explanation of their widely differing backgrounds. To give worthwhile opportunities to what he described as 'a very well chosen cast of talented new young actresses' the somewhat stiff documentary nature of the script needed humanising, for the characters were too static. To this end Leslie got both Aimée Stuart and Roland Pertwee, to aim for a lighter treatment and sense of fun.

On Adrian's recommendation, Leslie retained the original, young camera crew who had been up against such difficulties at Highbury: Cyril Knowles and Ray Sturgess. Ray was to have a distinguished career as cameraman, making *Hungry Hill*, *Seven Days to Noon* and Laurence Olivier's *Hamlet*. In a broadcast for the BBC on the North American service, Leslie later described the film, and the circumstances of his unexpected involvement with it, in these words:

'Early in July I arrived about midnight at my house near the Denham Film Studios to find a friend of mine, Derrick de Marney, waiting to see me. He brought with him a note from a mutual friend, Jack Beddington, with an urgent request that I should undertake the direction of a film about the ATS which de Marney was producing.

'My first instinct was to refuse because I was then very busy with the final editing of *The First of the Few*, my Spitfire film which was shortly to be released. Within a week, however, I accepted the invitation because I realised that here was obviously one of the most remarkable aspects of the war. The part played by women these days is so far-reaching and important that the least a mere maker of films can do is to express on the screen the significance of their work, both in gratitude to those already serving and in encouragement to the large numbers who have still to do so.

'This particular film is about the ATS, though it might have been about the WAAFS or the WRNS. Still it would be impossible in one short hour and a half to cover all three women's services, and the ATS have the distinction of being the first to be formed and of containing by far the largest personnel. The older generation will remember them as the WAACS more than twenty-five years ago and many girls are now in khaki whose mothers wore a similar if, perhaps, not quite so attractive uniform.

'We started shooting this film at a large training centre with 1,200 girls for our background. Our foreground is occupied by seven characters whose lives and stories we follow from the train journey which they take to join up until the final climax of the film, which I naturally shall not reveal to you. These characters are played by seven young actresses who had to go through the experience of undergoing all the preliminary training with the 1,200 real articles, and apart from the fact that they are talented actresses they are not different from the rest of the girls.

'The men in this film occupy small and inconspicuous roles, quite different from my Spitfire film when the reverse was true. This is a story about the women and the magnificent way in which they are doing their duty. For me, and for all of us concerned in the making of it, it has been a considerable privilege. I forgot to mention that after a variety of suggestions this picture is now called *The Gentle Sex*. After you have seen it and appreciated the valiant work which the ATS are doing you will probably agree that this is a rather gentle title.'

The large training centre Leslie mentioned in the broadcast was, in fact, Stoughton Barracks, Guildford, and here his seven leading ladies were enlisted, put on their uniforms for the first time and were indoctrinated into the gentle art of 'square-bashing'. It was the cause of much hilarity to the 'regulars' – 'Especially when film actresses were included,' as Rosamund John was to tell me. 'We were drilled by a Sergeant-Major who despised us all and frightened me into paralysis!'

Though Leslie enjoyed the fun of making *The Gentle Sex* he was scarcely stretched as director and Rosamund thought 'he was fairly bored and only did it because he genuinely wanted to help the MOI.' In devising a commentary for the film, Leslie appeared in it briefly, in silhouette, his back to the camera as he introduced the girls individually at the railway station from where they go to enlist. At other moments his voice acted as a bridge between scenes. 'Nevertheless by doing the commentary,' Rosamund said, 'he pulled the film together and his connection with it was largely responsible for its ultimate success.' As was his custom Leslie continued to improvise as he went along which Rosamund found unnerving with her 'assumed Scots accent.'

'I used to dash along to the set where John Laurie, a genuine Scot, who played my boyfriend, would put me right.' It must have worked quite well for many who saw the film complimented her on being the genuine article.

During production of *The Gentle Sex* Leslie continued to broadcast for the BBC. When he could not go personally to Broadcasting House they sent a recording car to Denham. He did several in Spanish and Portuguese for which he had a rather good ear and could deliver in an accent which sounded perfect. Rosamund recalled this facility with foreign languages, remarking on 'his uncanny skill to learn a speech in a foreign language phonetically and deliver it.' He also sat quite regularly on the panel of the *Brains Trust* –though he remained frankly puzzled why the BBC should want his 'services among such an auspicious body of experts'.

'I am not all that knowledgeable,' he admitted, and added: 'Still I have certainly learnt a good deal – it's been a form of education – since appearing with Julian Huxley and Malcolm Sargent as fellow panellists. Particularly, I have learnt when to keep my mouth shut!' Howard Thomas, the producer of the programme, said of Leslie: 'He was modest about his appearance in the *Brains Trust* and very much in awe of the others. Always deprecating his own ability, he was surprised that we kept him on. Often he said to me: "Just why *do* you keep me on?" '

While Leslie was working on *The Gentle Sex*, Noël Coward began his production of *In Which We Serve* which he wrote, co-directed and acted in. This epic story of courage and endurance was to do for the

Navy what Leslie had done for the Air Force in *The First of the Few*. The film was based on the true story of the evacuation of Crete and the part played in that heroic but disastrous rear-guard action by the destroyer flotilla commanded by Captain Lord Louis Mountbatten in HMS *Kelly*. Noël asked Leslie if he would speak the commentary which concluded the film. It was, in fact, the famous prayer – repeated on countless quarter-decks during the war – from which the title of the film sprang. It contained the words which I doubt if any sailor alive has forgotten: 'Be pleased to receive into thy Almighty and most gracious protection the persons of us thy servants, and the Fleet in which we serve.' Noël later said that Leslie's quiet voice speaking the lines of the prayer in the stillness following the violence of the action was one of the most moving things he ever heard.

*

In early October Leslie was approached by Basil Dean, then chief of ENSA, with a request to appear as Nelson in a special Trafalgar Day production *Cathedral Steps* by Clemence Dane. It was to be the full Technicolor spectacle of classic proportions staged live on the plinth and steps of St Paul's.

Dean had assembled a star cast of theatre and film people for this piece of theatrical showmanship which was expected to draw thousands of Londoners in addition to the Mayor and aldermen of the City. It was to be something of a morale-booster in this third year of what looked like a long war. Immense organisation was called for – the use of massed choirs and an orchestra conducted by Sir Henry Wood – and the whole area of St Paul's Churchyard and Ludgate Hill would have to be cordoned off, with traffic diverted, for a period of four hours so that a very large audience (estimated by Dean to be in the region of 100,000) could either see his production or have it relayed to them on amplifiers. Ten trumpeters of the Royal Household would open proceedings with a fanfare from a platform near the dome of St Paul's.

At the outset of this vast gala entertainment its germinating genius might well have seen himself, at its conclusion, arising Sir Basil. It was the sort of jingoistic effort that frequently accorded knighthoods and, I suppose, in the middle of a bitter war it was a laudable way of cheering people up. They could escape, for an hour or two, from drab surroundings and uniforms into a colourful world of somewhat outdated pageantry.

The artistes selected would, of course, offer their services without fee and the production took the form of selections from famous British poets and writers welded together by Dean into a patriotic spectacle illuminative of British virtues in times of greatness or adversity. The cast was to appear either in tableau groups, as in the style of miracle or morality plays, or singly as symbolic lay-figures. Eric Portman, dressed in scarlet, was to be 'Valour', attended by his 'Fighting Men'. Sybil Thorndike, in blue, represented 'Patience' – followed by her 'Men and Women of Peace'. Henry Ainley and Edith Evans as 'The Crowned Man' and 'The Crowned Woman' spoke for the Kings and Queens of England. As a kind of contemporary 'Everyman' there was to be a 'Mr Anyman', a role undertaken by Frank Cellier, who was to view these magnificent proceedings as he sat contentedly smoking a pipe of shag.

Immediately following the massed choirs' rendering of 'Rule Britannia', Edith Evans was to thunder out: 'Up my Britons – on my chariots, on my chargers! Not any Prince of Europe shall invade us. Pluck up your hearts! By your peace in camp and your valour in the field we shall shortly have a famous victory.'

This exhortative speech seemed to combine a stern warning to Hitler to abandon any invasion plans he might still be contemplating and a veiled reference, in Shakespearian terms, not so much to Agincourt as to another great battle then in progress, El Alamein, of which news was expected hourly. Miss Evans was to be followed by Robert Speight, in quieter mood, rendering Gray's 'Elegy'. Finally, Leslie was to appear as Nelson and, kneeling at the top of the Cathedral steps, speak the prayer before Trafalgar.

Since most of the actors, actresses, bandsmen, choristers and production staff were working here, there and everywhere in plays, films, concerts and other entertainments, Dean had to fit rehearsals in with the skill of ringmaster in charge of the Big Top. But he was well up to the assignment. Difficulties were overcome by Dean's flair for the 'big occasion', and with a minimum of preparation – a preliminary reading at Drury Lane, two rehearsals at the Albert Hall to fit in the music and a final run through at St Paul's on the day of production – the spectacle was presented with solemnity and panache. To the great crowds of Londoners who witnessed *Cathedral Steps* it must have seemed, for all its pomp, circumstance and panoply of the past, a stirring enough occasion that would be remembered for the boldness of its presentation. I don't suppose Dean was disappointed at the effect he had created, but it was scarcely an original way of presenting the British to the British in the

Planning the set-up – Jack Hildyard (cameraman), Adrian Brunel, unidentified, Leslie and Hazel.

Crisp and Mitchell shaping the Spitfire – David Niven and Leslie.

Leslie as director – *The of the Few*.

Reflections on a Merlin engine – Leslie as R. J. Mitchell.

third year of total war, and it was inevitable that some would find it irrelevant and distasteful while our Russian allies were dying in the ruins of Stalingrad.

Leslie's part in these grand proceedings seemed unpretentious, almost modern, by comparison. In a stillness, unbroken by trumpets or drums, he emerged from the Cathedral, a spare, almost ghostly figure in a silver-grey uniform that seemed to contain the last mortal remains of the victor of Trafalgar. There was a tomb-like pallor to his features. When he kneeled at the top of the steps a hush came over the crowds, as if, indeed, they were looking at a ghost. He seemed to hold them in the tight stillness of his clasped hands – and when he spoke Nelson's prayer quietly and simply, on that grey November day, he seemed to speak from the heart of England. It was a moment people remembered with a catch of breath. I think Leslie faithfully mirrored Clemence Dane's own image of Nelson when she wrote:

Nelson is everywhere,
He stands in the wreck of the road,
He sweeps up the broken glass,
He fights with fire and despair,
He feels for, he fingers your heart . . .

Leslie made few public appearances during the war, always happier to be a back-room-boy, and this was the last he was ever to make. Strange that he should say his farewell to London in the role of a hero killed by a marksman's bullet off Cape Trafalgar – for Leslie was to die less than eight months later the victim of German bullets off another Spanish cape, Corunna, in the Bay of Biscay. Though Leslie was scarcely a hero in the Nelson mould he, too, was to die at the peak of achievement, in the service of his country. Dismissing altogether the coincidence, I have often wondered if Leslie's death was due not so much to the haphazard mosaic of events, the way things fell together, but as the course of a more predictable destiny.

CHAPTER EIGHT

'The days are shortening . . . '
November 1942-December 1942

As the year declined and the sun dipped lower in the sky, summer gave way to autumn, October to November. In the garden at Monkseaton the last yellowing leaves of the poplars blew in little agitated spirals round the lawn and the rowan berries burnt bright red against a wind-swept, almost wintry sky. Of this autumn Leslie wrote:

> The days are shortening, the log fire is lit, the curtains are drawn early. These evenings are the most precious moments of all. Sometimes we sit at the oval table, the two of us, eating silently, a little too tired to talk after the long day's work and the confusion of many people and voices. Sometimes there are a few friends round the table . . . but generally it is alone . . .

Leslie, working hard to finish the film, drove home after each day's filming from Denham to Stoke Poges through now darkened, mist-shrouded lanes. He generally found autumns depressing and this fourth one of the war more so than others, chill and damp, the forerunner of a long winter. What summer there had been consisted of one brief heat-wave, lasting a week, during which he had been locked up at work in the studio. As the autumn days shortened into winter he confessed that both Violette and he were feeling more than a little tired and rundown. Professional achievement and satisfaction, he was later to write, had been 'brought at the cost of long gruelling hours in studio, office and study' and though it had brought them 'many highlights of inspiration, beauty and abiding love', it had finally brought them exhaustion.

In the second week in November Leslie developed a feverish cold and Violette rang the studio to say that she was keeping him at home for a few days. She nursed him as he lay on the sofa in the drawing room wrapped in blankets – bringing him pills and hot drinks. 'You have been ministering to me for three days. I cannot read for my head is too thick and my eyes too bleary . . . You are in and out of the room . . . standing over me with a cup of something hot and firm commands.' While she fussed over him to get him well again Leslie was more concerned for Violette than himself. He thought she looked tired and washed-out.

She had scarcely complained but there was a small spot on her nose that had swollen up and was hurting. 'It's nothing,' she told him, 'but it looks very unattractive.' And she put make-up on it to cover it.

In two or three days Leslie's cold was better but the swelling in Violette's nose had got worse. The infection, whatever it was, had spread, affecting her eyes and vision. The doctor who had seen Leslie ordered her to bed and prescribed the war-time anti-biotic, M&B. After a day or two, instead of responding to the drug, her condition worsened and Leslie became increasingly alarmed. A consulant was called in who advised that the doseage of M&B be increased and a day and night nurse were engaged so that there was always someone in attendance. Leslie later wrote of

> . . . the nightmare of those days with the dreadful barrier of illness between us . . . Hours spent watching you or concentrating on you – and wishing, praying, willing . . . The invasion of doctors and nurses – the frightening turmoil . . . and the utter futility and helplessness of the physicians and their drugs.

After six days the doctors began to admit defeat. They insisted she be moved to hospital in London. Leslie, entirely in their hands, agreed and Violette was taken there by ambulance. Leslie followed in his car, a journey which he described as

> the never-to-be-forgotten journey to London along that familiar route we had travelled together so often, so happily – now a dismal ca\.alcade on a grey English autumn Sunday. Nearly two hours of it, the ambulance crawling in front calmly, unconcernedly – and myself behind, alone, in the little car, clutching the wheel, eyes piercing the black monster in front, and praying, praying – for two hours praying without stop . . .

He saw her into the hospital – 'a ghastly, ugly building,' and into 'the gloomy little room with the bomb-proof bricked up window.' He remembered Violette's voice saying suddenly and very clearly: 'It's quite a nice room . . . ' – and the nurses smiling because her eyes were covered. Then, when they were alone, he sat with her, his hand on her head, trying 'with all the power of thought of which I am capable' to transfer to her the will to live. Later, he drove to Grosvenor House where his friend Filippo del Giudice had set aside a bedroom and sitting room for his use while he awaited further news from the hospital. Leslie had earlier rung Ruth to tell her the news, and she and my sister, without hesitation, hastily packing a few night things, had come straight from Stowe Maries to be with him.

The following morning, Monday, when Leslie reached Violette's bed-side, though her eyes were still bandaged, she knew instinctively that it was him and whispered his name. He turned towards the doctors, searching their faces. This time they did not avoid his eyes. They seemed a little more reassuring. There was a chance, a slight hope, they told him. Leslie, buoyed up at any turn for the better, went back to the hotel to tell Ruth and Doodie the latest news. Later, when he rang the hospital, they told him Violette was sleeping, apparently more comfortably – and Leslie felt suddenly hopeful that all would be well, that she had passed the crisis and would recover.

Ruth, without discouraging his optimism, was less sure and in her heart she wondered if the hospital was simply giving him a straw to clutch at. The last thing the hospital had said was that they expected her to sleep through the night and there would be no more news till morning. As Leslie had not slept properly for a week Ruth suggested he get undressed and go to bed, and she gave him a sedative. He protested he mustn't sleep too long in case the hospital rang. Ruth reminded him of what the hospital had said – that there would be no more news till morning – and that should they ring she would call him immediately. Leslie took the sedative and went to bed. He was soon in a deep sleep.

When Ruth went to her room she rang the hotel switchboard telling them that Leslie was not to be disturbed on any account. If there were any calls they were to be put through direct to her extension. If Ruth slept it was not for long. It was shortly after 2 a.m., Tuesday morning, that the phone rang beside her bed. It was the Matron at the hospital. She told Ruth that Violette had died at ten minutes past two, peacefully in her sleep. She said they had done all they could but the odds on her survival had been an outside one, and her condition had deteriorated rapidly in the past two days. Violette had died of cerebral meningitis.

Ruth lay awake knowing she would have to break the news to

Leslie and knowing how badly he would take it. But she was determined not to wake him till morning – protracting the moment and, perhaps, mitigating it. Leslie was later to write:

They did not wake me at ten minutes past two. I suppose they thought it best. I got out of bed at half-past eight, dazed and wondering. I heard voices from the sitting room. I went in and saw faces. Someone said: 'You'd better go back and lie down . . .'

Now began an exhausting calvary, a period of maceration and atonement. For all concerned it was as painful as having their emotions squeezed through a fine sieve. Leslie, in the extremity of grief, lay on the bed his hands over his face and began a catalogue of recrimination as he apportioned blame for his beloved Violette's death. First, he was supremely to blame for tardiness and indecision, then, the doctors and nurses for what now appeared to him their stupidity and negligence. No one, it seemed, was beyond the range of culpability for what had happened. None had been honest, no one had told him days ago how serious her condition was. Perhaps they didn't know, but why hadn't they admitted it? Why go on experimenting, using her body as a test-bench, a laboratory? All of them had been feeling their way in the dark, the consultant, an insult to medical practice, more stupid than the rest. There was no need for her to die if only he had been properly advised from the outset. Of course, it was *his* fault, in the first place, for not paying more attention to that friend at the studio who had mentioned a brilliant specialist in bacteriology, a man with a great knowledge of rare viruses. He could well have given the correct diagnosis before it was too late, instead of those other fools, messing about with their hit or miss methods.

Leslie was now, suddenly, face to face with the first major tragedy in his life. He had scarcely prepared for the role. No one is, of course, bolstered for tragedy and we all behave differently. Some absorb the blow better than others, finding reserves of strength to meet it. But Leslie was not this sort of person; he had no reserves on which to fall back. All his emotions were committed nearer the surface, the visible point of impact.

There were obvious reasons for this. Everything in his life had been relatively easy and uncomplicated, running smoothly and predictably, and he had never even remotely considered the possibility that there could be a darker side to the somewhat golden world he inhabited. In this he was quite naive. He had always been very much the master of his destiny, in control, making his own decisions, dictating the terms of both his professional and private life. He had also been somewhat cosseted and protected, and if there was something he didn't like he had generally walked away from it. He had never had to face an unremitting enemy who wouldn't budge. Now, forces beyond his power had snatched control, creating chaos, and suddenly this very reasonable man could no longer reason with events, alter their course – or walk away. The death of Violette had not only brought him his first major defeat, but brought him face to face with his own inadequacy. He simply could not cope.

In this moment of tragedy and expiation he seemed unable to listen to or even acknowledge the help of others. Shut off in his own private and disconnected world he could hear nothing but the voice of his own despair, his own self-pity. All Ruth's sympathy – her attempts to help and soothe – seemed inadequate, unavailing, the soothing words wasted. He stared blankly at his wife and daughter as if they were almost alien figures, strangers going through the motions of concern, trying to say the right things. In the over-stretched melancholy of his mood he even seemed to doubt their compassion – as if they had never properly understood what he felt for Violette. It was something private and personal they had never sympathised with. In a quite perverse, unbalanced way he imagined Ruth was stage-managing the obsequies, because she liked to be at the centre of things. He was utterly wrong – she was only trying to help in her strong, maternal way, to give him something solid to hold onto – but it didn't prevent a barrier rising between them that none seemed able to penetrate.

In the immediate wake of Violette's death that first hour in the hotel room dragged like an eternity. To relieve the tension and the claustrophobia of that small room where sensible communication seemed impossible, Doodie hopefully suggested a walk in Hyde Park, saying the fresh air might do him good. With a despondent shrug Leslie agreed and the two of them left the hotel and began pacing the Park.

As they walked about he talked incessantly of Violette, repeating much of what he had said in the hotel. He had not realised how selfless she had been, how constant, or how hard she had worked for his comfort and happiness. But he had asked too much of her, driven her too hard – and this was the ghastly result. Now there was no way he could make up for what had happened, for the one thing he wanted was her and this was the final, worst denial – her life thrown away, sacrificed – and for what? Film-making! Well, that was a miserable side-issue when the health, well-being and happiness of someone one loved was at stake. He had been blind not to realise how run-down and ill she had become while he had been concentrating all his energies on this idiotic film, a film he had not wanted to make in the first place. And she had never complained, not once – only thinking of him and finishing the wretched film. Well, he would give it up now – chuck it, once and for all. They could find someone else to finish it.

When Doodie interrupted this spate of words by agreeing, saying that what he needed now, above all, was a period of quiet and rest to recuperate, he looked at her in some amazement. How could he think of himself at a moment like this? What happened to him was supremely unimportant. As to rest and recuperation she was the one, poor darling, who had needed that but never got it – not him. He had only one duty now – to devote himself to her – for it was his failure to think enough of her that had contributed to her death. He must be with her now when she needed him, in the first shock of separation. Above all, he must be able to communicate with her spirit. His spirit with her spirit – that was essential. This was the only way he could live through the anguish of the next few months.

As Doodie listened to her father's outpouring of pent-up emotion, with its emphasis on neglect and guilt, she heard it like a confession to which no answers were expected or required. Whatever she said would make no difference. Despite the compassion she felt, she realised he was not really talking to her – he was simply communicating the reactions of shock to someone, anyone, whether they listened or not. He was simply talking to himself out loud. All she could do was to walk patiently beside him – hearing out a stream, of what seemed to her, quite unreasonable self-recrimination.

Violette had died through no fault of his, and he was in no way to blame. But Doodie knew her father well enough to know that the advice or opinions of an eighteen-year-old daughter were not what he sought. To say anything now might well provoke differences, but that didn't stop her thinking her own thoughts as they walked along. Though she had never seen her father quite like this before she was not unfamiliar with his frequently unpredictable moods or his avowed attitudes over emotional matters. Besides, he knew, as she knew, that her loyalties were unequally divided and that she had been critical of his relationship with Violette.

She had for a long time found her father's attitude on certain topics misguided, naive and biased: misguided towards her mother, naive in relation to other women and often biased by his more unconventional associates in the entertainment world. As a recently, and happily, married young woman my sister had little difficulty in being more conformist in her feelings about marriage and family than her father. Though they had for years been very close, experiencing a very strong father-daughter relationship, since her recent marriage they had become more remote and alienated. Not that he disagreed with her marriage, though thinking it premature – but he had, in a very real sense, lost her for good, the child he had known and loved, and the bond between them was never so strong again. Besides, he knew very well she disapproved of him, finding his liberalism in matters of sex quaint, to say the least, perhaps somewhat distasteful – and this expressed disapproval of his relationship with Violette which annoyed him.

Leslie had always been supremely selfish in emotional matters and Doodie found it unreasonable and unfair that anyone could pursue their own ends with such apparent lack of conscience for the feelings of others, in this case her mother's. Ruth's feelings had always come too low on his list of priorities. Leslie thought that so long as she had a home and the necessary creature comforts that went with it that was all he could do. He had not been ungenerous and, in return, expected her to accept an arrangement that gave him freedom of action to live his own life without criticism. He got criticism of course – he couldn't have expected otherwise. Perhaps, he should have made an end to his marriage years ago, giving Ruth a proper divorce settlement with adequate compensation. But he had not wanted that. He had wanted the marriage to continue but by his own terms of reference, his own ideas of freedom.

They had been silently walking now for some minutes, each with their own thoughts. Leslie's outburst of recrimination had burnt itself out, giving way to a kind of weary fatalism. They sat a few minutes on a park bench, unspeaking, Leslie staring glumly, abstractedly, ahead with blank eyes as if already communing with a ghost. In eight short days everything for him had come to an end. Five years of never-to-be-repeated happiness had been swept away at Violette's death, terminated by fate with cold, blind, heartless precision leaving him no more substance than memory. He seemed, indeed, to have become the man who, losing her, had lost himself – his life poised, in an almost posthumous sense, in a meaningless vacuum of time. He now only longed for the hand of destiny to move him on, to reunite him with Violette with the same impersonal precision that had torn them apart.

Watching her father as he stared, hollow-eyed, at emptiness, Doodie, for all their differences, felt a sudden, urgent, instinctive wave of pity and sorrow for all he had suffered, and reached out taking his hand in hers. After a moment, she said: 'Shall we go back? It's getting cold – and you look tired.' And, slowly, her arm linked through his, they walked te short distance back to Park Lane and the hotel.

When they reached his room, Ruth drew the curtains and covering him with a blanket left him to rest. But in his attenuated state sleep was impossible and after a while he called for her. He said his heart was behaving peculiarly. Ruth, suspecting his old extra-systole trouble, sent for the doctor. When he arrived he listened carefully to Leslie's heart, found its action rather erratic and gave him an injection of a calmative. It soon put Leslie into a deep sleep, and the doctor went into the sitting room to speak to Ruth. He was somewhat concerned, not with the heart, but with Leslie's symptoms of shock and fatigue. He ought really to go into hospital – but, if not that, at least home where he must stay in bed and be properly nursed. Ruth said at once she would take him to Stowe Maries, driving him there, and be responsible for looking after him. The doctor suggested that as he hoped the injection would last for several hours, it might be simpler for everyone if Leslie was taken home on a stretcher by ambulance. He also said he would prefer Leslie to be in charge of a nurse – who would be responsible and accompany him. Ruth agreed and the doctor arranged it.

A little later Leslie, still asleep, was taken by stretcher to an ambulance waiting at the back of Grosvenor House. Accompanied by a nurse he began his journey to Westcott. Ruth and Doodie followed him on that grey, November evening, driving behind the ambulance as Leslie had driven behind Violette's two days before. For Ruth it had been quite the most upsetting two days she had ever lived through. She had never in her life suffered so much for Leslie or felt his despair so keenly and yet, in a sense, felt so shut out, so unappreciated. It did not matter that he hadn't understood her sympathy or failed to appreciate that she had only come to help, and certainly not to stage-manage a tragedy. If he had been perverse about that, it was unimportant. She knew that Violette had been unique in his experience and quite irreplaceable. Except for Ruth she had shared more of Leslie's life than anyone else and for the past five years had been closest to him of all. Ruth was well used to taking second place in his affections – yet somehow, selfishly, he had always expected her to be there when he needed her and somehow, selflessly, she had always come – for, despite everything, deep in her generous heart, she still loved him dearly. But fate seemed to have designed her as the one who picked up the pieces, made the decisions, organised the retreats. If Leslie's problem was emotional, hers now must not be. It had to be immediate and practical, as was her nature – and, more than that, maternal and caring.

For the drugged man in the ambulance there was no question of decision. Ruth, who had come to London without hesitation, had made the decision to take him home – to nurse him and get him better. It wasn't a solution to any of their problems – simply an emergency measure. Whatever her feelings, she must now swallow them down, submerging them in his interests. There must be no differences. Yet, despite the uncertainties, as she followed in the dark behind the ambulance, Ruth found herself wondering, in her ever-optimistic heart, if, now that the pull of emotion was gone, Leslie might stay, settle down for a while, not rushing off once on his feet. If she had him at home might he find his way back to his old self again, regaining perspective in the quiet surroundings of Stowe Maries?

If this was unrealistic Ruth clung to it with some hope. It seemed to her that Leslie had reached the point of no return. There was no way back to what had been. If she could get him over the next few weeks the spell might finally be broken. Perhaps when he woke, bemused and rather surprised to find himself back in his old room again, in his old bed, he might be happy – relieved to be back in the storm-haven of home. He might even be grateful that Ruth had brought hime home. But, then, he might not. With Leslie, Ruth knew, it was always unwise to predict – even a few days ahead.

If Ruth's decision to bring Leslie back to Stowe Maries had been taken on the spur of the moment, it was the only conceivable solution in the circumstances. She could not know how long he would care to stay – that was for him to decide – but it seemed clear to her that his recovery would be slow, delaying any further decision, at least, for the immediate future. She could not anticipate the direction his mind would take or the strange limbo into which he would retreat.

For the first few days he remained remote, communicating in monosyllables, keeping to his room, not eating much from the trays that were brought. The nurse was cheerfully in attendance, though he scarcely noticed or spoke to her. However, it soon became clear, that in his abstracted state he could not continue with the film at Denham. For a few days production was suspended and Filippo del Giudice, fully aware of the tragedy and deeply upset, rang and spoke to Leslie. And Leslie confirmed what Filippo suspected – that he had no interest in going on and thought it best to call in another director. Leslie knew there was not much left to do and that three more weeks shooting would complete the film by Christmas. Adrian Brunel, the film's original director and Leslie's production consultant, was not, however, offered the job.

> The film had nearly come to an end, [he wrote] and there was no real need for him. In any case, he was in no fit state to carry on. When he retired, I did – though I would willingly have carried on for him. But I was not required.

Del Giudice, then, arranged with Phil Samuel a substitute director, Maurice Elvey, who seemed happy to complete the film without reshooting anything. The film, thus, remained essentially Leslie's work.

For the first week Leslie spent long periods alone in his room – not wanting to see or talk to anyone. He would shut his door and, sitting at his desk, appear to be staring blankly out into the garden. Occasionally he picked up a pencil and scribbled things down on scraps of paper. To Ruth and Doodie it was soon obvious that he was trying to communicate with Violette. These long, silent communions, during which he begged not to be disturbed, sometimes went on for hours on end with Leslie trying by sheer will power and concentration to make contact. As he was soon afterwards to write:

> Very quickly after you left me you took hold of my consciousness . . . and you aroused in me a sense beyond my physical senses, an inner sense of seeing, hearing, feeling. You made me know, beyond all doubt, that there is no death; that man, above all things, is a spirit – that the spirit once created is indestructible.

Later, he was to learn other, perhaps, more effective means to gain rapport and put himself in touch with Violette's mind. From now on, for some time, these arcane communications filled all Leslie's waking thoughts – and, perhaps, his dreams as well – and he remained remote and aloof, becoming no part of the life around

him. Though he now joined the family for meals his interest in
family affairs was confined to monosyllables.

It was only a few days after his arrival back that he attended
Violette's funeral at Mortlake Cemetery. Besides their many friends
from the film world who were at the short service of remembrance,
there were others, French friends of Violette's and Leslie's, who
stood a little apart from the film people. Some of these friends had
got to England in 1940, when France collapsed, others escaped
later. They were all now either in the Free French Forces, working as
interpreters and liaison officers, or employed by the BBC as
translators or broadcasters in their French services. Some were with
SOE and in direct contact with the Resistance movement. Through
Violette Leslie had got to know them well and met them often
enough at the Free French club off Lower Regent Street.

Some of these French exiles now became very close to Leslie and
it was through them that he took his first, uncertain steps towards
spiritualism. If his earlier, unaided efforts to establish rapport with
Violette had not been entirely successful he was, by the persistence
of these people, introduced to more well-tried methods. Through
these friends he met a number of mediums and was taught the
correct use of automatic writing and the planchette system. To these
means of communication Leslie devoted a large part of himself and
his time, in the early days of his bereavement, and developed an
intense, almost fanatical faith in their effectiveness. In company
with these compatriots of Violette he attended a number of seances,
in various places, where people – sitting in circles and holding
hands – faithfully awaited contact with their loved ones 'beyond the
Great Divide'.

As my sister recalled, Leslie spent hours seated at his desk,
composing messages to Violette and, apparently, receiving replies.
If these were mainly of a comforting or reassuring nature, Leslie
firmly believed that whatever actions or decisions he took were, in
the mysterious way of such beliefs, directly due to these communications – and were governed and controlled by them. It was as if he
was receiving direct advice and guidance from Violette. The few
examples of their spiritual contacts that I have seen are concerned
with comparatively mundane matters – but in these exchanges the
important thing is always his evident desire to please her and carry
out her wishes. Some are almost maternal in their consideration for
his well-being, their concern for his happiness and welfare. Indeed,
they read like living conversations – as if they were sitting side by
side on the sofa at Monkseaton discussing and recollecting the

ordinary, day to day events of their lives.

If these intimate communications were comforting to Leslie, they put him at a considerable distance from the solid, surrounding world. His retreat into this secret existence of the mind caused not only concern to his own family but to many of his friends in the film world. They felt he must be drawn back, encouraged to regain his normal outlook – as much for himself as his career. It seemed to his film associates that if he remained in this cul-de-sac of grief too long he would find immense difficulty in reorienting himself, in regaining those outward-looking, professional qualities for which he was famous.

Filippo del Giudice and Phil Samuel felt all this keenly, as did Tolly de Grunwald and 'Puffin' Asquith, a sympathetic concern and a compelling desire to get him back to normal. One over-riding feeling they had in common was to save Leslie from his friends – the French exiles, the mediums and seance-holders – who they felt were isolating him, prolonging his recovery with an almost gloating capacity for grief. I think as his film associates rallied round Leslie realised he, too, must make a more positive effort to cope and begin, at least, to find his way back.

If Ruth had hoped that Leslie would stay longer at Stowe Maries she was soon disappointed. He had decided, in spite of his initial intense reluctance, to return to Stoke Poges. He must make efforts to renew his professional interests and for this he must be near Denham and the people with whom he worked. They were doing everything to be helpful and considerate and it was time he responded.

Despite Leslie's efforts to come to grips with his professional life again, the move back to Monkseaton, with its heart-haunting memories of Violette, was far from easy. Yet he felt, somehow, she was still with him – her presence everywhere – when he wrote at the outset: ' . . . you made me know, on that first drive alone back to the little house, you were still beside me; you made me know that in the house I was not alone . . . and you made palpable your touch.'

As he began to pick up the threads again, he made irregular sorties to Denham and, with the help of his secretary, Rose Rutland, began to deal with the back-log of business correspondence and reply to the many letters from well-wishers and friends. He went along to the cutting-rooms to see how the editing of *The Gentle Sex* was progressing. With Maurice Elvey he saw a rough cut of the film, contributing useful advice and suggestions. Filippo del Giudice was regularly in touch, suggesting various projects to interest him.

One was a story about the nursing profession by Monica Dickens which Filippo thought Elvey might direct with Leslie in the not-too-taxing role of supervising producer. Leslie read the adaptation by Elizabeth Barron and thought, apart from the unpromising title *One Pair of Feet*, it had possibilities if some work could be done on the story to present the nursing sisters in a somewhat more attractive light. Filippo, entirely agreeing with Leslie's reservations, hoped he might give it further thought – with a view to production sometime in January. And Leslie, realising Filippo was trying to help by giving him something immediate to bite on which was not too demanding, said he would give it serious consideration.

Another person anxious to help was Alfred Chenhalls. Alfred had been close to Leslie right through the trauma of Violette's illness and death. I think it was Alfred who considered a change of scene might be the most beneficial answer for Leslie in the not too distant future. There had earlier been discussions about a trip abroad – possibly taking the form of a lecture tour similar to the one proposed over Sweden. In these discussions Spain and Portugal had cropped up as the obvious alternative – a kind of business-cum-holiday trip into the sunshine – and for this purpose Alfred thought he might accompany Leslie, promoting the sale of their own and other British war-films.

This had been talked about one evening over dinner while Violette was alive – but she had most vehemently opposed it. She felt it quite wrong for Leslie to have to leave the country. He was far too valuable as a film director and war-time propagandist on the home front. There were others who could better be spared for this sort of work. Besides, there was always a risk with the long journey out and back over water. A plane had been lost flying to Sweden. Leslie, tending to see it from Violette's point of view, was not particularly keen and the subject, once aired, had been dropped. Now, Alfred thinking it would do Leslie good at a time when his interest in film production was at a low ebb, suggested it again and Leslie, in an abstracted, vague kind of way, thought it might be an idea – but only as far as Portugal was concerned. He'd heard Estoril was nice in the spring.

He then told Alfred of Filippo's suggestion that he should undertake the production of the Monica Dickens story in a supervisory capacity, and Alfred did not think the ideas mutually exclusive. Once production was under-way, with Elvey directing and the ever-reliable Phil Samuel as associate producer, could they both not get away – away to Lisbon, at least, and leave Madrid open for the time being? Alfred thought both the MOI and the British Council would be extremely interested in the propaganda value of the trip. Leslie, without committing himself and remembering Violette's views on the subject, said it was interesting and he would certainly think about it. And there it was left for the time being. But after the New Year the idea became firmer and began to loom as a distinct possibility – but not yet to Leslie.

CHAPTER NINE

Powers of Persuasion

By the first week in January Leslie had agreed to Filippo del Giudice's idea of his producing the Monica Dickens film, now entitled *The Lamp Still Burns.* Production was to commence at Denham in the third week of January. Leslie realised the original story had limitations as a film script. The nursing profession as seen by Monica Dickens was not unrewarding, but it was bleak and intensely vocational. Was there some way, Leslie wondered, of mitigating the sterner demands of this somewhat closed order of sisterhood, making the world of nursing more attractive to those less dedicated.

Monica Dickens had worked as a probationer nurse in a hospital at Windsor, and on these experiences she had written her book *One Pair of Feet.* The conditions of service that Monica described were harsh and uncongenial. Long hours and hard work one had to accept, but the petty restrictions and Victorian attitudes towards discipline laid down by domineering Matrons had made nursing a profession to be avoided. The niggling rules about dress, appearance and hospital etiquette scarcely encouraged recruitment. As nursing was a profession of first importance and of special value in wartime, the film must succeed as an eloquent plea for better working conditions and a more sympathetic approach to the treatment of nurses. As a feature film it also had to appeal to the general public, so a love story was inserted to make its message more palatable. Leslie asked his old friend Roland Pertwee to come in and work on the scenario with Elizabeth Barron, hoping that Roland would soften some of the edges with humour.

The Lamp Still Burns remained in essence a recruitment film in the genre of *The Gentle Sex,* and it had been presented to Leslie by del Guidice as a kind of bridge back to film production. It was not the sort of film that would have fired him with much enthusiasm in normal circumstances, but these were somewhat abnormal. Phil Samuel thought Leslie took little or no interest in the production owing to his bereavement, and I agree it was probably limited. He had no directorial responsibility. Phil was always on the spot, so, I imagine, Leslie's regular attendance at the studios was neither vital nor completely necessary. Still very much in the grip of grief, Leslie groped his way back slowly, with his mind scarcely focussed on film production.

However, assisted by his sister, Irene, as casting director, he took considerable pains over the assembly of a fine medical cast headed by Godfrey Tearle as principal surgeon, and Cathleen Nesbitt as Matron. In her third successive role for Leslie, Rosamund John was cast as a young woman architect who sacrifices her career to become a student nurse. Also in the cast, making one of his earliest films, was Stewart Granger, playing a factory owner who, after being badly injured and burned by an explosion, is nursed back to health and falls in love with the student nurse. Supporting the principal players were Ernest Thesiger, Margaret Vyner and Aubrey Mallalieu, and in smaller roles Joyce Grenfell, John Laurie, Leslie Dwyer and Megs Jenkins, the last named appearing in the cast list simply as 'Plump Nurse'.

One morning, about a fortnight into production, Leslie was in his office at the studios when his secretary, Rose Rutland, brought an official-looking letter in and put it on his desk. Opening it, Leslie saw it was from Sir Malcolm Robertson, MP, Chairman of the British Council. It was a carefully-expressed letter, a kind of exploratory overture to the idea of Leslie considering a trip abroad on behalf of the Council, lecturing in Spain and Portugal. Leslie read through the amiable preambles describing Malcolm Sargent's successful trip to Portugal, from which he had just returned after conducting five concerts. It had been something of a musical bonanza for the Council, a considerable *succès fou* with many witty stories from the podium. Leslie, in his present frame of mind, felt little enough enthusiasm for film-making let alone lecture trips so he tended to hurry through the letter, skipping as much of the hyperbole as possible. The Council's target had been Sweden the year before; now it was Spain and Portugal, with the emphasis perhaps on Spain where democratic influence was sadly lacking. The Council desperately needed well-qualified lecturers and cultural personalities to visit these countries. Leslie noted that the Astronomer Royal, Harold Spencer Jones, was down to visit in April, and Rose Macaulay, the novelist. The letter, referring to Leslie as far the most popular actor in the Iberian peninsula by recent poll, suggested it would be a great propaganda fillip for the

Council, particularly in an Axis-dominated country like Spain, to have the use of his services. It would considerably benefit the British cause and war effort, and nothing but good could come of it.

Leslie put the letter aside on his desk and forgot about it for the rest of the day. That evening, before he left the studios, he picked it up and put it in his pocket. Then, collecting his script, pipe and tobacco pouch he vanished through the door on his way home to Stoke Poges.

The first thing he did the following morning was to reply to the letter. He thanked the Council for their invitation but confessed that, unlike the distinguished people who had been mentioned (and he was a good friend and great admirer of Sir Malcolm Sargent), he could neither conduct an orchestra, discourse on astronomy nor discuss the modern novel, and admitted that if he was called upon to tell a witty story he generally made a mess of it. What he meant was that all these people were specialists, and he wasn't. He could only talk about motion pictures, a sort of hybrid art, which almost anybody could do. He really had no technical skills, which he felt so important for a lecturer. Anyway, he had more or less given up acting and retired behind the camera, where he was still feeling his way. He was delighted, however, that they hadn't forgotten him in the Iberian peninsula – but he stressed he knew precious little about those countries or their peoples. He reiterated his technical deficiencies as a spokesman for the British point of view as he was inadequate at speech-making or any sort of official flag-waving. There were other actors far better equipped for this kind of platform work, some with a positive flair for making speeches. He ended by saying he still had a contract with Mr del Giudice which he felt he must honour.

Leslie asked Miss Rutland to get the letter off and went across to the set to see how things were going. There the matter rested – at least, for a few days. However, the British Council was not at all deterred by Leslie's modest letter, and soon other forces were at work behind the scenes. Jack Beddington (Director, Film Division, MOI) was one of them. Beddington was an old, respected film man with years of experience behind him – and he got on well with actors. He felt he had had quite a bit of influence with Leslie over *The Gentle Sex*. Besides, Beddington was extremely interested in the distribution of British films abroad, particularly in the 'neutral' markets where we were poorly represented. Knowing that these foreign trips were amicably arranged with the MOI, Malcolm Robertson conferred with Beddington – thinking he might give a shove in the right direction where Leslie was concerned.

Beddington thought the thing might tie up very well, if only Leslie could be persuaded what a contribution his presence would make in those countries. We were not only weak in Spain and Portugal with regard to cultural propaganda but our film-makers were finding it difficult to get distribution arrangements. We needed a better organisation and more outlets to the twelve hundred or so cinemas these countries boasted. They were mostly showing German or old American material. He agreed with Robertson we needed a spearhead, a quality name to fly the flag, someone with a first class reputation and internationally respected. They had little difficulty in agreeing that Leslie was the name they wanted.

Beddington, while appreciating the drollness of Leslie's reply, felt that his hesitation had sprung from his recent bereavement. He explained that his secretary, to whom he had been very attached, had died recently. Even so, in the best of circumstances, Leslie could be obstinate. If Beddington understood Leslie aright he must obviously have known how much he hated being any sort of 'front man' or cultural functionary. Though Leslie had been involved in a great deal of cultural and film propaganda – and he had been noticeably outspoken in his detestation of the Nazis – he had warily side-stepped any travelling ambassadorships, nor ever wanted to be the totem-image of British character-selling abroad. As a quiet, undemonstrative person he preferred to be left alone to make the films he understood and do the occasional broadcast for the BBC. He was not a figure-head or show-case personality and whenever he was needed for some sort of public appearance he had to be prised out of the studio and generally did so behind dark glasses, his hat pulled well down and a furtive hand covering what was left of his face. Crowded functions genuinely unnerved him and like a bat he escaped as quickly as he could to his secret hang-out, as if fearing the too-public glare of day. Leslie's escapist tendencies, though understood by his friends, were not altogether appreciated by those in official capacities as much time and effort could be wasted trying to nail him down to decisions involving public confrontations. In this instance, Jack Beddington, knowing him well, decided in his cheerful, easy-going way on a light-hearted frontal attack to overcome any pockets of resistance.

Beddington travelled regularly round the studios. He had a number of productions, connected with the war effort, in which he was interested – some which he had initiated – and on this occasion,

with Leslie at the back of his mind, he went down to Denham to see
how productions were progressing there. It was nearing the lunch-
break when he encountered Leslie, in company with Maurice Elvey,
on his way back from the set to his office. Elvey, who remembered
this meeting with some amusement, told me about it when we
worked together in 1947 on an early, post-war British film. He was
to recall a similar meeting with Alfred Chenhalls a few days later.

Jack Beddington greeted them in his usual, drawled 'ole-boy'
style, enquiring how the film was going and if they were on
schedule. Leslie said it was going well and on schedule, he believed,
though he should talk to Maurice about that as he wasn't directing!
As the three of them strolled towards the office, Jack asked what the
stop-date on the production was, and Leslie glancing at Maurice,
said: 'Ought we to tell him – isn't he a spy from the MOI?' Once
inside, Leslie explained they hoped, optimistically, to complete
production in May. Was that any help? And Jack, quickly warming
to his subject, then broached the lecture tour.

'Oh, that!' said Leslie. 'They always want me when I'm busy!'
Leslie had already sensed the drift of the wind and when Jack
remarked that it was felt he was being over-modest about his
capabilities, Leslie confessed he was fairly inarticulate when it came
to lecturing. But Jack persisted, seeing Leslie in a far more
important role than that – a film-ambassador, no less, opening
doors into big, potential markets. Leslie, realising what he was in
for, knocked his pipe out and suggested they all go to lunch.

As they walked towards the studio restaurant Leslie felt he was
being officially manoeuvred into a corner from which he might
have some difficulty in extricating himself – and he was grateful for
Maurice's presence over lunch. As soon as they sat down, Jack
reopened the somewhat one-sided discussion, airing all the advantages of Leslie making the trip a very personal mission, winning
friends and influencing people wherever he went. All the pros, in
fact. Leslie countered with a number of contras. Maurice recalled
Leslie felt a bit selfish about his objections and that the central
question, to go or not to go, reminded him of the 'To be or not to be'
soliloquy in *Hamlet* about 'conscience making cowards of us all'. It
seemed to Leslie that he had been listening to his own conscience
which advised him 'to bear the ills he had than fly to others that he
knew not of'! Maurice felt he wasn't listening to Jack whose voice
droned on about the importance of it all. Was it thus, Leslie
remarked to Maurice later, that 'enterprises of great pitch and
moment' were turned awry and 'lost the name of action'?

During lunch, Leslie restated his own problem – if such it was – in simpler words. However attractive the Spanish bonanza, he was in the middle of a production he must guide through to its end. He had a contract with Two Cities to that effect. 'My business, God help me, is making pictures – and I have few talents in other directions.' He also had plans for other films, and when Jack asked him what they were, he told him about *Hamlet*. This puzzled Beddington.

'As a war film?' he asked, slightly drop-mouthed. And Leslie began to explain his theories: how Britain like Denmark was on a war-footing; how Fortinbras, about to attack Denmark, turned east to attack Poland. There were parallels everywhere in Shakespeare's text.

It was now Jack's turn to look bored and crumble his bread. He was only listening to Leslie with half an ear. Then, suddenly Maurice recalled, he made a classic riposte.

'Hamlet's a loser, Leslie. He dies. We're going to live and win. It's bad propaganda material!' Leslie said he appreciated all that, but even losers like Hamlet were more interesting to him than film-ambassadorial trips to Spain and Portugal, and he half rose to go, saying they had to get back to the set. But Beddington, determined to have the last word, detained him a moment longer, drawing his attention once more to the vital role he could play in the Iberian peninsula, now from the propaganda angle the primary target of our Foreign Office. Surely he could spare himself for a month for this vital task, and still be home before the film was finished? At this point Leslie, remarking drily, 'How can I refuse!', managed to rise from the table and Jack, laughing, resumed his cheerful, nonchalant character. He patted Leslie's arm affectionately. 'Anyway, ole boy, think on't – as the Bard says!'

Leslie did think on it – but not, as yet, very deeply. And he came to no conclusions, keeping his options open. He was still much intrigued with the *Hamlet* idea and wanted to make it his major production for 1943, though so far he had not been able to arouse much financial enthusiasm for the subject. It was to remain a concept never to be realised – as tempting a challenge, in its way, as the ghost that beckoned Hamlet from the castle-turrets of Elsinore. In the meantime, this less attractive challenge was being dangled before him.

A few days after the meeting with Beddington, Leslie was in his office with Maurice Elvey discussing the following day's shooting arrangements. On his desk was a model of the 'Operating Theatre' set. Leslie had invited Maurice home to dinner that evening at Monkseaton. Earlier, there had been a call from Alfred Chenhall's secretary to say that Alfred would be at the studios on business and would drop in on Leslie about six.

While Leslie and Maurice were immersed in their discussion, there came a tap on the door and Alfred strolled in followed by an aroma of Havana cigar smoke, looking like an outsize cherub. Nodding quickly at Elvey, with a certain benign indifference, he enquired of Leslie how things were going. Leslie said everything was fine – and on schedule, thanks to Maurice. He was delighted with Rosamund as the probationer and thought Cathleen Nesbitt a wonderful piece of casting for the Matron. Then, he drew Alfred towards the set model, describing the tricky operation scene with Godfrey Tearle as the surgeon and Stewart Granger as 'the body' which they hoped to start in the morning.

It was not long before Alfred switched the conversation to the point of his visit – the much talked about though scarcely agreed upon lecture trip with which Elvey was familiar. Alfred said that, following Leslie's luncheon, Jack Beddington had been on to him and the project was now being discussed at high level. Brendan Bracken, the Minister of Information and Beddington's boss, thought it would be a huge propaganda boost for Britain if Leslie could be persuaded to go. According to Elvey, Leslie was still far from keen and, though flattered at Bracken's enthusiasm, thought that a more extrovert personality, with a flair for the public occasion, was needed for this kind of showmanship; he suggested Noël Coward as ideal or, failing him, someone like Godfrey Tearle.

At this point Elvey interposed: 'They can't have Godfrey, Leslie. Had you forgotten – he's working for us!' Leslie laughed, saying what he really meant was that Godfrey was the type they needed – English to the core, with a marvellous theatrical record – whereas he was only a kind of up-graded Hungarian who'd pinched the Emperor's clothes! Alfred, then, drew the conversation into more business-like channels – discussing the wider distribution of British films which was to be an important part of the envisaged trip. Arrangements in the United States were now pretty good – Sweden very difficult because of German pressure – Norway, Holland, Belgium, Denmark, out of the question: enemy occupied. That left Spain and Portugal – plus the Latin American countries – as a much needed and potential market for our film products.

When Alfred said he'd been preparing a memorandum on the subject for the Treasury, Leslie intervened saying he didn't quite see where he came into this promotion campaign, which was basically salesmanship. He was a film producer not a distributor. Alfred, a little surprised, reminded him that he had made some pretty important war films – and that del Giudice and GFD wanted to get *his* films in as well. When Leslie said anybody could handle distribution arrangements Alfred replied that he was being naive – 'anybody' wouldn't do. They needed a name – and a world star name, like Leslie's, was needed to set the drums rolling and get the necessary publicity. Alfred, then, said that he was prepared to go with Leslie, as general dogsbody under Treasury cover, to deal with the business side of the distribution arrangements and be, he hoped, a not disagreeable travelling companion.

Elvey recalled that at this moment – after studying Alfred's rubicund, smiling face – Leslie appeared to give way, saying that if they travelled together it wouldn't be such a bad idea. Alfred replied that was precisely what he meant and he was sure it could be fixed. Certainly, Jack Beddington seemed to think so. 'I'm the sprat to catch a mackerel, Leslie.'

At this point of near-agreement, Leslie threw a small spanner into the works. He said that, on consideration after talking to Bedding-ton, he was reasonably convinced about Portugal but, in view of the time element, as he didn't want to be away too long, they should limit the trip to Portugal. He reminded Alfred that he had never been keen on Spain. He had recently discussed it with some friends and he had heard that Madrid was an intimidating place and positively at its most Anglophobe at the moment. They would scarcely be received there with open arms. The fact that he had made a number of outspokenly anti-Nazi films and broadcasts was not guaranteed to make his face fit particularly well with Falangists. From what he heard the atmosphere in Madrid was bound to be hostile – indeed, they might well both be putting themselves at risk for there was always the chance, slight though it was, that some idiot might take a pot at them. At this Alfred laughed loudly.

In answer to Leslie's Spanish objections, Alfred pointed out that the British Embassy in Madrid would make quite sure they were only involved with the right sort of people: they'd vet them very carefully. And as for being at risk because of anti-Nazi views, Leslie must surely realise there were lots of English people living in Madrid who shared indentical views and survived quite happily, without being shot at! Leslie then reminded Alfred that most of these had diplomatic immunity and were careful what they said – which he and Alfred mightn't be. Besides, with no diplomatic immunity, there was always the risk of internment; he'd heard people had been interned for quite trivial political infringements, and he didn't fancy a one-way trip.

Alfred thought Leslie's reservations over Spain theatrically amusing but somewhat exaggerated. So far as he knew, in the last three and a half years of war, no visitor to Madrid had either been interned or assassinated. It seemed to him a million to one chance it would happen to either of them. Anyhow, he assured Leslie, if he wasn't exactly a cordon sanitaire, he was certainly a bigger target! And on this note, Alfred rose to go – thinking he had, at least, achieved something.

Standing by Alfred's car parked outside the office block Leslie restressed that he was quite prepared to accept the assignment as far as Lisbon. It was simply a question of fixing a suitable date. 'Mr Figures', as Elvey called Chenhalls, leaned towards Leslie like a large friendly bear assuring him, once more, that his fears over Spain were really quite groundless. Still, if they only went to Portugal it would be something, for Portugal was beautiful in the spring, particularly Cascais and Estoril. He reminded Leslie that it was a long time since he'd had a holiday in the sun, and it would do him a world of good. Then, slipping into the driver's seat of the car, he looked up at Leslie.

'Anyway, have a quiet think about it, and if you have a sudden change of heart over Spain, get in touch with me.'

As Maurice Elvey walked with Leslie towards his car, Leslie remarked that Alfred, for all his brash pushfulness, was right about one thing. The sun might well be what he needed after the long, cold and miserably sad winter. In Portugal the orange trees would soon be in blossom. As they drove towards Stoke Poges, Leslie spoke of a recurring dream he had had. He was in the Santa Fe train, the old 'Chief', as it chugged slowly down through the orange groves into San Bernardino. Even in his dream he could hear the far-off, wailing hoot of the engine and, what was more surprising, he swore he could actually smell the first, unforgettable smell of the orange blossom after the long, dusty journey across America.

Just before they reached Monkseaton, Maurice recalled that Leslie turned to him and said that however much he hated journeys they usually had their compensations. Even so, as far as this propaganda trip was concerned, he wasn't going to be pushed or hurried. He had one golden rule, Leslie said – never be forced into doing anything against his own judgement.

*

If Leslie's attitude to the idea of the Iberian journey may have
puzzled official minds at the MOI and the British Council, to others
who knew him better his indecision seemed the direct result of his
bereavement. If he had dug his toes in over Spain, it was not entirely
due to his own native obstinacy. At a sensitive time, he had listened
carefully to the views of friends who thought it inadvisable for him
to visit Spain due to the predominantly anti-British attitude of
government circles in Madrid. They felt he would achieve little
there in the present political climate and only expose himself to
unnecessary risks. As a result, Leslie's attitude continued to harden
towards Spain in the next few weeks.

On the other hand the official view at the MOI and the British
Council was that there was no place more needful of British
influence, both culturally and politically, than Spain. If it was
important to influence Portugal, which was basically friendly, it was
doubly important to influence Spain which was not. To the MOI
and the British Council, Portugal was the least important half of the
cake, and they naturally hoped Leslie would amend his views on
Spain. To this end our Foreign Office was to lend something more
than its benign, blanket influence.

Since the Torch Operations and the Allied landings in North
Africa in late 1942, the Iberian peninsula was becoming a highly
sensitive area and the Germans were worried about our possible
military intentions. They had therefore been increasing pressure on
Franco and Salazar with the aim of inflaming anti-British, anti-
American and above all anti-Communist feelings.

Maintaining the neutrality of Spain and Portugal was vital to our
war interests. With Portugal, an ancient alliance had hedged our
generally amiable association; with Spain the situation was very
different where the government was predominantly Fascist and
pro-German. From the point of view of our diplomacy it was vital to
keep Spain, if not entirely neutral, at least non-belligerent.

The rock of Gibraltar, that little tail of Spain jutting into the
Straits, was ever the source of historic dispute, and it was important
that Gibraltar should not become the tail that wagged the sleeping
dog of Spain into open belligerence.

When Hitler abandoned the invasion of Britain he had substituted,
in its place, Operation Felix, the assault on Gibraltar. Hitler was
quite specific: 'Gibraltar should not be considered of secondary
importance but as one of the main blows against Britain.' By
November 1940 the operational orders were complete and Franco's
brother-in-law, Serrano Suner, travelled to Berchtesgaden for a

conference with the Führer. It was more a harangue than a conference. 'I have decided to attack Gibraltar. I have prepared the operation. The only thing left is to start – and start we must.' There was to be a bargain – or a bit of blackmail. Spain was short of food – Hitler promised the immediate delivery of 600,000 tons of grain. All Spain need do was declare war on Britain. 'As for recompense in Morocco, this would follow naturally once Gibraltar had been taken and the German forces had crossed over to North Africa.' Suner contrived to give Hitler the impression that Spain would soon be entering the war.

In December an impatient Hitler decided that Admiral Canaris, his Chief of Intelligence, should go to Madrid to help Franco make up his mind. Canaris wasted no time telling Franco that Hitler intended sending his troops into Spain on 10th January for the attack on Gibraltar, and economic assistance would commence from that moment. Franco felt this too coldly deliberate, too high-handedly Teutonic. It was scarcely the way to treat the head of the Spanish state – as if he was some kind of menial. Franco continued to prevaricate and delay.

It must have been a considerable relief to our Ambassador to find Franco so sulkily obstinate in the face of German demands. In February, Hitler made up his mind that in Franco was imbedded all the quixoticism of Spain. Better to have Franco as a happy, pro-German neutral than an unhappy war-participant. At this moment, Hitler switched his attention to the long-dreamt-of attack on Russia. Perhaps 'Barbarossa', the lightning campaign for the liquidation of communism would convince the wavering Spaniard that he and Hitler were fighting the same enemy. For the time being Gibraltar would have to wait. In fact, it did not re-enter Hitler's strategic thinking for the best part of two years – and with it, Spain.

As a result of Operation Torch Hitler – now in difficulties in Russia – saw the danger to the Iberian peninsula. Spain could now become the back-door to Europe, the way in to Hitler's Fortress. He needed to be sure that his sluggish ally would be ready to assist the assault whenever and wherever it came. There were other vital considerations that would follow an invasion by the Anglo-Americans – as Admiral Raeder was careful to point out to Hitler. Germany would be deprived of important raw materials: he quoted, 'A million tons of iron ore, 3,500 tons of wolfram, 200 tons of lithium, tin, mica, beryllium.' Clearly, Admiral Raeder had little faith in Franco's ability to resist a determined Allied assault. The only way was to forestall the Allies, to get in first and take over the entire Iberian peninsula.

'Germany must be ready to seize Spain and Portugal by force and integrate them into the economic life of Europe *at the very moment* when the danger of an enemy seizure of that Peninsula is imminent.' (This was the last paragraph in the official German summary of the conference of 22nd December 1942). As a result, preparations for Operation Gisela were put into immediate effect. This took four weeks to perfect and was ready by 1st February 1943. It involved the immediate occupation of the Cantabrian coast from San Sebastian to Vigo by seven infantry divisions. It envisaged Spanish consent to the use of airfields by the Luftwaffe, and an Italian division was to be landed at Barcelona to link up with the Germans.

It seems clear from the plans of this conference that Hitler was seriously considering a pre-emptive incursion into the Iberian peninsula before the Allies might do so. As Sir Samuel Hoare, our Ambassador in Madrid, noted: 'Hitler's intentions were so blatant that no one could mistake them. By hook or by crook he was determined to embroil us with Spain. A definite breach between the British and Spanish governments would give him a Spanish welcome and liberty of action in the Peninsula. With liberty of action he could move at will through Spain to Gibraltar, Africa and the Mediterranean.'*

Our Foreign Office was not unaware of the mounting tension and that the German propaganda machine seemed determined to spread rumours that the Allies would not respect Spanish or, for that matter, Portuguese neutrality. Yet it was difficult to mount any effective counter-propaganda against the German war of nerves and rumour-mongering for it was not only aided and abetted by the Spanish Press and Propaganda Department but any attempts to counteract it were silenced. In an Aide Memoire, referring to various acts of provocation, our Ambassador in Madrid stated:

> I need not go into details – but the main complaints are that the British press is banned in Spain, the British radio is jammed, correspondence from HM Embassy and the UK is often seized and destroyed, on frequent occasions employees of HM Embassy and Consulates have been violently maltreated by officials of the Falange and there is a constant policy of discrimination against our war news on the Spanish radio, newsreels and in the Press ... All this is serving no other interest save German Propaganda.

* *Ambassador on Special Mission,* Collins 1946

CHAPTER TEN

Enter Anthony Eden

When, towards the end of March, Anthony Eden returned to London from Washington, he soon realised how confused and acrimonious the Iberian situation had grown in his absence. He had been well aware before he left, of the mounting irritations to which our representatives had been exposed and it was now to further reports of discrimination by Spaniards and mis-representations by Germany that he had to listen. It was an increasingly tiresome catalogue of complaints and frustrations, and one to which there seemed to be no effective answer. The Germans seemed to have a stranglehold not only on the Spanish administration but on their propaganda machinery.

Of course, Spain and Portugal represented to our Foreign Office no more than a section of the global war which daily engaged its attention and, though it had to be seen in the perspective of other more vital confrontations with the primary enemy, Eden was aware of a new and more dangerous factor which had been looming. This was the possibility of a German pre-emptive bid in either or both of the countries. By March 1943 concern about this, and adjacent problems, had become a high priority and in a spectrum of departments from the Ministry of Economic Warfare to the MOI and the British Council, more active policies were put into effect.

Within the perspectives of these counter-policies and preparations, ranging across the Iberian canvas from the threat of invasion and the seizure of tungsten and iron ore mines vital to German war industry to lesser questions of censorship and pro-paganda, it seemed to Leslie that the services of a Denham film-producer had about as much importance within that canvas as one scattered dot of paint in the composition of a pointilliste. Certainly he could be forgiven for seeing himself as fairly unimportant within those larger perspectives. Perhaps he underestimated himself, but he was obviously shrewd enough to realise that his services as lecturer and film personality could have little influence over the complicated picture of political and diplomatic intrigue which was the state of affairs in Spain. He seriously doubted if, in that hot-bed of turmoil and unrest, Madrid, much attention would be paid to the posturings of a film actor come to pour a little cultural oil on troubled waters. His only use, it seemed, was to be paraded as a kind of theatrical distraction from grimmer topics.

However, now he was caught up in our propaganda machinery, he had agreed – at any rate in principle – to undertake a modified tour as far as Portugal. Since he had accepted that part of the assignment, it was felt at the MOI and the British Council that he would in due course overcome his objections to Spain, and preliminary arrangements were put in hand for both countries. Towards the end of March Leslie wrote to the Council clarifying his position. He said that after discussions with Mr Beddington and Mr Chenhalls he was happy to offer his services as far as Portugal was concerned, but that was all he could do in the circumstances. Owing to his film commitment and the final editing of *The Lamp Still Burns*, he must be home by the second week in May at latest. He, therefore, regretted that in view of the time element he would be unable to go to Spain.

On receipt of the letter the Council and Robertson, its chairman, were pleased to find that Leslie had, at least, overcome some of his scruples. Still, it seemed a pity that he could not be persuaded to go on to Madrid. It cut the most important place out of the programme and reduced considerably the propaganda value. Heads were once more put together and, in agreement with Beddington who had now spoken again to Brendan Bracken, it was decided to approach the Foreign Office to exert more persuasive power. And this would give the whole undertaking a more important cachet.

To Anthony Eden the importance of Spain at this moment was certainly paramount. He had had a letter from Samuel Hoare in Madrid stating that the Embassy was passing through a very difficult time:

Like everything else in this irritating country the position is not at all simple. My natural impulse would be to push matters to an extreme. At the same time, we are not yet finished with Africa and the naval base at Gibraltar remains extraordinarily vulnerable. It does not therefore seem wise to use our last sanction, namely the economic sanction . . . I feel also that we must not forget the fact that the Falangists are becoming desperate and that they are obviously stoking up a campaign against us for the purpose of

embroiling us with the Spanish government . . . The events of
the last two or three weeks have irritated me more than words can
say, and for many personal reasons I should like to be quit of
Spain and Spaniards.

Eden, in his reply, though regretting the difficult time the
Ambassador had been going through, did not feel the moment had
come for 'economic retaliation' despite 'the mixture of mulishness
and quixotry' of the Spaniards who were not 'being as quick as we
should wish in drawing the proper conclusions from the improve-
ment of our prospects.' Nor had the time come 'when we can cease
to regard Spain as a vital point in our strategy and therefore of first
importance to the war effort.'

In the course of dealing with official correspondence, Eden's
attention was drawn to the correspondence from the MOI and the
British Council regarding the envisaged lecture tour of Leslie
Howard. He noted the recommendations and, himself appreciating
the value of Leslie's trip at this time, saw that some sort of
sponsorship on his part was requested, and wrote to Leslie
accordingly. The letter expressed pleasure at Leslie's acceptance of
the British Council's invitation in so far as Portugal was concerned
but indicated some surprise at his reluctance over Spain. Eden
enquired if there were any matters in which he might help to set
Leslie's mind at rest as he felt that, unless they were insurmountable,
it would be a great shame while he was already in the Iberian
peninsula if he did not extend his visit to Madrid where he was sure
Leslie could do so much for Anglo-Hispanic relations.

On receipt of this letter Leslie composed a reply to Eden. Since he
had agreed about Portugal it seemed but a small matter to cross the
frontier into Spain. It was not quite as simple as that. He had heard
disquieting reports about Spain and, though he had no official
information, he understood it was becoming a pretty ruthless
country, almost a police state. As far as the Germans were
concerned he was a well-known anti-Nazi which would make him
in Spain not only anti-Fascist but anti-Falangist. Leslie stressed that
he had no desire to meet the leading Falangists or hobnob with
them at official functions, which might be unavoidable. Another
thing that worried him was that the Russians might misunderstand
his motives for the journey, particularly if it was reported that he
had been seen in the company of members of the Spanish ruling
party at official gatherings and so on. He ended the letter on a
lighter note, mentioning the opening of his film *The Gentle Sex* on 23

April which he hoped Eden and his wife might be able to attend as
his personal guests, and, finally, he suggested it might be a good
idea for them to have dinner together one evening and, perhaps,
discuss things generally.

Leslie thought the letter summed up his feelings about Spain and
only hoped Eden would not think them exaggerated. He had so far
only expressed his inner feelings to one man, his close friend Alfred
Chenhalls, and he felt some trepidation that he was now revealing
them to a man who was technically the second most important
official in the country. Leslie's letter was dated 12th April and, as the
British Council were already making arrangements for his flight to
Lisbon – in fact, they had made provisional bookings for Alfred and
Leslie a week earlier – he waited somewhat anxiously for Eden's
reply. It reached the studio on 20th April, and was headed Personal
and Confidential, Foreign Office, SW1. It read:

My dear Leslie Howard,

Many thanks for your letter of 12th April about your
forthcoming visit on behalf of the British Council to Spain and
Portugal.

I can quite understand your scruples about hobnobbing
with any Falangist leaders in Spain, but I do not think they need
worry you unduly, or affect your plans for the journey. The
Falangists although tiresome and influential are only a minority
in Spain, and it is I think unlikely that you will come into contact
with many of them. On the other hand it is very important just
now to fly the British flag in Spain and to give encouragement to
our many friends there, who are to be found in all classes. On the
whole I think it would be best to avoid Spanish internal politics as
a subject of conversation, and to concentrate on explaining the
British war effort. First hand reports on this subject are of special
value in a country like Spain where the Axis have succeeded in
reducing our publicity to a minimum. As for the reactions in this
country I feel sure that it will be understood that your visit has
been undertaken at the request of the Government and in the
General interest of the war effort of the United Nations.

I do not think either that you need fear that your journey will
be misinterpreted by the Russians, who take a realistic view of
Spanish affairs and of the importance of Spanish neutrality to the
United Nations war effort.

I hear that the preliminary arrangements for your trip have
already gone quite far and I think it would be a great pity to

interrupt them at this stage. I am sure you can do a lot of good for us in Spain and Portugal,

> Yours sincerely,
> Anthony Eden.

Eden had added, as a footnote to his letter, in his own handwriting: 'We shall certainly be delighted to dine with you one evening if this letter doesn't exasperate you too much!'

Leslie might have guessed that would be the answer. In a formal, yet perfectly friendly way, Eden had dealt with nearly all his objections – and neatly dismissed them. Leslie had set his face, and his heart, against going to Spain, yet here was the Foreign Secretary putting all his fears to rest and dismissing all his reservations with infuriating reasonableness! The letter exasperated him yet, because it was so reasonable and blandy reassuring, Leslie felt suddenly ashamed of his protestations and the difficulties he had created, like a schoolboy caught dodging taking his medicine. The letter was, in its way, a diplomatic tour de force – with its gentle insistence that plans should in no way be affected, nothing be interrupted, by personal scruples or unrealistic fears. It would be foolish to try and argue round it. The least he could do at this stage was to go through with it and make the best of it. Leslie decided, there and then, not to interrupt arrangements any further. He would tell Eden that he was going to Spain reluctantly and hoped his visit there would be as brief as possible. The truth of the matter was that he hadn't thought very seriously about the Iberian trip. It had been pushed aside, deferred. Now it had suddenly overtaken him – more or less organised, as far as he was concerned, in absentia – and with precious little consultation or instruction. No one had suggested anything more precise than flying the flag, giving encouragement to our friends abroad and explaining the British war effort. However, if Eden, with all his other manifold cares, had rationalised the whole thing, so now must he. If he had ever wanted to do something more positive for his country – in the way Wink was doing – this, he supposed, was the opportunity.

Before he left his office Rose Rutland gave him some messages. Mr Chenhalls had rung and would meet him as arranged at the Savoy. They were to have drinks with a Spanish film producer and distributor in the American bar before supper, but Alfred said he needn't brush up his phonetic Spanish! She also had a note from the British Council saying they had re-booked his flight with Alfred for 28th April, a final alteration due to the Trade Show on the 23rd.

They were to spend the night of the 27th at the Grand Spa Hotel, Bristol, as the flight took off at 9 a.m. and the airport was some distance away. Well, that was it, thought Leslie – sealed, signed and delivered – one actor for onward transmission. With Eden's letter in his pocket, he couldn't back out of this one. Alfred would have a fit!

Later that evening, something caught Leslie's eye as he entered the Savoy. Chalked on a news-vendor's board by the doorway were four words: 'British Civil Air-Liner Attacked'. He hesitated a moment, as he later told Ruth, to read it a second time. There were no papers to be had so he passed on into the hotel, vaguely wondering where it had happened.

Alfred was in the American Bar with a small, round, olive-complexioned man, Senor Rodriguez from Madrid. He spoke English quite well and they were all soon engrossed in a light-hearted discussion about film production in London and Madrid. Being a distributor as well as a producer, Rodriguez was interested in getting some of Leslie's films for release in Spain. They agreed there was difficulty with dubbing and the Spaniard thought Leslie's idea of making films in several languages, using the same sets, both practical and economical. He said he was a friend of the Duke of Alba, who was Spanish Ambassador in London, and that the Duke was very interested that a film should be made about Christopher Columbus. Alfred thought the idea might have strong attractions in America and that the production money would be available through the Hispano-America Bank. Rodriguez considered a co-production of this intriguing subject, with its famous voyage of discovery, would certainly have a very wide appeal. Leslie thought the subject of interest but scarcely of value in war-time.

'But *we* are not at war,' said the Spaniard. 'And we have big studios, San Martin, in Madrid, with all facilities . . . ' He described to Leslie how Columbus' ship could be built in Cadiz from the original design. In fact, everything could be built in Spain – except Columbus. And he gestured at Leslie in the friendliest way: 'You could be the great explorer – you, Senor Howard – perfect casting!' Leslie, not quite expecting this, said Columbus was Genoese. Did he look Genoese?

'No matter,' said Rodriguez. 'Some make-up – a little different hair – perhaps, a beard . . . ' It was not important. Leslie was a great actor – and very popular in Spain – that was why he should do it. '*Soberbio, soberbio!*' he said, carried away by his enthusiasm for the idea. Leslie remarked it would take a bit of planning – but there was certainly a great deal in what Senor Rodriguez had said.

Finally, Rodriguez said he would like them to be his guests at the studios in Madrid, where they could discuss the Christopher Columbus film in more detail. When he had gone, Leslie remarked he hoped the Spaniard wouldn't spread it around Madrid that he had cast him for Christopher Columbus, as he might have to disappoint him. Alfred, laughing, said it wasn't his suggestion. Still, Rodriguez could be very useful over distribution – so he thought a little encouragement sensible. Leslie considered that a splendid idea – as long as he didn't have to be Christopher Columbus to encourage him!

Over dinner the conversation turned to the forthcoming trip. Leslie gave Alfred Eden's letter to read. Perusing it, Alfred showed no surprise – he had felt Leslie's hesitations a bit of a storm in a tea-cup. The letter had come at a timely moment, spurring Leslie's indecision. No need to dispute Leslie's reasons for Alfred knew well the shifting, unpredictable moods that had followed Violette's death. And he felt immense sympathy for Leslie. One had to do one's best to keep him occupied and cheerful for he was very much a chameleon taking colour from surrounding events. In this respect the trip would do him good, getting him out of himself. He would come back refreshed.

Alfred had ordered champagne and, when the wine was opened, proposed a toast – *The Gentle Sex* – 'I think it'll be a winner, Leslie.' Leslie hoped they would give it a good press at the Trade Show. He said he had sent the Edens an invitation and hoped they would be coming. Returning to the question of the trip, Leslie supposed he should feel flattered that he had been asked to visit Spain and Portugal 'at the request of the Government and in the interests of the war effort of the United Nations', but flying the flag was scarcely his cup of tea and how, he asked Alfred, was he to explain the war effort? Alfred thought Eden obviously meant through his experience of war-time film production. That should not present any problem. Leslie agreed – but what about the second lecture, the important one at the National Theatre in Lisbon. Did Alfred think a sort of modern actor's approach to *Hamlet* would fill that part of the bill? Alfred, knowing Leslie's particular interest in *Hamlet*, thought it would do very well – and agreed with Leslie's use of soliloquies by way of illustration. He suggested Leslie pack his notes on the subject, bring them in the plane.

At this moment Leslie remembered the four words about the airliner. Had Alfred seen it? Alfred said casually he'd read a brief report of it in the stop-press of an evening paper, but it contained no details. When Leslie asked where it happened Alfred, keeping a straight face, replied: 'Somewhere in the Bay of Biscay – off Portugal.' Leslie made some sort of interjection and Alfred added: 'The plane landed safely in Lisbon. It couldn't have been very serious – nobody got a scratch.' Leslie wondered if it was their plane, which made Alfred chuckle a bit.

'Our plane! How could it be?' Leslie said what he meant was it a KLM flight – like the one they were booked on?

'It didn't say. Reuters were waiting further details from their Lisbon correspondent.' Alfred shrugged. 'Probably one of those Pan-Am 'Clipper' flights. Have some more champagne.' And Alfred filled their glasses. 'I don't think they were gunning for us, old boy!' Leslie looked serious a moment before he got the joke. Then, he smiled, raising his glass.

'Well, here's to a couple of confirmed fatalists. I suppose it'll be in the papers in the morning.'

'Very likely,' said Alfred. 'You'll be able to read about it over breakfast!' And Alfred steered the conversation away from the subject, opening his brief case to show Leslie some of the memoranda he had been preparing for distribution agreements in Spain and Portugal. Leslie made some suggestions and it was nearly one o'clock by the time they walked out of the restaurant. Leslie had agreed to drop Alfred off on his way home.

As they drove along Alfred reminded him of their Foreign Office briefing on Thursday morning – and, as he got out of the car, his last words were:

'See you at the Trade Show'.

Leslie had heard the FO briefing was a thorough one – mainly on matters of security, normally a routine affair for travellers proceeding abroad and expecting visas. As was the case with most VIPs, he and Alfred would be expected to agree to be questioned on their return on matters concerning their visit and their general reactions. Their 'sponsor' at the Foreign Office would probably let them know, when he saw them on Thursday, roughly the sort of information that would be of value. There might, indeed, be other matters of a more special nature on which they might be expected to report. Leslie, with his sensitive intelligence and quick, actor's memory, might clearly be a useful sounding board.

It was too late when Leslie got home to get a news-bulletin regarding the attack on the airliner and he went to bed, with a slight suspicion that Alfred was concealing something.

Normally Leslie never bothered to buy a paper but the following morning he picked one up on his way to Denham – and read a report on the attack. Reuter's correspondent in Lisbon said that a KLM air-liner, in flight between UK and Lisbon, had been intercepted by German long-range fighters off Cape Corunna. It had been badly shot up by cannon and machine-gun bullets –losing part of a wing – but the pilot, after taking evasive action, managed to reach Lisbon. There seemed to be no reason why the Germans had attempted to interrupt the flight. It had taken place on 19th April.

Leslie felt a little stunned at the news – more so, perhaps, because he seemed to remember that he and Alfred had been provisionally booked to fly on the 19th. It had to be cancelled because of the Trade show, and also because Leslie had not heard from Eden till the 20th in reply to his demurring letter over Spain.

When Leslie reached Denham it was inevitable that someone would make a passing, though light-hearted, reference to the attack on the plane. It had been on the radio and in most of the morning papers. However, Leslie managed to forestall Phil Samuel with the 'news when he saw him on the set. Though Phil, at first, made light of it – pulling Leslie's leg – when he saw him later in his office he was concerned about Leslie flying and said: 'Leslie, do you think it's worth the risk?' And Leslie replied, with a certain mock serenity, 'Well, Phil, what the hell – you know I'm a fatalist anyway.'

What neither Leslie or Phil Samuel realised was that the plane attacked was the same plane that Leslie was to fly to Lisbon in on 28th April. But of this Leslie remained fortunately unaware till the day he flew when, as the passengers boarded, a number of uneasy jokes were made about the repairs to the bullet holes in the passenger cabin. Finally, it was this same plane, G-AGBB – or *Ibis*, as she was known – that was to become, by a strange twist of coincidence, the machine of Leslie's destiny when the last line of his life story was written over the Bay of Biscay. It was in this plane that he and Alfred were shot down on 1st June.

*

The KLM, or Royal Dutch Airline, had been operating its service, under BOAC, for three years. It had carried over 5,000 passengers between the UK and Portugal without loss and almost without incident. It was a wonderful record by these flying Dutchmen who had originally left Schiphol Airport in May 1940, getting their planes out under the noses of the German bombers.

There were to begin with six DC3s, and these formed the squadron that flew from Heston. Their new British names were *Aigrette, King Falcon, Curlew, Buzzard, Heron* and *Ibis*. The Commodore of the air-line was the celebrated Dirk Parmentier, who had come second in the England-Australia air-race of 1928, and the senior pilots were Quirinus Tepas and Theo Verhoeven. *Ibis*, named after the sacred bird of the ancient Egyptians, made the first flight to Lisbon on 25th July 1940, piloted by Tepas, who in 1942 was to receive the OBE from the King for his services to the Lisbon line. She was, with rare exceptions, to be piloted by Tepas for the remainder of her flying life, till she was shot down into the Bay of Biscay in June 1943. *Ibis* was the only plane of the line to be lost in flight due to enemy action.

Built in 1936 by Douglas, she flew on the Jakarta run to the Dutch East Indies till she was brought back to Europe to fly the European network. From September 1939 she operated between Schiphol and Shoreham in Kent. On 9th May 1940 she was damaged by German bombers at Schiphol and was got away to Shoreham after emergency repairs. From Shoreham the squadron moved to Heston, operating from there to Lisbon, but on 20th September Heston was taken over by Fighter Command and the wing moved to its final home at Whitchurch, near Bristol. One of the planes, the *Heron*, was written off due to an accident at Heston and the *Curlew* went up in flames as a result of a bombing raid on Whitchurch. Of the remaining four only three were still in service by 1943.

Ibis remained the only plane in the service to be attacked in flight –on no less than three occasions. The first of these appeared to be a freak attack and not an attempt to interrupt the service. It occurred in November 1942, shortly after the Torch landings. *Ibis* was attacked by a single Me110 on her flight north from Lisbon and only 240 miles from Barnstaple. It appeared to be an error of judgement by an unbriefed pilot.

There had been, from the outset an unwritten agreement about the service of these planes which amounted almost to a guarantee of safe conduct. They were often shadowed but were left alone once they had been identified. This understanding extended to the Germans operating Lufthansa Section Madrid-Berlin and the Americans flying Pan-Am 'Clippers' across the Atlantic. The KLM service between Lisbon and the UK had certain attractions and advantages. Agents of all descriptions, both single and double, travelled regularly and freely on the line, so long as they had presentable passports, and flew unhindered whatever might have been their fates at either end. M15 and 6 used the service as well as representatives of the Abwehr and, as far as Franco and Salazar were concerned, it was the one open link with Britain for diplomatic purposes. Newspapers came out from London daily on the Lisbon line and were on sale in the streets of Lisbon the evening of the day of publication. Couriers came and went on the planes and the diplomatic bags of the Spanish, Portuguese and British governments. It was quite obvious that both Franco and Salazar, as neutrals, had achieved an apparently happy modus vivendi with the Germans over the operation of this service for it continued without let or hindrance, as if surrounded by an invisible cordon sanitaire, until that isolated attack on 15th November 1942.

Five months later on 16th April Tepas decided to abort his flight to Lisbon and returned to Whitchurch. He was one hour out over the Channel – whether this was due to enemy shadowing or mechanical failure is not known (a similar incident occurred on 23rd April). Tepas had been worried by enemy shadowing before, thinking they were after him. His fellow pilots had pulled his leg about it. Tepas took off again later the same day and flew to Lisbon without incident, returning the following day. On his arrival back it was decided by the Commodore, Dirk Parmentier, to take Tepas temporarily off flying duties and rest him. Normally pilots were rested in rotation for three or four days after three weeks operational. On this occasion Tepas was rested for eleven days which was somewhat exceptional. He did not fly again till 28th April and Parmentier brought himself in as relief captain.

With the coming of the longer days and clearer weather over the Bay, Parmentier had been worrying about the possibilities of interception. All his pilots had reported greater aerial activity over the Bay, more Kuriers and Kondors and Ju88s about. He had discussed the matter in some detail with both the Ministry of Civil Aviation and the Air Ministry. He pointed out that German technocracy, with radar and beam assistance, was reaching a point where interception was becoming more feasible and more likely. He wanted a route further west, say 11 or 12 degrees west, or, better still, a change-over to night-flying. But, as usual, nothing had been decided. Re-equipping for night-flying was difficult due to the supply position, and, anyway, meant pulling planes out of service. Heads of departments agreed to look at the matter of re-routing, but the unbroken continuity of the line must not suffer. However, as there had only been one interception, and that without loss, officials questioned whether such elaborate precautions were necessary. Parmentier had heard it all before and he would hear it again – but it didn't make him any easier.

On the 19th, three days after Tepas' return from Lisbon, *Ibis* flew south again with its usual crew, this time piloted by Parmentier. There were only three passengers, plus the newspapers: a priest, a courier and a business man. There had been cancellations for the plane should have carried fourteen passengers, a total of 1,600 kgs in pay load including freight. Parmentier was surprised at the sparsity of passengers. It was fortunate, the way things turned out, that the plane was so lightly loaded.

Parmentier was airborne shortly after 9 a.m. and the flight proceeded uneventfully till *Ibis* reached a position approximately 46 N. by 9 W, a distance no more that 150 miles north by east of Cape Corunna. Then, de Koning, Parmentier's co-pilot and navigator, drew his attention to six or eight planes coming out of the sun on their starboard beam. As the planes drew closer Parmentier recognised them as Ju88s and he held his course steady expecting them to sheer off as soon as they read his civil markings – but they didn't. They opened fire instead and Parmentier, seeing no cloud bank close enough, put *Ibis* into a steep dive as the first tracer bullets swept across him deciding to get as near the wavetops as possible in case he had to ditch. It was an unequal struggle with Parmentier man-handling the plane fifty feet over the Bay, jinking this way and that, as the Junkers came in at wave-top height raking him with cannon and machine gun bullets. Van Brugge, the wireless operator, just managed to get out the attack signal before his aerial disconnected. The running attack over the sea lasted six minutes which Parmentier later described as 'the longest six minutes in my life' – and, then, more by luck than good management, he found cloud – not much, but ten-tenths, enough to pull *Ibis* in a shuddering climb off the wave-tops. It was fortunate the plane was only lightly loaded and, with her engines flat out, had given Parmentier the extra speed he needed. He thought afterwards the German pilots must have been amazed at his display of aerobatics in an air-liner.

As soon as Parmentier found cloud he flew a course for Cape Vilano, the nearest point of land, and from there nursed the badly-mauled *Ibis* at reduced speed to Portela, the Lisbon airport. On landing he was met by Van der Vliet, KLM's Lisbon manager, who had picked up the first part of the attack signal. Together they examined the damage to *Ibis*: left wing-top shot away two feet back into main wing, left aileron badly damaged by cannon shell.

Machine gun bullets had pierced the cabin section of the fuselage and shrapnel had penetrated the left rear tank draining it of petrol, and the aerial was hanging loose. But why had he been attacked? Or was it just a chance interception? Parmentier did not think so. One plane, one pilot can make a mistake, but an error of judgement by a squadron meant the compound error of six to eight pilots not only in RT communication with themselves but with base. They could not all have failed to see his civil registration letters two feet high on the sides of the air-liner, or the red, white and blue bars which distinguished it from the roundels of a war-plane. The Germans were not that stupid. As they discussed the time it would take to effect temporary repairs, Parmentier noticed the Lufthansa mechanics had left their service bay to have a look at the bullet-holes in *Ibis*.

On arrival back at his office, Van der Vliet picked up the passenger manifest. He wondered if there was anybody specially interesting on the plane. He noted the light cargo and the three passengers. The names meant nothing. Too many people in wartime travelled under assumed names. Even the priest could have been an M15 man in clerical mufti. The manifest proved nothing yet could hide everything. Fruitless to pursue that line of enquiry. It led to dead ends.

Parmentier wanted repairs carried out that night and Van der Vliet agreed to signal Whitchurch so that Verhoeven could bring out a spare wing tip the following morning. The rear tank could be repaired at Whitchurch. Parmentier would fly home on one tank, topping up at Oporto for the journey over the Bay. He told Van der Vliet he meant to put in a stiff report, demanding immediate re-routeing or night-flying operations. It was just too risky. He'd been lucky flying a lightly loaded plane, as he said, by the seat of his pants for six of the longest minutes of his life. But if there were to be more interceptions, with fuller pay-loads, the planes would be sitting ducks for destruction.

On 21st April, Parmentier, with a patched-up plane and a new wing tip flew home. He was carrying twelve passengers, plus diplomatic bags and freight. And he made his stop at Oporto for fuel. Then, he went out over the Bay, not without trepidation. But he saw no German patrols, nothing – the sky was clear. When he landed at Whitchurch *Ibis* went straight into the service bay and Parmentier went to his office to make out his report. Taking Tepas' place, as relief captain, had taught him something. He now had first-hand experience of what interception meant.

The following day he received a letter from the Superintendent of Routes congratulating him and his crew on 'their most fortunate escape'. He appreciated the letter but doubted if his flight plan would be adjusted or night-flying instituted. Parmentier's report covered the circumstances of the attack, the damage to the plane and added: 'It is certain that the enemy aircraft had sufficient opportunity to recognise our plane as a civil aircraft.' Later that week a note was appended to the report:

> Captain Parmentier has taken up the whole question of operation of the service with the Air Ministry – it may even be decided to fly at night. He has had one meeting at which KLM requirements were quoted and expects a second this week at which as he said, 'we shall be told what we can have'.

It will be seen from Parmentier's comments that he was far from optimistic about getting his requirements met. Those for night-flying involved fitting astrodomes for taking night-sights, cowls on exhausts to reduce the chance of night fighter interception and black-out scuttles for port-holes. It looked to Parmentier like the same old question of buck-passing and delay. The Air Ministry had to meet both the RAF and Transport Command requirements for night-flying equipment. KLM priority was well down the list. The official view was that, on the basis of one interception, the service should not be interrupted and so Parmentier had little option but to continue daylight flying.

As the mechanics worked on *Ibis* to bring her to full flying readiness by 28th April, Leslie Howard at Denham was tying up production details on *The Lamp Still Burns* and preparing for the Trade Show of *The Gentle Sex*. Then, there would be the dinner with Eden, and a day later he would travel to Bristol for the flight south in *Ibis*. The Iberian journey was about to begin.

*

As the last images faded from the screen of the Odean, Leicester Square, at the conclusion of the first public showing of *The Gentle Sex*, there was prolonged applause. Then, the curtains were drawn and the footlights came up. There was an expectant hush and, a moment later, Leslie's slight, bespectacled figure appeared from the side of the stage, held in a single spot-light. At his appearance the applause started again as the specially invited audience of press and show people, Foreign Office and MOI officials, paid tribute to the film's co-producer and director.

Leslie began his short speech by thanking them all for coming, hoping they had enjoyed the film – as he put it – 'about the girls who, as you will have seen, having something to offer besides the men in their efforts to grapple with Armageddon'. He admitted that though he might be accused of picking pretty girls as his leading ladies this was far from the truth 'for they all look magnificent in uniform and one could not tell the actresses from the real thing'. He was only sorry that the WRNS and the WAAFS had not been included in this tribute to 'the wonderful women', but as the ATS were the successors to the WRACS of the first world war one had to remember that they were the first of their sex to be enlisted. 'I need only add – the first of equals.' He concluded by pointing out that the film had been made through the effective cooperation of the Army and the Chief Controller of the ATS, not to mention 'those stern-voiced though gentle fellows, the sergeant majors, who had put his theatrical platoon through their, at times, hilarious paces.' He thought that after what they had seen they might, perhaps, consider the title a trifle too gentle.

Leslie went from the Odeon to the press reception at the Savoy Hotel where he was joined by Doodie and Major Dale Harris. He chatted with many who had been at the Trade Show and was congratulated on his brief appearance, in backview, at the railway station from where the girls go off to enlist. A lady member of the audience felt it was a pity he hadn't appeared more often to which Leslie replied: 'I may be gentle, Madam – but I'm the wrong sex!' Alfred came across to congratulate him on his silhouette performance and Jack Beddington complimented him on the commentary he had both written and spoken.

However, what delighted Jack most was that Leslie appeared to have overcome his scruples about the lecture tour which was, Jack felt, bound to be a huge success – and he wished him well. Maurice Elvey, who had helped Leslie complete the film, was there and also Puffin Asquith and Tolly de Grunwald. Puffin, in the uniform of an aircraftman, would insist on calling Bob Dale Harris 'Sir', which amused my sister. Tolly and Leslie stood a few minutes in deep conversation. Tolly knew well what Leslie had gone through at Violette's death and the distraction of spirit that had made him almost a stranger to his friends. In the ensuing months they had met from time to time, though not often since *The First of the Few*, and Tolly found him at least halfway back to his old self and, apparently, coming to terms with his bereavement.

He made Leslie laugh, telling him some funny stories about the filming of *The Demi-Paradise*, his production starring Laurence Olivier which Puffin was completing at Denham. It was a sophisticated comedy, full of Tolly-esque satirical twists and turns; its subject was friendship and cooperation between England and Russia and was, interestingly, the first war film with an Anglo-Russian theme. Leslie mentioned the subject of a film Two Cities was interested in his making, *Liberty Ship*, which had a Russian end product for it involved the journey of the ship from the Halifax to Murmansk with a cargo of munitions. It would also tell the story of the piecemeal construction of the ship on the west coast of America – for such ships were delivered in pre-fabricated sections – and its initial journey through the Panama Canal. It was to be made in conjunction with the Americans, have an international cast and Leslie thought he might have to go to Hollywood for consultations. To Tolly it seemed an odd subject for Leslie and he asked if there had been any progress with the idea of his *Hamlet* film. Leslie said there had been but it was still not a very 'hot property' with distributors, and he thought Larry Olivier's idea of doing *Henry V* seemed more appropriate to the embattled times. For the time being the nearest he would get to *Hamlet* was to make it a subject for his lecture tour.

The following morning Leslie rang Ruth to say he would be coming down to Stowe Maries for a couple of days prior to his departure for Lisbon. He had now only his dinner with Eden before he and Alfred left for Bristol on the first leg of their journey. Though Leslie's visits to Stowe Maries had for the past two or three years been marked by their brevity they had since Violette's death been more frequent. He seemed to need the comfort of the family and be leaning towards it more. As the initial shock of the tragedy receded family relations had improved and, with everyone putting on a cheerful face, were certainly less of a strain. Still, he was not the most predictable of men, and my mother had to be ready for quixotic shifts in the emotional barometer; on this occasion before the journey she felt there might be need for more oil than usual on troubled waters. So she decked herself in one of her more resilient moods. Fortunately, my sister and her husband were at home at the time and would help to make it something of a family occasion.

Ruth was determined that these two days should be happy ones. She had tried very hard to come closer to Leslie – to fill the void, as it were – but it was a formidable task. Happily, she had the ability to rise above her feelings, disguising them in a buoyant manner. Leslie was not a man of disguises where his emotions were concerned and could never successfully dissemble his feelings, even for an occasion. Yet I think he admired Ruth for the very qualities he didn't possess. If admiration hadn't taken the place of love, then it was a very special kind of love that Leslie felt for Ruth, a love reserved for the admirable, the stoic qualities she possessed – and had to – for they both knew that the essential passion of a man for a woman had long been absent from their relationship. It seemed unlikely they would find it again for when he lost Violette the place she had occupied in his heart remained untenanted. For Ruth it had for years been a kind of battle of attrition for the lesser affections, the soothing, cosseting, maternalistic approach that he had come to expect. If it was poor reward for devotion, it was one she had accepted with understanding.

Ruth did not have to use much intuition to know that he was going to be a reluctant traveller. He always hated journeys, but on this occasion from the moment he arrived his discomfort seemed heightened by foreboding, as if an ill fate attended the whole thing. Though admitting, with a certain bravado, that he was a fatalist, he was clearly a little worried about the attack on the plane the previous week. If Ruth had any qualms about that she kept them in perspective, thinking it a slight chance that such a thing could happen again, and did everything to assure him that all would be well – and that the trip would do him immense good. 'You'll feel better about the whole thing once you're there,' she told him. At which he shrugged gloomily and went off to explore the garden.

The following morning, after an early night, he was more cheerful and, dressed in an old jersey and slacks, he went for a walk through the Deerleap with Doodie and Bob. When they returned an hour later the exercise seemed to have shaken off his Hamlet mood. Ruth greeted them with champagne cocktails and, by lunchtime, most misgivings about the journey had evaporated in the laughter and leg-pulling round the table, only to return briefly at the moment of separation, as he sat in his car saying goodbye. Though he seemed resigned to the journey, it took him some time to break away, to drive off, holding onto Ruth's hand like a life-line. Finally, as he put the car into gear, he said:

'I don't know why – but I have a queer feeling about this whole trip. Still, what the hell!'

These were the last words Ruth remembered as he drove off down the lane on his way to London.

Leslie was returning to London for his dinner with Anthony Eden, but where it took place or what was discussed on this private occasion one will never know. The two men who sat down together are both dead and there is, so far as I know, no living witness to their conversation. It may well have touched on some important facet of Leslie's journey – may, indeed, have involved some other commitment not connected with the apparently innocuous lectures. On the other hand, it may simply have been a social occasion, involving no more than pleasantries and trivialities.

It has been suggested in some quarters that Leslie was to bring back a private report for Eden (*vide* Adrian Brunel's autobiography, p 195), a sort of unwritten memorandum of his observations while in Portugal and Spain and committed to his actor's memory. If this was the case they were never imparted and died with the observer. Though Leslie might have had his uses in the sphere of political warfare and even in terms of strategic deception (*vide* the occupation of Azores which was hatching) we have to this day only German suspicions as to his activities. The Germans always remained deeply sceptical about 'cultural' trips – thinking they were simply a cloak for other activities. They could not believe that he had gone to Lisbon and Madrid just to give lectures and asserted he was a British agent. Our departments have remained silent or resisted any suggestion that his British Council activities served any other than cultural purposes – or were, in any sense, a cover for espionage.

IBERIAN JOURNEY

CHAPTER ELEVEN

Flight to the Sun

Two days later, on 27th April, Leslie and Alfred Chenhalls travelled to Bristol. They spent their last night in England at that staging post, the Grand Spa Hotel, Clevedon, where all travellers to the Iberian peninsula assembled for their flights. In the dining room that evening their presence was observed by Wing Commander Jack Schreiber, the British Air Attaché in Lisbon, and his dining companion Martin Blake, in charge of the British Council's Foreign Division. They would also be flying to Lisbon the following morning. It is far from improbable that others, in the pay of our enemies, observed them as well for the Germans were known to have agents and transmitters in the Bristol area, and few travellers were not observed by these watch-dogs.

Early the following morning, as the flight took off at nine, Leslie and Alfred joined their fellow travellers outside the hotel to board the small airport bus that plied between the Grand Spa and Whitchurch aerodrome, five miles south of Bristol. There were ten passengers on this occasion and as it was a chilly morning Leslie wore a hat and tweed overcoat. He carried some notes, random jottings for his film lecture and 'An Actor's Approach to Hamlet'. All his other requirements were packed in two smallish suitcases. One item he had not brought, which was considered *de rigueur* for all official soirées in Spain and Portugal, was a dinner jacket. His only concession to formality was a double-breasted dark blue suit.

Once they had gone through passport control and were walking across the concrete apron towards the plane Leslie knew he had reached the point of no return. The Air Attaché, Schreiber, walking beside him told him the plane on this occasion was the *Ibis* and the pilot the celebrated Quirinus Tepas OBE, and that the flight plan would take them out several hundred miles into the Atlantic. Schreiber had flown out and back many times and assured Leslie it was a very straightforward journey – it took roughly seven and a half hours – and might be described as what the Americans called 'a commuter service'. Leslie felt reasonably reassured though he had a certain distrust of flying over large expanses of water: a fortune teller once told him that the watery sign in his horoscope indicated some danger.

However, it was something else that attracted his attention as he approached the steps into the plane: a series of indentations like pock-marks in the metal fuselage of the DC 3, which appeared to have been hastily-patched-up and painted over. They looked a bit like bullet-holes, and his suspicions were confirmed when Schreiber, jokingly, admitted that these, in fact, were what they were – bullet-holes from a previous attack. Leslie now realised this was the plane there was all the fuss about in the paper a few days before. As the passengers boarded there was some jocular bravado about the plane's war-wounds and when Leslie took his seat across the aisle from Alfred he noticed, on looking up, some repairs to the floc-padding interior of the cabin. He was about to remark on this to Alfred when a member of the crew put his head into the cabin and asked them to fasten their seat-belts. A moment later, the plane's engines started up with a roar and they were soon lumbering across the bumpy airfield, taxiing for take-off.

As *Ibis* lifted slowly into the air over Dundry beacon to begin its journey down the Bristol Channel, Leslie probably wished he were anywhere but in this aeroplane. However, it was too late now for second thoughts.

Shortly after take-off, as was common practice, the Flight Engineer (Rozevink), who acted as cabin steward, instructed passengers in the use of life-jackets and how to inflate and board the life-raft *Ibis* carried in case of ditching. For the first hour or so it was not possible for passengers to see out of the plane. The port-holes were covered by fabric panels which let in light but prevented any observation of the coast-line, military installations or airfields over which the plane passed at low altitude. As many foreigners – and some agents – used the Lisbon line information about our defences could have been gained in this way. When the panels were removed sunlight flooded the cabin and passengers looking out saw only the wrinkled mirror of the sea far below. It was generally expected passengers would report any planes they saw through the port-holes, and the Flight Engineer reminded them of this.

Gradually, at a speed of 170 knots, *Ibis* edged her way out into the Atlantic, climbing – since she was unpressurised – to an optimum, cruising ceiling of 9/10,000 feet. Somewhere off the Scillies she turned south to begin her run across the Bay of Biscay. This was the most exposed part for possible interception and whenever there were clouds over the Bay – often the rule at this time of year – the KLM pilots kept near them. Clouds had their uses in the event of shadowing by enemy planes. It was understandable if passengers glanced a little apprehensively through their port-holes – but, on this flight, they saw nothing except, where the clouds shredded back, occasional glimpses of ocean. Save for *Ibis* the sky seemed uninhabited.

How Leslie occupied himself during the 7½ hours of the flight no one knows and if he had any misgivings they have not been recorded, save one admission, in a letter to Ruth, that 'the flight was smooth' and 'Alfred slept happily – but I'm afraid I didn't'. It seems probable that, as the flight proceeded uneventfully, he began – in his mind – to give some shape to the lectures he was to deliver, particularly the important one on *Hamlet*. Leslie had a great ability to detach himself from his immediate surroundings, and putting his mind to work very quickly, with little peripheral exploration, get straight to the centre. He was also a quick 'study', being blessed with a photographic brain. He knew most of the Hamlet soliloquies by heart, but it was on Professor Dover Wilson he had long leaned for textual advice. In fact, his copy of Dover Wilson's monograph *What Happens In Hamlet* was marked with Leslie's pencilled notes from beginning to end.

Years later Walter Starkie showed me the Penguin edition of *Hamlet* that Leslie had used – the slips of paper marking the soliloquies still in place. The first passage noted began with Hamlet's arrival at court in mourning for his father, the soliloquy 'O, that this too, too sullied flesh would melt' and the condemnation of his mother's hasty marriage with its 'frailty thy name is woman'. A few pages on Leslie had marked 'Remember thee? Ay, thou poor ghost while memory holds a seat in this distracted globe . . . ' And then 'It is adieu, adieu, remember me.'

Another passage marked was the warlike reference to an impending battle for 'a little patch of ground' that was to be defended to the death by its garrison. Dover Wilson, in his notes, thought it relevant to the defence of some sand-dunes near Ostend in 1601 by Sir Francis Vere against the Spaniards – 'two thousand souls' pitted against 'the twenty thousand men' of Spinola's army – fighting 'for a plot whereon the numbers cannot try the cause, which is not tomb enough and continent to hide the slain.' And Leslie had carefully underlined the fate of this predominantly Spanish army that 'for a fantasy and trick of fame go to their graves like beds'.

It was about 4 p.m. that Van Brugge, the radio operator, appeared in the doorway between the cabin and cockpit. As the plane was beginning its descent into Lisbon, he asked the passengers to fasten their seat-belts. A few minutes later, they saw the Tagus gleam, serpentine, beneath them as it wound its way to the sea. *Ibis* was soon skimming over sun-lit cork and olive orchards, farms and villages. When the wheels touched down at Portela, Leslie felt a surge of relief. It had been a smooth flight – but he was heartily glad it was over. If progress on 'An Actor's Approach to Hamlet' had been limited, reflecting on the play had concentrated his mind – suspending his thoughts in the uncertain air.

As *Ibis* taxied towards the airport control tower Leslie noticed other planes dotted about, some Spanish, some with Lufthansa markings and swastikas, some American. When *Ibis* came to rest, Van Brugge opened the rear door – and a hot breath of Lisbon air entered the plane. Leslie had no need of his overcoat as he and Alfred walked across the tarmac into the airport building. It was quite stiflingly hot for so early in the year – 'Hot as Albuquerque in June', as he wrote to Ruth. Apparently, Lisbon was in the grip of an early heat-wave, with temperatures well into the eighties.

When they reached the Portuguese passport control and customs, George West, director of the British Institute and his assistant, David Shillan, were there to meet them. No sooner had West steered them quickly through the arrival formalities than Alfred said he felt like a glass of port to celebrate their arrival in Portugal, and it might buck up Leslie a bit who had wilted in the heat. So they went to the bar. No sooner had they swallowed some port than they were whisked off to a limousine to be driven to the Aviz Hotel. As they drove into Lisbon, West told them there was to be a press reception at 7 pm in the offices of Vitoria Filme, and he would call for them just before seven.

The Aviz, in the Avendia de Liberdade, though one of the smaller was one of the more luxurious hotels in Lisbon with an attractive, galleried entrance hall. Its better appointed rooms faced onto a terraced garden where a fountain bubbled. To one of these rooms Leslie was conducted; Alfred's was directly adjacent. Leslie had scarcely had time to look round and, whether it was the sudden, unexpected and unfamiliar heat or the unwisely and quickly swallowed glasses of port he did not know – but he felt a wave of giddiness and had to lie down. He thought it was his heart – his 'damned heart' that always let him down on journeys – and after a few moments he rang Alfred, saying he wasn't feeling too good. Alfred came round, had a look at him and called a doctor.

The doctor examined Leslie and listened to his heart. There seemed nothing serious the matter. It was probably the journey and the heat. He gave Leslie some pills and told him to rest for an hour.

When they arrived at the Press reception, Leslie assured his sympathetic host, Rafael Seruya, that he was feeling better, and apologised to the assembled journalists and photographers for keeping them waiting, confessing 'the climate had taken him rather by surprise'. A journalist describing the scene said:

> The man in grey moves round the table from this knot to that of journalists. The cameramen have taken up new places of vantage . . . flash after flash of magnesium illuminates the glasses on the table. The well-laden buffet receives scarcely any attention so great is the news appeal of the quiet man in grey who looks so tired after his journey.

Alfred, keeping a watchful eye on Leslie, stood in the background talking to Anthony Haigh, the 1st Secretary and Cultural Attaché at the Embassy. They discussed the distribution arrangements Alfred hoped to come to with Senor Seruya for a wide portfolio of British films. They would have more detailed discussions later at the Embassy. After about an hour George West, mindful of Leslie's health, had a few words with Seruya and the reception broke up.

On the way back to the Aviz, it was suggested that as Lisbon was in the middle of a heat-wave it might be a good idea to find somewhere cooler to stay. West, said he would try in the morning, but the better hotels were rather booked up. When Leslie reached his room he sent Ruth a telegram saying he had arrived safely – it was like California 'including heat' and he was 'drinking a large orange juice to them all at Stowe Maries'. Later that evening Alfred and he took a short walk along the Avenida, intrigued at the brilliantly lit city, with its neon signs and flashing advertisements, after the long years of the London black-out.

Next morning West was in touch, and was happy to report that, after some difficulty, he had managed to book them into the Atlantico at Estoril. He warned them, however, there were a number of Germans in residence, either 'tourists' or Embassy people – so one had to be fairly discreet. Large numbers of expatriate Germans were returning through Lisbon from Brazil and other South American countries, the younger ones to be conscripted, and being flown home by Lufthansa. There was a wide-spread feeling among English residents in Estoril that the manager of the Atlantico, if not actually German, was distinctly Germanophile. A secret transmitter had recently been discovered there. Leslie, taking note of West's warning, didn't mind so much about the Germans so long as he could breathe some fresh air and, the following day, he and Alfred moved out.

At the Atlantico Leslie had a room with a balcony overlooking the beach and the broad sweep of the open sea. Alfred was just down the corridor. It felt and looked a lot like California, reminding him of San Luis Obispo. After the sticky heat of Lisbon Leslie revived rapidly, 'breathing gulps of ocean air'. Since the first lecture on films was to be given the following Tuesday he asked George West if he could have the services of a secretary to take dictation. It was arranged that Miss Gwyneth Williams, West's secretary at the Institute, would come out to the Atlantico. When she arrived Leslie and Alfred went to meet her at Monte Estoril station. They escorted . her back to the hotel entering it somewhat unconventionally by the rear instead of the front entrance. To achieve this they had to climb over a high, padlocked gate. Whether this was part of the policy of discretion suggested to them and they wished to slip in unobserved, I do not know. Gwyneth said it was the quickest way into the hotel – though I dare say she found the gymnastics somewhat novel.

Settling Miss Williams on the balcony outside his room Leslie disappeared to change into shorts. He always believed in combining work with the acquisition of a sun-tan whenever possible. Thus suitably attired, and lying comfortably in the sun, he began dictation of the film lecture. 'He dictated straight out without corrections,' Gwyneth recalled to me years later. 'He knew just what he wanted to say, no fumbling for words.' And this, indeed, was always Leslie's method – straight out as if he was talking to his intended audience and, in the case of the more conversational film lecture, with no previously prepared notes. He described the problems of making films in war-time, from first script conference to production, lightly and amusingly, straight out of his head.

After the first dictation session, Alfred joined them and they all went to lunch together. They took a table by the wide windows that overlooked the sea and Alfred, glancing round, grimaced slightly. 'Don't look now,' he said, 'But we *should* be lunching with them!' And he indicated, with a backward nod of his head, some Embassy people at another table. Perhaps they had forgotten, immersed in the lecture details and dictation, and Alfred went over to apologise.

There were to be other lapses of memory, particularly in Madrid, which were the subject of more unfavourable comment. However it must be remembered that neither Leslie nor Alfred lived in the conventional, somewhat closed world of diplomatic protocol, and they did occasionally in the demanding six weeks ahead of them get their wires crossed and miss appointments. Alfred, without the lecture responsibilities, had more free time and tended to make his own arrangements – often for both of them – which caused some friction.

I think the principal difficulty the Council faced with Leslie was that their representatives had had no experience of this kind of visitor before, either with the charisma Leslie generated or the power he had over broad masses of people. They had, in the past had principally to deal with 'specialists' – professors, scientists, judges, medical men, leaders of the Church and so on – whose appeal was to scholarly people in similar or adjacent professions. They arrived well-briefed with specific formats. But the personality of an actor overflowed these tidy and containable limits. The Council people found themselves a little bewildered and intimidated by the sort of 'fan' worship and idolatry that Leslie attracted. This remained a problem not only for the Council but for Leslie – for there were too many interested parties, too many people scrambling for patronage – and he was over-lionised and torn between too many commitments.

By Friday evening Leslie had completed the dictation of his film lecture and spent most of Saturday in the sun on his balcony or exploring Cascais and Estoril in company with Alfred. On Sunday they both went across to the Casino to join the Shillans and Martin Blake for dinner. After dinner they attended a violin recital at the College of Music given by Philip Newman. Newman, an expatriate Manchester violinist, was professor of music at the Conservatorio Nacional. Leslie became very attached to Newman, describing to him the lessons he had received from Jascha Heifetz during the making of *Intermezzo* and the dismal squeaks he obtained from the violin while Heifetz played the sonata for the film track, more or less behind his back.

Monday found Leslie dictating the more important lecture on *Hamlet* that was to be presented at the Teatro Nacional. As this was to be given in front of university professors, drama critics and other Portuguese writers Leslie was more anxious about its reception than the film lecture. He expected they all knew more about *Hamlet* as a literary work than he did, and so he stuck mainly to his modern actor's approach. He just hoped that those who remembered more formal productions would not find his comments too unconventional.

Leslie linked the soliloquies he was using with an amalgam of Dover Wilson's textual comments and his, Leslie's, ideas on how the play should be staged and presented by modern actors. He concentrated on the seven soliloquies he had selected and, following the course of the play emphasised its extraordinary timelessness, its then and now sense, which made it contemporary with the current world scene. Yet he avoided any direct reference to the present war. Nor did he forget the 'little patch of ground' speech wherein a small garrison, by attrition, brought a vast army to its knees, though perhaps this was to prove more effective in Madrid as veiled counter-propaganda. He had much fun with the player scene in which Shakespeare's advice to actors might have been written yesterday. He added part of the Yorick scene with the lines 'Now get you to my lady's chamber and tell her, let her paint an inch think, to this favour she must come' and, finally, he included 'the readiness is all' speech where Hamlet throws procrastination aside. 'Not a whit, we defy augury. There's a special providence in the fall of a sparrow.' It was Hamlet's philosophy of necessity and fatalism – a man must be ready to act, at all times, where he feels like it or not.

As Gwyneth Williams later told me, Leslie worked with great thoroughness over the play and had given it a most original emphasis. It is strange, with the hindsight of what happened, how parts of the play had almost the shape of his own destiny – even to the 'Not a whit, we defy augury' speech with its philosophy of fatalism in 'the fall of a sparrow'. Leslie wound up, quoting Shakespeare's sources in the translation by Florio:

It is uncertain where death looks for us . . . A man should ever, as much as in him lieth, be ready booted to take his journey. What matters is it when it cometh, since it is unavoidable.

*

When Leslie arrived at the Teatro Politeama in Lisbon the following evening, escorted by George West, there was a big audience in attendance. It was composed largely of Portuguese film people – scenarists, directors, actors and so on – and Leslie was introduced from the stage by Dr Gustavo Ramos, president of the Institute de Alta Cultura. Leslie regretted he knew little Portuguese – except what the chambermaid who looked after his room at the hotel had taught him – and he hoped his descriptions of filming in wartime in England would be understood. Referring to film people in the audience he felt 'their common problems gave them, perhaps, a common language – a sort of filmic Esperanto'. As it turned out there seemed to be no great difficulty in the communication system between one set of film makers and another. As one journalist put it:

> ' . . . the immediate response to his jokes showed how closely his words were followed. From its unexpectedness his manner was just the kind to captivate a public rather surfeited with Gallic esprit, verve and what not. Leslie Howard just moved or sat around and took the audience into his confidence. He chatted pleasantly about the pitfalls in film-making and touched lightly but forcefully on the peculiar difficulties of producing under bomb, fire and imminent invasion. He got his audience every time.

Eugenio Navarro, a leading Lisbon critic, wrote:

> Leslie Howard is not an orator – he is an actor. His lectures or talks were neither one thing nor the other. Leslie Howard does not discourse nor does he demonstrate. The actor represents. His 'talks' were 'representations'. The artist simply acted a new part and may, perhaps, have created a new genre – that of the representational lecture, a kind of intellectual and cultural interlude, without the insensitiveness of the ordinary lecturer and with all the attractions of a living and varied performance . . . Without any magisterial manner, in lively colloquy with the audience whom he kept in constant laughter, the artist explained his idea of a film, how one wrote the plot and the dialogue, how one planned, acted, directed and produced it.

Leslie went on to describe the resources of the American cinema by way of comparison and ended his talk with a manifestation of his faith in the future of European film production.

Alfred had not been idle while Leslie had been preparing his talks. It had been agreed that Rafael Seruya of Vitoria Filme should have the agency for the distribution of the majority of British war films. This would give him a big – if unleavened – portfolio and, as an encouragement, he would receive a number of outstanding films like *We Dive At Dawn*, *Cottage To Let* (directed by Anthony Asquith) and *49th Parallel*, plus the whole output of Two Cities Films and Leslie's films. And Alfred gave both Seruya and Haigh copies of a very clear memorandum on the present state of negotiations.

Since 1941 there had been some increase in the number of British films shown in Portugal. On the other hand, those that had been passed for public exhibition rather than private Embassy showing, had been heavily censored owing to representations by the German Embassy to Salazar on the grounds of bias or other unfairness to the Third Reich. Despite the ancient alliance Salazar had had to move warily and, as a neutral, was constantly having to light candles to both God and the Devil.

On Wednesday there was an urgent enquiry from our Embassy in Madrid as to when Leslie was leaving for Spain. It came from Arthur Yencken, the British Minister, anxious to complete his preparations for Leslie's arrival and make arrangements for various dinners and functions he was expected to attend. The Director of the British Institute, Walter Starkie, also rang so that he could complete his programme. As was frequently the case with Leslie, the myth was preceding the man and everyone was furiously at work exploiting this valuable export.

On Wednesday Leslie was guest of honour at a luncheon, given by the Royal British Club, presided over by HE The Ambassador (Sir Ronald Campbell). On Thursday afternoon he was back in Lisbon for the more important of his two lectures 'An Actor's Approach to Hamlet' when he was introduced by Sir John Balfour HM Minister in Portugal. This was a somewhat different audience from the one he faced for the film talk. There would be no filmic wavelength of communication and, it would seem, little latitude for light-hearted sallies. His audience composed of professors and their wives, producers of classical repertoire and serious drama students had taken their seats in the Teatro Nacional Donna Maria II – and as Leslie surveyed them, stretched to the back of the theatre, not a seat vacant – and, certainly, no mind – the stillness of their expectation may have caused him some qualms. He was not a Shakespearian scholar and scarcely a Shakespearian actor of any repute. Leslie had written to my sister the day before expressing some uncertainty about his fitness to lecture at the National Theatre on 'so sacrosanct a subject as *Hamlet*, which they are all very serious about, and about which I don't know much – and have forgotten most. Unfortunately, it has been put about that I am the great English Shakespeare expert, which God knows I am not. I think I shall come clean and admit all.' (Despite the jocular vein of these remarks, Leslie was far better equipped to talk about *Hamlet* than he pretended.)

Leslie needn't have worried: they proved no more frightening than the film audience and just as unconstrained when he made them laugh, which he did quite often. They seemed quite willing to accept his modern actor's approach which presented Hamlet with no trimmings, pre-conditions, props or costumes as a contemporary investigation into human psychology. If in the search for a modern *Hamlet* he had divorced the play from its Elizabethan trappings, he had only done so to explore its underlying motives which were universal and eternal. It was the human relations that fascinated Leslie and on these elements Shakespeare had certainly built the play. Leslie's approach need not have concerned him. As one journalist remarked: 'The memory of *Hamlet* as played in Lisbon at the turn of the century is naturally a little dim.' And the same journalist went on to say, not without humour:

> Those Irvingesque productions gave only two popular quotations to current language, viz: '*Ser ou nao ser*' and, surprisingly, '*Vai para um convento*' – though a few days ago an evening paper, à propos of something or other, opined that there was something rotten in the state of Denmark.

Of the *Hamlet* lecture, Eugenio Navarro said:

> We saw a new Hamlet, heard another Hamlet, original and unmistakeable – a Hamlet-Howard. His unaffected style of speaking, with its gentle, yet clear, enunciation, worked the miracle. Without scenery, without unity, without theatrical illusion ... he told us how an actor of today, dressed in an ordinary suit and clean shaven ... ought to perceive the part of Hamlet. He gave us ... an unforgettable performance, in the profoundly poetic voice of Shakespeare, of the collective spirit of England.

As Leslie and Alfred were to leave for Madrid on Saturday 8th May it was arranged that *Pimpernel Smith* should be shown to a specially invited audience at the Embassy Cinema (Estrella Hall). At the conclusion of the film Leslie spoke from the stage, admitting he had had some difficulty arriving at a satisfactory end to the film. He hoped they had approved of the one he had decided on. According to Sir Michael Stewart, KCMG, then our Press Attaché in Lisbon, Leslie had remarked, apropos of Professor Smith, 'I wonder where he is now?' Sir Michael's guest, the American Cultural Attaché, replied: 'Well, he's dug up half of Germany already – I guess he's digging up the other half!' Later that night, after a reception at the British Institute, Leslie dined with Michael Stewart at his flat in Lisbon.

One of the invited journalists, Jose Ramalho, wrote of the film show:

> *Pimpernel Smith* was the first war film produced in England. Many others have followed . . . but this first work will survive because it puts moral above material values and because it represents the victory of intelligence over brute force. The timeliness of the film's concluding prophecy, though written in 1940 at a time of uncertainty and adversity, is today being impressively confirmed.

The prophecy referred to was Professor Smith's parting remark at the frontier station, as he leaves Germany behind a puff of cigarette smoke: 'We will be back. We will all be back.'

CHAPTER TWELVE

Journey to Disenchantment

As the long, slow, green Lusitania Express crawled out of Lisbon station Leslie and Alfred were on board. Gone were the days when this train could be called an express. The creeping journey now took nearly twenty hours, four hundred miles at an average twenty miles an hour. Leslie was scarcely looking forward to it – or Madrid. George West and several of the Embassy people waved them away, wishing them luck. Leslie, depressed at leaving Lisbon, felt they'd need it.

They had both enjoyed those eleven days in Lisbon and Estoril – particularly Estoril with its sun and bracing air. If Leslie had enjoyed the sun more than Alfred, Alfred had had some fun in the Casino. They had got on tremendously well with the Portuguese, the lectures had gone down well and the distribution arrangements would please British film producers. Alfred and Leslie would have further talks with Seruya and Haigh to finalise negotiations when they got back from Madrid, and the deal would be tied up once they returned to London.

If they reflected with misgivings on the train journey ahead, it was the only way to get there. The Lisbon-Madrid air-service, which took two hours, had been terminated due to petrol shortage. It was, however, the thought of Madrid that Leslie found the least appealing. He was travelling away from a friendly country towards one whose political doctrine he had long hated. Though he might find friends in Madrid, there was always the dichotomy – who was friend and who foe? Uncertain of his reception, he was conscious of political distinctions he had never thought about in Portugal – and this troubled him.

Beyond the Sierras, lay a country not only in the grip of Fascism, but to a large extent in the grip of the Germans. This would make it difficult for Leslie to like anything about Spain or, for that matter, to trust any Spaniard. Eden was certainly right – Spain was where our influence was needed most. But Leslie wondered if he would not just be another voice crying in the wilderness. If this was a challenge, it was a thorny one and he would have to be extremely careful not to speak his mind. Alfred, a more flamboyant character, enjoyed this sort of challenge, facing it with a truculent light of battle in his eye.

At the Atlantico, Alfred had out-stared – or out-glared – most of the Germans with his 'glacial glance'. It seemed to him unlikely the Germans would come any closer than glaring range in Madrid. Leslie hoped so as he was not very good at glaring and might say something unfortunate instead.

The journey through the night as they climbed the Sierras and passed through the province of Estremadura had been cool and pleasant. The following morning, as the sun rose above the scrub and desert, the heat increased with each eastward mile. At 10.15 as the train rolled into Madrid Central the temperature had reached 80°F in the shade.

Dr Walter Starkie, their host in Madrid and head of the British Institute – author, traveller, violinist and scholar of all gypsy languages – was on the platform to meet them. A short man, of stocky build, with a remarkably wide, broad head, he had been resident British Council representative since the summer of 1940 and had lived through trying and difficult times. His small, merry eyes twinkled geniality. He greeted Leslie effusively, with all his Irish charm, but was a little nonplussed at Alfred's presence, whom he had not heard about from the Council. He assumed at first he was Leslie's travelling manager.

As all customs and immigration formalities had been dealt with at the frontier, he hurried them to a waiting car, talking loquaciously as they went. He hoped that they had become acclimatised and that the early heatwave in Madrid would not discomfort them. Once in the car, he launched into a detailed explanation of Leslie's programme which he had prepared very carefully. He regretted that, unlike Lisbon, where Leslie had spoken in public theatres to large audiences this would not be possible in Madrid – unless specially invited to do so by the Spanish authorities. Also if one engaged a private theatre or cinema one would have to submit scripts of the lectures to the censorship which was, unfortunately, dominated by Axis sympathisers and fellow-travellers. There was also the danger the Security Police might step in and stop the show, or Falange elements start a row.

As the Ambassador, Sir Samuel Hoare, was against taking risks of any sort, Starkie said he had been obliged to limit Leslie's public appearances to the somewhat narrow confines of the British Institute. He had sent out invitations to a number of distinguished and pro-British Spaniards connected with the theatre and cinema and, also, from the worlds of art and literature. However, as it was impossible to seat more than eighty people at a time in the Institute – and, he added, there were many English people who wanted to hear the lectures as well – it would be necessary for Leslie to give repeats. At this Leslie's face dropped somewhat, but he said nothing. Starkie, then, went on to explain that he had also arranged a Tertulia, a fortnightly gathering of literary men and artists, who were looking forward to meeting Leslie and discussing professional problems. He had also arranged a special Flamenco party in his honour. In this careful and well-balanced plan of operations Starkie said he had worked closely in conjunction with the various Embassy functions and dinners Leslie would be expected to attend. And he presented Leslie with a typed copy of this elaborate and detailed scenario. Perhaps, he had picked the wrong moment.

Leslie listened to all this with a blank face and mounting scepticism. With a distinct tendency to wilt on arrival in unfamiliar places, particularly when accompanied by high temperatures, he suddenly found himself not only feeling positively uncooperative but positively anti-British Council. The programme seemed grossly over-loaded. They were clearly expecting too much of him. He had had a certain amount of free time in Lisbon – here, it seemed, he would scarcely have time to look round, let alone breathe. And the place was already like a steaming cauldron. What with all the Press and Embassy functions, visits to studios etc, the typescript in his hand looked like the programme for an athlete on a treadmill – and a very fit athlete at that.

By the time they reached his room in the Ritz Hotel which, though a little noisy, had been tastefully arranged with flowers by Mrs Starkie, Leslie, whose obstinacy when presented with a fait accompli was well known, decided to put a spoke in official wheels – in which Alfred joined. Starkie at first listened with mounting disbelief.

Leslie accused the Council of trying to accomplish far too much – the programme was too big and far too strenuous for him. Portugal was one thing, but, at least, he had had some free time there. The truth, however, of the matter was this – and he might as well be frank about it – he had never wanted to come to Spain in the first place. In fact, he had written a letter to the Council saying he would not come to Spain for he suspected the place was antipathetic from the outset, and he had only meant to go as far as Portugal. Now, without consultation, there was all this extra work, this onerous programme.

Starkie, a sympathetic man, was a bit stunned and listened with increasing chagrin and bewilderment. He had heard from George West that Leslie was only regarded as in transit through Portugal and that he was really meant for Spain. There seemed to be some contradiction in what Leslie was saying, or someone had his wires crossed. For some reason both Leslie and Alfred then proceeded to criticise the earlier handling of the tour. What had been done to arouse their ire remains to this day problematical. Perhaps they had not been told of the repeat lectures that had apparently been agreed with Starkie, or they had not understood it. Whatever the case, Leslie flatly refused to give repeats and proceeded to tear Starkie's typed programme, figuratively, to pieces. As the tickets for guests were already printed and in their envelopes this was unfortunate. According to Starkie, Leslie changed the lecture dates, cancelled the Tertulia and telescoped his visit, saying he could not stay so long in Spain and wanted to get back to Portugal.

When things simmered down Leslie said he was sorry to make these alterations but he was simply not up to such a strenuous programme, and Starkie, trying to see it from Leslie's point of view, and swallowing disappointment, went back to the Institute to dismantle and rearrange his programme. All he could now hope for was the minimum, the two lectures and the Flamenco party.

If Leslie's introduction to Madrid had started on a note of conflict over his programme, the official machinery soon got to work to smooth down any ruffled feathers. If Leslie's temper had flared, due to heat and the long train journey, soothing words were soon spoken and the inauspicious start forgotten. Though his stay in Madrid was scarcely cut short – it lasted twelve days – Leslie remained disenchanted and never settled down. His own pre-conceived hostility to the place was partly the cause: to Leslie it only confirmed what he had always felt.

It was, however, understandable that Starkie should have felt 'some qualms about the visit of this celebrated actor and film star' whose name 'was such a household word in Spain' for Leslie turned out to be the only visiting lecturer who did not stick closely to the arrangements made for him. Starkie felt, in a country like Spain where the situation was so delicate, it was imperative that visitors do as they were asked by the Council Representative. What complicated things was that there were too many rival interests, and Starkie thought Leslie's and Alfred's main purpose was to get in touch with their commercial ventures. In this he was wrong: their interests were those of the MOI and British films generally. I think Starkie's axe was ground in the direction of Alfred whom he seemed to regard as a distraction.

After Starkie's departure, they spent the rest of Sunday (9th May) settling in and having a look round Madrid. They walked in the Prado Gardens and down to the Puerto del Sol and back. Later, they went to the Ritz bar where they noticed and were noticed by a number of Germans. As newcomers they were obviously of interest and Leslie was sufficiently well-known to be recognised without much difficulty. Alfred, as usual, either simply out-stared or out-glared them. Later that evening, Leslie wrote to Ruth remarking on the early heat-wave, that his room was comfortable if a little noisy and despite what he had heard about the Palace being the Herrenvolk's hotel there seemed to be a fair sprinkling of them at the Ritz. He and Alfred had encountered them in both the lifts and the bar where, apart from icy-eyeballing, everyone had maintained discreet diplomatic silence. Alfred referred to it as 'heel-clicking *Uberlegenheit*!' Referring to the Germans, Leslie said: 'They are a grim looking lot, men and women, and they don't like us much. We get dirty looks and they seem to resent the idea that we can have a good time. English laughter is the last thing they want to hear . . . '
Leslie also told Ruth in the same letter that he was convinced someone had searched his luggage while he was out walking with Alfred –which, apparently, was common practice at the Ritz. He confessed that he had forgotten to lock anything – but it intrigued rather than worried him for the suitcase so disturbed only contained clothes and some notes for his *Hamlet* lecture. Perhaps they had been photographed and sent to Goebbels in Berlin. What fun he would have deciphering the soliloquies for secret messages! In fact, he felt his letters in the diplomatic bag were a lot safer than himself – who had no diplomatic immunity.

The following morning, a car called for them and took them to the Embassy. They were welcomed by Arthur Yencken, the British Minister, who took them along to meet the Ambassador. Later in Yencken's office Leslie apologised for making changes in Starkie's programme. Yencken, brushing it aside, said he had already heard about it. But Leslie was not to worry. Both the Embassy and the

Council were prepared to lighten his burden. His first official engagement would not be until Tuesday, a luncheon given by the British business community at the Cork Club, at which Starkie would take the chair. Alfred explained that he wanted to meet various film distributors and both he and Leslie had been invited to visit the San Martin film studios. Yencken said he would like Leslie to attend a Press reception on Thursday and this was agreed. The first lecture was to be given on Friday at the Institute.

While at the Embassy Leslie and Alfred heard the news that the Germans had surrendered at Bizerta and Tunis – and that we had 250,000 prisoners of war including von Arnim, the German general, and his staff. The Spanish press had been noticeably silent and any British reports had been bluepencilled by the Censor. Though this was indeed cheering news Leslie and Alfred were advised that the new situation might cause some tension. Rumours were already flying about as to the Allies' next intentions.

The German Embassy, fostering unrest, suggested that the next Allied moves would be against Spain and the British Ambassador gave assurances that 'HM Government did not intend to . . . invade Spanish territory . . . Yet, in spite of this . . . the Police were treating British subjects and Anglophile Spaniards as if they were conspirators engaged in plots to stir up internal revolution and to organise a foreign invasion.'

Count Jordana, the Spanish Foreign Minister, was under constant pressure to squash invasion rumours stretching from the Pyrenees to the Mediterranean frontier with France. Franco, himself, was on a speech-making tour of principal cities and military installations to see that everyone was on their toes.

The bulk of the German anti-Allied propaganda and invasion-scare-mongering was fabricated daily in the office of the German Press Attaché, Hans Lazar – of whom Sir Samuel Hoare wrote:

This representative of Aryan racialism had been born a Turkish subject. . . In Vienna he had faithfully served Hitler as a fanatical propagandist in support of the Anschluss. Since then he had become . . . the eminence grise of the German Embassy in Madrid. A mysterious figure of strange tastes, his bedroom was decorated as a chapel with two rows of twelve figures of saints and an altar upon which he slept. In spite of his repulsive appearance he was popular in a certain society in Madrid and particularly with ladies. From the German Embassy, where he had more authority than the Ambassador himself, he daily directed not only the general course of the Spanish press, but even the actual words of the news and articles. Not a word reached the Spanish public that had not been subject to his sinister approval.*

Walter Starkie had had problems with the German Press Attaché, and in a letter he wrote to me Walter said: 'I, myself, as British Council Representative, had great trouble owing to the intrigues of Hans Lazar . . . a close confederate of Josef Goebbels whom I remembered when I was in Hungary and Rumania in 1936 . . . ' Earlier, staying in the same Madrid hotel, Starkie had had his phone tapped by Lazar.

Though neither Leslie nor Alfred were, so far as I know, to come into contact with this sinister propagandist, they were to become well aware of his reputation and power. Against such press corruption and suppression our propaganda had an impossible task, and the fact that neither Leslie's presence or his lectures were given coverage in the Falangist press considerably neutralised the effect of his visit. Starkie admitted: 'The longest articles which appeared about him in the press here were an interview by one of our teachers, Sr Balbuena, and another which I got him in *Primer Plano*.'

On Tuesday Walter Starkie accompanied Leslie to the luncheon at the Cork Club. As they drank sherry in the ante-room Walter introduced him to members and luncheon guests. Among those he met, in the unexpected way of destiny, were three men, F.G.Cowlrick, G.T.Maclean and W.J.B.Israel – his travelling companions on the fatally interrupted journey home to England three weeks later. Cowlrick, a director of Babcock and Wilcox, was on a final tour of Spain and Portugal before his retirement. He was intrigued to meet Leslie and later begged Walter to use influence to get him transferred from the BOAC sea-plane, on which he was booked, to the KLM flight with Leslie. Gordon Maclean, a slightly built man with iron grey hair, as Inspector General of Consulates was touring round British establishments in the Iberian peninsula. He also turned up in Lisbon three weeks later, booked home in the same plane. Perhaps the most interesting was Wilfrid Barthold Israel, travelling in Spain and Portugal on behalf of the Jewish Refugee Mission. His connections with Germany were long and deep-rooted. In the thirties his family had owned a department store in Berlin. They had, in due course, been black-listed by the Nazis

---

* *Ambassador on Special Mission*, op cit.

Leslie at Press Reception in Madrid with Spanish actor, Hierro Nieto.

Leslie and Alfred Chenhalls at Press Reception in Lisbon given by Rafael Seruya (Victoria Filme) and British Council. Photo includes, *l to r* Martin Blake (Director Foreign Division, British Council), Rafael and Mrs Seruya, George West (Director British Institute) and Anthony Haigh (1st Secretary and Cultural Attaché British Embassy).

Flamenco Party, British Institute, Madrid – the Duke of Alba in dinner jacket on Leslie's right.

Reception after Hamlet lecture, British Institute, Madrid – Leslie talking to Arthur Yencken (British Minister, Madrid).

and dispossessed of their business. Since 1937 Wilfrid Israel had been in and out of Germany many times, actively plotting the escape of Jewish refugees and saving many families from gas-chambers and death-camps. Israel got out of Germany on the edge of war, with a false passport under an assumed name. On reaching London he set up the Jewish Refugee Mission which became the Jewish Agency for Palestine in Great Russell Street. Since 1940 he had been described in the Wehrmacht Confidential Book on Britain as a British agent. It seemed to Leslie, who had only acted the role, that this man was, indeed the true modern Pimpernel.

Israel had come out from London to organise the movement to Palestine, then a British mandate, of the 1,500 Jewish refugees waiting in the transit camps of Spain and Portugal after being smuggled from Europe.

The Germans later became suspicious that among the refugees on Israel's lists, under assumed identities, were scientists and engineers with knowledge of German heavy-water installations in Norway and the experimental rocket-station at Peenemünde. But, try though they might, this was never successfully proved. Israel's death in the plane disaster was a great loss to the Agency for no one, not even Dr Bloch in Madrid, had the persuasive power, magnetism or extreme mobility of Israel who, as the central figure in the Agency, had so successfully coordinated all its activities in concert with world-wide Zionist organisations.

Leslie was still talking animatedly to Wilfrid Israel when Starkie shepherded the members and guests into the luncheon room. In the centre of the dining table, decorated with silver goblets and trophies, stood the club's symbol – an outsize cork from a Jeroboam bottle. Leslie was just taking his seat next to Starkie, with Israel beside him, when he noticed there were thirteen at table and suddenly started up. Starkie later told me: 'I remember the trouble we had with Leslie's superstitious nature: he discovered we were thirteen at table when we sat down. We had to call in a parson friend to make the fourteen!'

Not normally a superstitious person, Leslie could have become one after the death of Violette and his connection with spiritualism – or simply because he was uneasy about being in Madrid. Not only had he been sleeping badly and having nightmares but, he confessed to Walter, since he'd been in Spain he'd been getting a strange recurring dream. 'Someone with a message for me . . . In this dream a dead person is trying to tell me something important – and I cannot understand what it is.' Was it some sort of warning of mischance associated with thirteen? Certainly, it was curious that the four men among those thirteen at table were to be among thirteen passengers who perished in the plane three weeks later. It was an incident long remembered by others at the luncheon – for Arthur Yencken, who was also a guest, was killed a year later flying his own plane in an accident between Barcelona and Madrid.

On Wednesday Leslie and Alfred accepted an invitation to the San Martin film studios on the outskirts of Madrid. A luncheon was given in Leslie's honour and he met once again the producer-distributor so keen on the co-production of *Christopher Columbus*. Beside Leslie sat Conchita Montenegro, a popular Spanish film actress, with whom he had worked in Hollywood.

During the visit to the studios there was much talk of General Franco's return to Madrid that evening. He was to make a broadcast clarifying Spain's careful neutrality. Leslie and Alfred had earlier noticed that the buildings and houses were draped with flags and tapestries. When they got back to the Ritz they heard that all performances at cinemas and public entertainments were to terminate, and all cafés and restaurants were to close their doors, by 8 p.m. until the Caudillo's procession had passed.

There were two objectives in Franco's speech-making tour with its important termination in the capital: to bring the country to a state of readiness in the event of an invasion of Spain by either the Allies or the Germans, and to tighten up and enforce security. Our Military Attaché in Madrid was reporting extensive Spanish troop movements in coastal areas which seemed to indicate fear, encouraged by German propaganda, of immediate Allied invasion. As early as 8th May the area Biarritz-St Jean de Luz-Hendaye was declared a military zone by the Germans. Our Ambassador reported: 'The Police are seizing the opportunity of imprisoning anyone against whom they have a grudge . . . If the prisoners ask the reason they are told nothing or it is hinted they are accused of being British agents.'

To whip up anti-Allied hysteria, the Falange concocted the story of an imminent Allied invasion in Rosas Bay, Catalonia. And there were to be simultaneous landings at three other points on the Spanish Mediterranean coast-line. 'Behind these alarms and excursions,' wrote our Ambassador, 'there is constantly emerging the black hand of the Nazis. German propaganda is being directed more ruthlessly than ever at Spanish nerves and a frantic attempt, perhaps a final attempt, is being made to embroil us with Spain. . . . In this way the Germans are trying to work up Falange hotheads to take advantage of tonight's proceedings to attack this Embassy . . . '

In the midst of these military and political manoeuvres, and the backwash of hysteria created by them, Leslie's presence in Madrid must have seemed of small consequence – yet was, in its way, a useful antidote and variation on the general theme. From the British point of view his arrival in Madrid was not only well-timed as a distraction from the German war of nerves but was useful counter propaganda. Not only would his presence boost British morale, but, his presence would appeal strongly to Spaniards in all walks of life. Here again, as in Lisbon, the myth had preceded the man. Indeed, this charming English export epitomised for many Spaniards the best and most admirable of British qualities.

To the Germans, I doubt if Leslie's visit was seen in so simplistic a light as sheer cultural propaganda. They were suspicious that it might conceal a more than cultural emphasis. They could not believe that Leslie had been sent all the way to Madrid solely to lecture on *Hamlet* and films. It seemed to them too naive an explanation. What was white to us was often grey or black to them and the film personality of Leslie Howard, with its much published charm and apparent political ingenuousness – to the point of vagueness – suggested to them a clever British cover-plan for other activities. As evidence will later show, they listed him as a British secret service agent and, I am convinced, they believe this to the day they shot him down.

At the Ritz Hotel, employed in the beauty parlour adjacent to the barber's shop, was an attractive young woman of mixed Polish and French descent who watched Leslie's comings and goings with some interest. There is now little doubt that she had been placed there by the Abwehr to report on the foreign visitors to the hotel. She had taken up her appointment not long before Leslie's arrival.

Her background is obscure. Ian Colvin, in *Flight 777*,* referred to her not as Polish but as 'the daughter of a small Argentine farmer . . . (who) played extra parts in Hollywood and then . . . met a Belgian who seemed to offer her security until this German Count came along touring America . . . ' The German Count married her, and they settled in Berlin just prior to the war. Presumably she used her maiden name at the Ritz Hotel. Her marriage to the German Count did not survive the German collapse and shortly after the war she married a wealthy Englishman. Referred to, apocryphally, as 'the Countess', she was apparently a wavering spy with a predilection

* Evans 1957.

for Englishmen. In his book Colvin suggests that 'before the end of the visit he (Leslie) must have known that she was an enemy agent and that she was, apparently, ready to quit the Axis cause.' This theory, like his theory that Leslie was attempting 'to dislodge a spy', may well be anchored in some fact. Unfortunately, Colvin's documentation, which was thorough, painstaking and generally accurate, became inextricably mixed with a romanticised version of their relationship in the genre of journalistic spy-fiction.

However, it seems clear that the Polish girl was reporting on his activities, for this she frankly admitted to Nevile Kearney, the Films Director of the British Council, when he saw her in Madrid after the shooting down of the plane.

When the Madrid papers published the German communiqué on 2nd June announcing that the plane had been shot down with Leslie Howard on board the woman came to me in the greatest distress. She sank to the floor sobbing and confessed that she was an enemy agent who had been specially charged to watch the movements of the film star in the Spanish capital ... and although she had reported on his activities she swore she had never meant to harm him. Others of her service had been acting similarly in Portugal, she said, and she passionately blamed them for his death*

Certainly, Walter Starkie was never in any doubt as to the job the girl had at the Ritz nor, as it turned out, of the extremely hostile interest the Germans took in Leslie. In a letter Walter wrote me in August 1974, he stated categorically: 'The Germans, I am convinced, were out to get Leslie Howard and they used the beautiful Polish girl at the Ritz as agent.'

With these words in front of me it is hard to dismiss Colvin's theories out of hand, though hard to take too seriously the cat-and-mouse game played out between them at the Ritz hotel. Any positive attempts to dislodge 'the Countess' or make her change sides would have put Leslie in a most compromising situation and, perhaps, in a rather different category to that of propagandist. This and the theory of the Polish girl's wavering allegiance to the Germans must, to my mind, remain an interesting theory – and yet

* (Nevile Kearney in an interview with Sidney Rodin, *The Sunday Express* 17th December 1950).

a theory, nevertheless, to which the Germans could have paid some attention. They could well have wanted to believe he was attempting to dislodge their agent in the interests of British intelligence – an extension, as it were, of his 'Pimpernel Smith' character – and this would clearly give them a motive against him.

My theory, for what it is worth, is that the Germans in Madrid – without doubt on instructions from Berlin and, very possibly, Goebbels himself – may well have wanted to establish a motive for liquidating Leslie. He was Britain's most powerful and effective propagandist, he had ridiculed the German hierarchy in *Pimpernel Smith*, he had broadcast against them and he was, certainly, on Goebbels' black list as William Joyce had announced to the world. The justification from the German point of view was that his British Council activities were simply a cover for those of the Foreign Office and British Intelligence, and they had reason to believe he had been trying to 'turn' one of their agents. A letter written by Leslie to the Countess from Lisbon, and delivered by Nevile Kearney, in which he said he hoped 'she would be able to reach England soon' goes some way to support the dislodgement theory.

Whatever the convolutions of this game of intelligence supposedly being played out in the honeycomb of the Ritz hotel, I do not doubt that Starkie was right in thinking Leslie had become a marked man. Another factor that worried Starkie was Leslie's involvement with 'foreign film companies behind the Iron Curtain' that, according to Starkie, Leslie 'controlled'. In his 1974 letter to me, Walter wrote: 'I had private information about Leslie Howard's and Chenhalls' interest in the film companies behind the Iron Curtain and that worried me a lot during the visit . . . '

Apart from Leslie's own production companies and those of Alfred's concerned with distribution, I know of no other companies Leslie 'controlled' or was even interested in behind the Iron Curtain. It may be that Leslie wished to get in touch with democratic film-makers in the occupied countries, and may also have wished to get our propaganda films into the Russian zones of interest. He always remained deeply interested in the exchange of ideas, the breaking down of barriers, and wished to establish artistic links with friends of democracy even in the German zones of occupation. If those contacts could be made through democratic film connections in Madrid, so much the better. It would prove that the voice of freedom could still be heard even in Falange-dominated Spain.

Whatever Leslie's views regarding his effectiveness in Spain as an instrument of propaganda, it was rapidly becoming clear from German reactions that the persuasive mystique of his personality was having some effect on their propaganda. And, with his Hamlet lecture I believe it had more.

On Friday evening Leslie gave his film lecture at the British Institute using *Pimpernel Smith* as example. As in Lisbon, the invited audience was largely composed of producers, directors, actors and scenario-writers in the Spanish film industry. There was a reception and discussion afterwards.

As I mentioned earlier, the programme for Leslie and Alfred in Madrid was a pretty heavy one and gave them little free time. A résumé of their engagements between Saturday (15th May) and the following Wednesday, the day before they left, reads as follows:

Sat, 15th May . . . Reception at RAC Club, 1.15 pm.
Cocktail party at Ritz, given by Mr Cowlrick, 8 pm.
Flamenco party at British Institute, 12-4.30 am.

Mon, 17th May . . . Further discussions about *Christopher Columbus* production. Lunch with Spanish co-producer at Ritz.
Cocktail party given by HM Minister and Mrs Yencken, 9.15 pm.
Attended Spanish Film premiere, 11 pm.-1.30 am.

Tues, 18th May . . . Further visits to studios. Luncheon at San Martin. Appointments with distributors, pm.
Leslie and Alfred attend dinner given by Mrs Yencken. Present HE and Lady Maud Hoare and forty guests – Members of Diplomatic Corps and Spaniards, including Senor Luis Escobar, Director of the National Theatre, 9.30-3.30 am.

Wed, 19th May . . . Leslie lectures on *Hamlet* at British Institute, 10 pm. Party and reception at Institute following lecture, 11.30-2 am.

Apart from the above list there were a number of appointments that

Alfred made himself direct with the people concerned, involving film-sales and other distribution arrangements. These were quite outside the official programme. Even so, according to Starkie, a number of receptions and dinners had to be abandoned at short notice – and some without notice at all, which resulted in a certain amount of bad feeling. At a dinner arranged by the Marques de Aledo, governor of the Hispano-America Bank, neither Leslie nor Alfred, the principal guests, turned up and no explanation was given. Such engagements, Starkie pointed out, had nothing to do with the Embassy or Council 'and were made by the people direct with Chenhalls, but they constituted set-backs to what might have been such a magnificent success'. This, finally, led Starkie to express the opinion that it would have been better if Leslie had come out alone and unencumbered.

Nevertheless, an immense amount of negotiating work was carried out by both Alfred and Leslie in the interests of British films. Despite one or two missed dinner engagements, Starkie had every reason to be delighted at the success of the lectures and particularly the Flamenco party he had arranged in Leslie's honour. At this the Duke of Alba, the Spanish Ambassador in London, was present and a number of distinguished artists, theatrical and literary people – Zuloaga, Sebastian de Miranda, Cristobal and others – and the evening was adjudged one of the highlights of the tour.

As far as Starkie was concerned, there was only one fly in that particular ointment. A slightly discordant, and perhaps upsetting, note was struck in the unexpected arrival of 'the Countess' who was presumably not on the official list. It is suggested by Ian Colvin that some photos taken at the party by a Madrid agency 'were whisked round to the German Embassy and they saw their own agent close to the British propagandist'. I must add that the photos I have of this occasion do not appear to include the lady in question, though Colvin states that Starkie was well aware of her presence and somewhat put out by it. Starkie was genuinely worried that the Germans were trying to compromise Leslie with this girl. As to German reactions about her presence at the party Colvin wrote:

It was one thing to spy on the enemy in the hotel but quite different to be seen openly at the British Institute. She was, after all, the wife of a German officer and plainly this was a gesture of independence or of defection ... The outcome was that 'the Countess' had to surrender her passport and so remained a hostage to her masters.

At this distance from events it is difficult to hazard anything more than a guess about that relationship, except to say that Leslie obviously felt 'the Countess' was working for the wrong side and, apparently, ready to change.

On the final evening in Madrid (Wednesday) Leslie gave his *Hamlet* lecture to a specially invited audience of professors, dramatists and critics packed into the narrow confines of the Institute. Describing Leslie's charisma and style Starkie wrote:

> He became like the visitor from another planet. He had a strange mystical quality that communicated itself to people the moment he entered a room . . . and enabled him to sway the crowd as a great artist would upon a responsive instrument . . . and to make an impact on men and women in a tragic evocative sense. Upon women he always had this subtle effect but I noticed how he was just as able with men.

There was a further significance to the lecture and it lay, I think, in Leslie's selection of the passage which begins 'Good sir, whose powers are these?' (*Hamlet*: 4.4.9) and contains the 'little patch of ground' speech. I don't think this was an entirely random selection, a mere illustration of poetry or plot, for the kernel of its argument contained a warlike, an almost perceptible contemporary relevance. My conjecture is that he selected it on purpose, with an eye to its political undertones making it analogous to the present war. Certainly, the implications of the sequence and its soliloquy gave it a new significance in Madrid. If I had made this the German case against *Hamlet*, there is support for this view in the immediate German reaction to suppress it.

In the 'little patch of ground' speech and the soliloquy 'How all occasions do inform against me', Leslie drew the analogy of the defeat of a large army by a small garrison. I think he did so as a comparative illustration – and a warning. Here was a reference germane to Gibraltar and a case-history of what might happen. Would not the Germans – and even Franco – be wise to ponder how Spinola's army was once sacrificed, 'even for an eggshell', among the polders and dunes of Ostend, the defence of which had excited so much admiration in Shakespeare's day? Might not history repeat itself if the ambitions of the Falangists got out of hand?

> Witness this army of such mass and charge
> Led by a delicate and tender prince,

Whose spirit with divine ambition puff'd
Makes mouths at the invisible event,
Exposing what is mortal and unsure
To all that fortune, death and danger dare,
Even for an egg-shell. Rightly to be great
Is not to stir without great argument,
But greatly to find quarrel in a straw
When honour's at the stake . . .

Well, Gibraltar was certainly a thorn in Spanish honour and if
Franco, egged on by the Germans, committed his soldiers to an
attack on the Rock, might he not live to regret it, however righteous
his cause? Could not his army, like the Spaniards before Ostend,
'for a fantasy and trick of fame, go to their graves like beds' and at
Gibraltar 'fight for a plot whereon the numbers cannot try the
cause, which is not tomb enough and continent to hide the slain'?
And, finally, when the battle was over, what might be left but an
'egg-shell' victory, a pile of rubble and thousands dead?

Allied strategy was aimed at keeping Spain non-belligerent.
Franco must not, under German pressure, be provoked into an
attack on Gibraltar whose defence would divert us from 'Husky',
the Sicilian operation. To this end the words of a visiting actor might
serve a purpose and not seem oblique to an intuitive audience. I
think, in his quiet way, Leslie was serving this purpose.

The subtle propaganda value of Leslie's *Hamlet* lecture was clear
to Starkie and many members of the audience that night at the
Institute, yet not a word of what he said ever reached the press or the
Spanish radio. Starkie issued a translation which he handed to
members of the Spanish press and radio with the hope that it might
be published and broadcast. The result was an immediate clamp-
down. It was forbidden to be printed, broadcast – 'or even
mentioned in the Spanish press on a directive from the German
Embassy'.

There is little doubt that Hans Lazar, the instrument of Nazi
propaganda, was behind this directive. Whatever Lazar suspected I
think his action, in concert with the Spanish Censorship and Press
Department, to suppress the lecture indicated a suspicion that it
contained some 'message' relevant to the war. Why otherwise
bother to suppress an innocuous lecture on *Hamlet* – on the face of it
Hamlet was not particularly good British propaganda? It could of
course be argued that agents frequently used phrases from books or
lines from poems as a means of communicating information to

their friends.* Quite apart from this, *Hamlet* was intensely interesting to Germans (the saga of Amleth was a Jutish legend) and German scholars had spent much time deciphering its mysteries. Even Goethe had reclaimed Hamlet for Germany, remodelling him into a German hero in Wilhelm Meister. Doubtless the Abwehr employed specialists whose time was devoted to a systematic search for double-meanings, and even codes in material submitted for publication, and certainly *Hamlet* was a mine of such conundrums. To the sinister and suspicious Lazar the British propagandist, Leslie Howard, might well have slipped in something with a double-meaning, even a secret code in a rhyming pentameter – it had been done before – for the attentive ears of a British agent. It might well put Leslie into a different category – even of agent himself.

Without carrying this too far into the realm of spy and counter-spy, it seems clear that Serrano Suner, and his henchmen Aparicio and Salgado, in the Press and Propaganda Department not only hated the British because we had fought on the side of the Communists in the Civil War and were allies of the Russians in this one but because our occupation of Gibraltar was a serious military disadvantage, to say nothing of a historically unjust seizure of Spanish territory. In this crusade for 'Spanish Gibraltar', aided and abetted by the Germans, even the most innocuous activities would be investigated with a ruthless efficiency worthy of a better cause.

To this end Hans Lazar cannot be accused of stupidity or aimlessness of purpose. This monocled, pudgy propagandist, the connoisseur of wine and women who was 'so popular with ladies' was wary and watchful, crafty and cunning. Whatever propaganda or message he suspected in Leslie's lecture is unimportant. What is important is that he suppressed its wider circulation, so that no one, beyond the invited guests in that room at the British Institute, would know of its existence.

If this was no more than a wise precaution, it was very much in line with German annoyance at the success of Leslie's visit. There were other reasons for German uneasiness. The British propagandist was in process, with his associate Chenhalls, of negotiating a very large sale of anti-German propaganda films into Spain, which

---

* *SOE Codes:* 'In the early years every operator took with him . . . a personal code which he had memorised; this might be as simple as a Playfair code based on a single word. A rather more elaborate system . . . followed; this was based on a phrase, usually a line from a poem, chosen by the agent because it could easily be remembered.' *SOE in France* by M.R.D. Foot, HMSO 1966

would hurt Germany not only culturally but financially. These negotiations, if successful, would leave considerable frozen assets in Spain, in the form of credits, which could be used for the purchase of war materials, such as iron and tungsten. Leslie Howard was also making arrangements for a joint Anglo-Spanish production of *Christopher Columbus* which would be good propaganda in the Latin-American countries and the USA – and a strong argument for closer Anglo-Spanish cultural alignment.

Another factor which was worrying Lazar was the relationship with their woman agent at the Ritz Hotel. It was also worrying his associates in the Abwehr. Whatever the nature of the association, if Howard was using persuasion to dislodge or turn her was he not, then, dabbling in more dangerous waters – and might this not be his heel of Achilles? On this ground Lazar might have reason to study *Hamlet* more closely.

Were there not certain 'riposte' values in *Hamlet* that could be turned to German advantage? Could it be played back, as it were – for Hamlet dies at the end of the play, brought down by an envenomed foil? Possibly at night, stretched out on the altar of his bizarre chapel – surrounded by his 'saints' – Lazar saw how he could be revenged on the British propagandist, in a sinister way, by simply following the course of Shakespeare's text: Laertes and Claudius plot to kill Hamlet with a poisoned foil – a slight scratch in a pass of practice.

And for his death no wind of blame shall breathe,
But even his mother shall uncharge the practice
And call it accident.

If the Germans, as Starkie stated, were 'out to get Leslie Howard', then, one can see how the plot of the play, with its catastrophic conclusion, might serve as illustration. I can, of course, only suggest this is how they thought on the theory that the interest to the Germans – the affinity between Leslie's and Hamlet's situation – lay in the possibility that revenge, once achieved, could be attributed, quite simply, to accident.

Leslie met his death by water, a danger about which he had been warned. There is a story that an attempt was made on his life during a sailing trip on the Tagus so that it might look like an accident. What truth there is in this, I cannot say – one heard so many stories, after the event, in the search for motives. What I do know is that he died, probably by drowning, in the Bay of Biscay as a result of an attack by Ju88s – and the Germans, exonerating their pilots, put it down, finally – after a variety of excuses – to 'an error of judgement'.

Horatio, at the end of the play, speaking to Fortinbras and the Ambassadors from England, says:

> And let me speak to the yet unknowing world
> How these things came about: so shall you hear
> Of carnal, bloody and unnatural acts,
> Of accidental judgments, casual slaughters,
> Of deaths put on by cunning and forced cause . . .

If my *Hamlet* theory of a German plot against Leslie seems too frail and 'accidental', I have simply presented it as a possible motive in my search for truth. I have always believed in the link between Hamlet's and Leslie's death and that the 'slaughters' of innocent passengers in *Ibis* were far from casual and were indeed 'deaths put on by cunning and forced cause'. In this I entirely agree with Ian Colvin's belief that the shooting down was deliberate.

Whatever the motives for the assassination of an aircraft, and the deaths of men, women and children in that unwarlike encounter, I can only re-echo here the strangely apt truth of the words of Fortinbras when he said, just before the final curtain fell on *Hamlet*:

> Take up the bodies: such a sight as this
> Becomes the field, but here shows much amiss.

CHAPTER THIRTEEN

Return to Lisbon

Thursday, 20th May was Leslie's last day in Madrid and the *Hamlet* lecture the culmination of his visit. Only one duty remained – an informal talk to the children at the school run by the Institute. Leslie was to arrive at three o'clock and the children were gathered in the main reception room. By three-thirty, as Leslie had not arrived, Walter rang the Ritz, but the hotel reception was unable to trace him. By half-past four, as he had still not arrived or rung, the talk was abandoned and the children sent home. At about five, the telephone rang – it was Leslie. He was abject in apology, admitting the children's talk had entirely slipped his memory. Later, when writing to Walter, he asked him if there was anything he could send the children from England 'as an apologia'. Of his forgetfulness, he wrote: 'Of all my shortcomings it is the one I most sincerely regret.'

At 8 o'clock that evening Walter accompanied Alfred and Leslie to the station. The Lusitania Express was to leave at nine for Lisbon. A number of friends from the Embassy, including the British Minister, Arthur Yencken, and most of the staff from the Institute were on the platform to see Leslie and Alfred off. Also returning to Lisbon was Martin Blake of the British Council. As they stood in their compartment saying goodbye, Leslie told Walter he was going to have a week's rest in Estoril before flying home. He admitted the twelve days in Madrid's heat had left him feeling jaded, but he was deeply grateful to Walter for not over-burdening him and particularly wanted to thank Mrs Starkie for her genuine concern for his health. In the letter he wrote Walter, he said: 'If I had cracked up she would have been the first person to whom I would have turned.'

I think, for several reasons, Walter Starkie was greatly relieved when the train drew out and the mission was officially over. It had been a great success but a considerable strain for everyone. Walter knew Leslie had travelled reluctantly to Madrid and had come mainly to please him. Walter confirmed this when later he wrote to me: 'I always felt deeply concerned with the visit of your father – for I had been pressing the British Council to persuade him, if possible, to visit Madrid.' Certainly, Malcolm Robertson knew Leslie had been far from well when he began the journey in April, and in his letter of sympathy to my mother, after the tragedy, said: 'Mr Leslie Howard undertook his journey to Spain and Portugal . . . at great inconvenience to himself and at a time when he was over-worked and not in the best of health.'

Now at least Leslie would get a holiday in Estoril before he flew home to supervise the completion and final editing of *The Lamp Still Burns*. While Leslie and Alfred had been in Lisbon earlier, they had purchased a number of gifts, mainly nylon and silk stockings unobtainable in wartime England, for relatives and friends at home. Forgetting they were dutiable items, they had taken the package containing them in the train when they left Lisbon for Madrid. At the frontier, they had to declare them and rather than pay the high duty they had left them in charge of a Portuguese customs officer. Alfred reminded Leslie they would have to pick them up when the train reached the frontier.

At lunch on Friday they joined Martin Blake in the dining car, and this was the last Blake saw of them for by the time the train reached Lisbon they had vanished. What happened was this. When the Lusitania Express reached the frontier post at Valencia Alcantara, Alfred spoke to a customs officer who boarded the train. The man said he remembered the package, but it had been sent to a bonded warehouse for sake keeping. However, it was some distance from the station and he had no authority to hold the train. Rather than leave the stockings behind and being rather bored with the train journey – Leslie and Alfred took a taxi the rest of the way. The only reason I mention this story of the stockings is that they figure again, perhaps more importantly, when they were nearly forgotten later at Lisbon airport.

Leslie and Alfred had probably reached Estoril in their taxi by the time the Lusitania Express creaked its way into Lisbon station. On its arrival, Blake no doubt explained to a surprised George West, the situation regarding the missing travellers. When West phoned the Atlantico later he was relieved to hear they were once more installed in their rooms overlooking the Atlantic. To Leslie it was a great relief to be able to unpack his things, to the sound of waves breaking on the beach, knowing there would be no more official engagements.

Staying at the Atlantico, a few doors down the passage from Leslie, was Nevile Kearney, in charge of the British Council's Film Division. He had flown out recently from London, and was later going on to Madrid. In a general discussion about film negotiations, at which Alfred was present, Kearney discovered that one of Leslie's most important films, *The First of the Few* had not been seen in Lisbon. He felt this omission should be rectified. Could a print be obtained in London and flown out so that a showing could be arranged at the Embassy cinema? It would be something of a fillip for the Council – especially if the Portuguese Propaganda Minister, Tavares d'Almeida, would agree to attend. Leslie thought it a good idea if the whole thing could be arranged in a week. Leslie said he would advise his production manager, Phil Samuel, if the Council would arrange the collection and shipment of the film.

By Monday, as Leslie relaxed on his balcony above the sea, Kearney was in touch with the Council in London, and the film would be sent out by air freight on the earliest plane. If it arrived by Wednesday, invitations could be sent out for a showing at the Embassy cinema on Saturday. On this basis, Leslie and Alfred would leave for home by Sunday, or at least Monday – and provisional bookings were made by the Air Attaché's office. In fact, provisional reservations were made for the Sunday KLM flight as there was no flight home on Monday.

While Leslie rested in the sun at Estoril, he and Alfred were invited out to Cintra as the guests of a Portuguese family called Santos Mendonca. They seemed to have several pretty daughters, one of whom, Maria, was intensely stage-struck and wanted to become an actress. Leslie cautioned her, saying it was world's most unstable profession. He enjoyed his day with this amiable Portuguese family in the hills above Cintra, admiring the Moorish castle and palace and the breathtaking views to Cabo da Roca and the distant Atlantic. He said it reminded him so much of California, even to the scent of the eucalyptus trees.

From Estoril Leslie wired Ruth: 'Having few days rest Estoril while waiting transport. Expect to see you all soon.' This was sent on Wednesday afternoon – the day he hoped the film might arrive –just after he had spoken to Bill Collett who worked in the Press Attaché's office. Collett ran the Embassy cinema at the Estrella Hall and had called on Leslie to tell him the film had, so far, not arrived at Portela. As people needed three days notice the Embassy could not get out the invitations – until it had. Enjoying his break in the sun, Leslie was quite prepared to play the whole thing by ear – though he wasn't quite sure how Alfred would play it! Alfred wasn't so fond of the sun and was getting restive. He had an office to run and clients to see in London and hoped they would be able to get away early the following week.

Waiting for the film to arrive, Leslie wrote a number of thank-you letters to hosts in Madrid. To some he apologised for turning up late and others, like the Marquis de Aledo, for not turning up at all. With a number of functions to attend his diary-keeping had become deficient and he hoped they would forgive him. While composing these letters on his balcony Bill Collett called. The print of *The First of the Few* had arrived at the airport. The Press Attaché's office could now get the invitations out – but as it was Friday the earliest the film could be shown was Monday evening, 31st May, and this was rather short notice. A firm booking could now be made for the flight home the following week and, allowing for any possible delay with the film showing, Leslie thought Wednesday would be best.*

As a small accolade for Gwyneth Williams who had helped him in getting his official letter-writing tidied up, Leslie invited her out to dinner. They went along to the Casa Laura, a small, attractive fish restaurant, in Cascais, situated on the site of an old fort overlooking the dunes and sands of Guincho. While they were dining Leslie spotted old Mr Cowlrick, his acquaintance from Madrid, who came over and spoke to them. He mentioned he was flying home on Tuesday and hoped Leslie would be on the plane.

Leslie thought it unlikely – he had the film show on Monday, he said – and thought it would be too much of a rush. Anyway, the arrangements were in the hands of the Air Attaché's office. He

---

* The reservations were made by the Air Attaché's office and a passenger manifest in my possession confirms that Leslie's and Alfred's booking numbers, U/1675 and U/1676, were, in fact, for Wednesday, 2nd June. Yet, as will be seen, a final change of plan was to be made by the Air Attaché's office as late as Monday afternoon when Leslie's and Alfred's names were brought back from Wednesday's flight and substituted in place of two other passengers for the flight on Tuesday. This last minute change of plan is also confirmed by Ian Colvin (*Flight 777*, p 166) when he wrote, referring to Tyrrel Shervington's booking (Priority A for 1st June): 'His name was there (Saturday 29th May) – and the passenger list was made up but the names on it did not include those of Howard and Chenhalls.' According to Colvin their final booking was only made as late as 5 p.m. on Monday. This information was unearthed by Colvin in his researches into the BOAC ledgers at Lisbon after the war.

Last week-end, Lisbon – Leslie and Alfred at picnic party, Praia das Macas.

Leslie with Santos Mendonca family at Cintra.

Leslie delivering film lecture in Lisbon (*seated right*) Seruya, Dr G. Ramos, George West.

Leslie and Alfred at Aviz Hotel with Calouste Gulbenkian and Madame Theis.

would fly sometime next week – nothing more definite than that.

After Bill Collett's call, the Press Office was not left with much time to organise a list of guests and get invitations out. In view of the week-end, many people had to be contacted at home by telephone. An important guest was Tavares d'Almeida, the Portuguese Propaganda Minister. He said he would be glad to attend and would even be happier if Mr Howard would be guest of honour at a dinner after the film show at the Aviz Hotel. Another invitation that reached Leslie just before the week-end was to a beach party at Praia das Macas, an informal picnic to be given by the Air Attaché, Jack Schreiber, and his wife. As Leslie had originally been booked to fly on Sunday, the picnic had been arranged at short notice due to the changed flight schedules.

Towards the week-end the Atlantico was popular. It had a fashion-able cachet – adjacent to Estoril's more expensive shops and close to the Casino – it attracted an international set. At lunch-time the bar was crowded, with dotted here and there the crop-headed, punctilious Germans – Embassy staff, soldiers in mufti, Abwehr men on arcane missions.

Leslie, in one of his letters to Ruth from the Atlantico, remarked: 'The Herrenvolk are not hard to recognise and whenever they see us approaching they drop their voices and stare icily.' Alfred had a rather resonant voice coupled to a gusty sense of humour – and he was scarcely a respecter of Germans. One lunchtime standing near a group of them in the bar, he was expatiating happily on our recent victories at Tunis and Bizerta. He hit the words Tunis and Bizerta with, perhaps, too much brio. Leslie, who observed the Germans' reactions, said in the letter to Ruth: ' . . . if looks could kill, Alfred would have been stone dead!' George West had had to warn them several times about speaking too loudly; apparently one of George's friends, having lunch at the Atlantico, easily heard what was being said at Leslie's table, even to hearing West's name mentioned. West had reason to believe their movements were being closely watched by German agents. Nevile Kearney was also worried on that account.

On May 29th we met before lunch in the cocktail bar. Also in the bar was a tall, attractive, thirty-year-old Hungarian titled woman, married to an Austrian. I immediately spotted her as a known enemy agent. I checked by telephone with the first secretary of the British Embassy in Lisbon – an old friend – and he, as I expected, advised me to warn Leslie and Chenhalls.

Whether Leslie or Alfred had spoken to this woman, Kearney did
not say – but she was obviously a security risk and may, indeed, have
been placed at the hotel to listen to and observe the movements of
interesting visitors. Sometime during lunch on Saturday, at which
Cowlrick was present, there was talk of flying dates and, later,
Kearney, in the privacy of Leslie's room, 'told him he had been a
little indiscreet – but he was so modest about himself that it never
occurred to him that anyone would be interested in his movements.'
I somehow doubt that Leslie would have discussed 'openly', as
Kearney put it, his return journey. He had, after all, been warned. It
seems more likely that one of the others at the table – possibly
Cowlrick who knew he was flying on Tuesday – suggested to Leslie
and Alfred that they could switch their booking arrangements,
thereby saving a day. I believe Colvin was nearer the truth when he
wrote of these final days in Lisbon: 'It seems that Leslie was not
quite certain about his movements or his departure altogether.
There was something erratic about his behaviour.'

One thing that is certain is that neither Leslie's nor Alfred's name
was on the original passenger manifest for Tuesday, 1st June. This
was complete by Saturday morning and technically closed. The
passengers proceeding to the UK on KLM's flight 2L272 had been
made up by the Air Attaché's office according to priority – Priority A
passengers, the official or Embassy allocation, being the highest.
After them came passengers who had reached the top of the waiting
list, special consideration being given to women with children,
children alone or in custody. The final list contained the names of
the following fourteen passengers:

I.J.Sharp . . .	Director of the United Kingdom Commercial Corporation.
F.G.Cowlrick . . .	Continental Director, Babcock & Wilcox, (Sponsored by Dept of Overseas Trade)
T.M.Shervington . . .	Shell Manager in Lisbon (Sponsored by Ministry of Fuel & Power)
G.T.Maclean . . .	Inspector General of Consulates
K.Stonehouse . . .	Washington Correspondent of Reuters.
Mrs Stonehouse . . .	Wife of above.
Mrs C.A.Paton . . .	Wife of the Cuban Consul, Liverpool.
W.J.Israel . . .	Travelling on behalf of the Jewish Refugee Mission.
Father.A.S.Holmes . . .	Vice-President of the R.C.English College.
Mrs R.Hutcheon . . .	Wife of Lt.Col Hutcheon, R.A.

Petra Hutcheon . . .

    and   Daughters of Col & Mrs Hutcheon

Caroline Hutcheon

Derek Partridge . . .   Son of Major F.Partridge, OBE, (The Foreign Office)

Dora Rowe . . .   Nanny accompanying D.Partridge.

Of the last five passengers on the list, Mrs Hutcheon and her daughters had been living in Canada. They were returning to join Colonel Hutcheon in England. Derek Partridge and his nanny, Dora Rowe, had been in America since 1940. They had arrived the previous week in the *Serpa Pinto*, a Portuguese ship, from New York. All had been evacuees.

Of the top priority passengers Ivan Sharp, a mining engineer of the UKCC, had been negotiating wolfram exports to the UK. This valuable mineral (tungsten) was a principal steel-hardener in the manufacture of armaments, and Sharp's job had been to achieve a bigger allocation from producers in Spain and Portugal. Cowlrick, of the well-known firm of marine engineers, had been on a trip round their Iberian establishments. Shervington, Shell Oil's manager who lived in Lisbon, was going home on business and to see his son before he was posted on active service. Stonehouse was on his way to take up an appointment as war correspondent with the American forces, and Mrs Stonehouse was coming home to join the WRNS. Of the others, Israel had completed his job for the Refugee Mission and Father Holmes was going to London to discuss the appointment of a new President of the English College with Monsignor Cullen. Mrs Paton was a late addition – having been put on the passenger list the day before the flight by Geoffrey Stow, the Assistant Air Attaché.

The particular DC3, in which these passengers were to fly, was fitted with fourteen seats (seven a side) and this was regarded as the de luxe flight. The planes could carry up to twenty-one passengers, according to load, when fitted with extra seats. The plane on this occasion was *Ibis* – the one previously attacked and in which Leslie had flown out – and was to be captained once more by Quirinus Tepas, the senior pilot. His air crew consisted of co-pilot de Koning, radio officer van Brugge and flight engineer Rozenvink. *Ibis* had reached Lisbon, after an uneventful flight from Whitchurch, late Monday afternoon. It would be serviced and ready to fly back at 9 a.m., Tuesday.

On Sunday Leslie, accompanied by Alfred, joined the beach

party at Praia das Macas, a long sandy strip backed by dunes, and among the many guests were Philip Newman and Tyrrel Shervington. Among some photos I have of the picnic, Leslie is seen bare-legged, in shirt and shorts, and Alfred – somewhat incongruously for a warm day – in a city suit. Though hastily arranged the party was a great success and Sam Herbert, the Assistant Press Attaché, long recalled 'the enthusiasm about it afterwards'.

Sometime before luncheon on Monday, Leslie heard from the Press Office that everything was set for the film show that evening. The Press Office was delighted with the response to the invitations, and a large Anglo-Portuguese audience was expected.

What now seems clear is that sometime on Monday Leslie and Alfred conferred about their flying arrangements. Since both the film show and dinner were to take place that evening, there was no need for them to stay any longer. Why could they not fly home first thing on Tuesday in the 9 a.m. plane? To Alfred it seemed a sensible suggestion. He had a back-log of work piling up at his London office and Leslie wanted to get back to see progress on the film at Denham. If it was possible to squeeze on the morning flight, along with Shervington and Cowlrick, it was worth trying. They would be home just after tea and in their offices by Wednesday morning.

Sometime on Monday afternoon, and I am here quoting Colvin who said it was as late as 5 p.m., the Air Attaché's secretary had a telephone call from the booking clerk at the BOAC offices in the Avenida da Liberdade. The clerk said he had two passengers, L.Howard and A.Chenhalls, who wanted to be booked out on Tuesday's flight. They were claiming priority. The Air Attaché's secretary answered that the list was already made up: 'Why can't they wait until 2nd June?' The clerk said they were insisting, to which the secretary replied: 'Well, I suppose, you'll have to take off two others.' The two passengers removed from Tuesday's flight to accommodate Leslie and Alfred were in fact Derek Partridge and his nanny Dora Rowe. Finally a third passenger, Father Holmes, was taken off board the aeroplane due to a last minute telephone call. These rearrangements took place at Portela – delaying the plane's take-off by thirty-five minutes – and it is possible they did not pass unnoticed by interested observers.

The young boy, Derek Partridge, was looking forward keenly, after three years in America to being reunited with his mother and father in Limpsfield, Surrey. It was extraordinary that, years later, I was to meet Derek – quite by chance – at a friend's house. He told me the whole curious story. To begin with – when he and his nanny first arrived – they were put up at a small Estoril hotel on the seafront. 'I know we stayed in Estoril and that I spent several days on a narrow strip of beach with fine, light-coloured sand and rocks.' While the boy Derek wandered on the beach waiting for his flight home, Leslie not far away waited at the Atlantico. Neither knew of the other's existence – yet Derek owed his life to a last minute change of plan by Leslie.

Derek, before writing to me in 1975, discussed the circumstances with his mother.

All she could add to what I will set out below is that (1) my father (Major Frederick Partridge, OBE) handled the whole matter – (2) that my nanny and I were taken off the flight at the last minute – and (3) that my father had apparently contacted the Consul in Lisbon regarding us and was then informed that we had been removed from the plane and were therefore safe.

Discussing his arrival at the Portela airport the day they were to fly, Derek said:

My first memory is walking out from an airport building to a plane with a rear entrance. I also seem to remember seeing the tails of two other planes behind ours and that they had some sort of German markings on them. I believe we were seated almost opposite the entrance door as I have a memory of looking over my left shoulder at someone who came into the aircraft and, after speaking to Miss Rowe, caused us to leave the plane with him.

What happened then was that they were sent back to Estoril to await another flight. In fact, it was a week later before they finally left Lisbon and by then, owing to the loss of *Ibis*, the schedules had been changed to night-flying.

On Monday, after Leslie and Alfred had moved from Estoril to the Aviz in Lisbon, they received an invitation for drinks from Calouste Gulbenkian, the Armenian oil millionaire. Gulbenkian arrived in Lisbon after the occupation of France and assembled his art treasures there, setting up the Gulbenkian Foundation. He occupied a suite of rooms at the Aviz. Over drinks they were joined by his secretary, Madame Theis. Kenneth Clark described her in *The Other Half* as 'a large, pleasant looking lady in early middle age who led, I should imagine, a very restricted life.' There is a picture of the four of them seated together, Leslie looking dubiously at a drink he is being offered by Gulbenkian – while Madame Theis and Alfred look on, smiling broadly.

That evening at the Embassy cinema Leslie, in a short speech to the audience, introduced *The First of the Few*. They seemed to enjoy every minute of Leslie's depiction of Mitchell's life and when the lights went up afterwards, crowded round to offer congratulations. Among those who attended the film show was Samuel Mervyn Herbert, the Assistant Press Attaché, who wrote:

That Monday was, in fact, another immense success. Leslie, who was after all thoroughly accustomed to star treatment, was himself surprised by the strength of emotion and the enthusiasm he aroused in the Portuguese, and was interested in our explanation of it. Someone suggested it was because he was not only a great actor but because he fitted so precisely the Portuguese idealised picture of the perfect Englishman. Leslie laughed at this and said: 'I suppose we do not have to tell them that I began as a Hungarian.' This was certainly the first I had heard of his Hungarian origin and I could hardly believe it, though I know I have since read it.

While Leslie was attending the screening of his film, two other passengers for the morning flight were sitting not far away under the trees in the gardens that divide the Avenida – Kenneth and Evelyn Stonehouse. *The Evening Standard* correspondent in Lisbon wrote:

We sat under illuminated trees at tables on the Avenida Liberdade, Lisbon's main thoroughfare which is lit up at night like the Bois de Boulogne in peace-time – and talked about old days in Fleet Street and the new, grimmer London he would find on his return. Mrs Stonehouse said her ambition was to join up in the WRNS – 'I only want a week to look up old friends,' she said, 'then I will be glad to take my part in the war effort'.

Later that night, speaking to a Portuguese journalist friend, Stonehouse said: 'I'm not normally frightened but somehow I feel bad about this air-trip. I wish I could go to sleep here and wake up at some English airfield.'

After the film show Leslie went back to the Aviz to join the dinner party given by Tavares d'Almeida. During the dinner the Portuguese

Minister made a speech and presented Leslie with a gold medallion for the finest film of 1942. Leslie replied thanking not only the Minister but 'his many friends in Portugal for making his visit so memorable and enjoyable'.

The following morning Leslie and Alfred were up early. Not long after eight Leslie had a phone call from Gwyneth Williams wishing them both *Bon Voyage*. A little later they went along to the BOAC offices in the Avenida to collect their tickets which had now been altered and revalidated for Tuesday, and their names were inserted on the passenger manifest. Shortly afterwards, accompanied by George West and the Press Attaché, Michael Stewart, they left by car for the airport.

When the KLM airport staff arrived at Portela the passenger list for Tuesday's flight had still not been amended, and did not contain Leslie's or Alfred's names. Arrangements had been made to collect Mrs Hutcheon and her young daughters, Derek Partridge and Dora Rowe. They were the earliest to arrive and, after their tickets had been checked against the manifest, they were allowed to board the plane which was ready to load. By half-past-eight all the other passengers had arrived, their reservations verified and baggage loaded. They sat or stood about in the departure area only waiting for the signal to board. The flight was due out at nine, but by now it looked as though there was going to be a delay. As someone observed, Tyrrel Shervington was pacing up and down, puffing at a cigar and looking a little irritated.

Other people from the Embassy and British Council were now arriving, to see Leslie off. Most had driven out in their own cars, among them Sam Herbert and David Shillan. Several Portuguese friends of Leslie's and Alfred's had come out to wish them *Bon Voyage*, and there were one or two local press people and photographers. Just before Leslie reached the airport the KLM Manager, Van der Vliet, received a call from BOAC in the Avenida. Two top priority passengers would now be flying in place of the boy Partridge and his nanny. Van der Vliet amended his passenger list accordingly. He was not unfamiliar with last minute revisions due to people changing their minds, VIPs claiming priority, or simply security, to keep important names off the passenger list till the last minute. He asked the boarding officer to go out to the plane, take off the two passengers and bring them to his office. He would apologise and put them on the next available flight.

When Leslie reached Portela those waiting to board Flight 2L272 were a little surprised to discover he was a fellow passenger. Some had heard he was flying the following day. Van der Vliet welcomed Leslie and Alfred cordially if briskly and once their baggage had been loaded they joined the small queue of passengers filing out onto the tarmac. As Leslie walked past the barriers his Portuguese friends spotted him. They waved excitedly as they bade him farewell. He paused momentarily to allow a few photos to be taken in the bright, early morning sunshine. Then, with a final wave, he caught up with the others on their way to the plane.

It was, of course, impossible at Portela not only to keep the movements of air-liners secret but also the movements of passengers. However security-minded officials might be, the passengers were always in full view, either arriving or leaving. Nobody as well known as Leslie would pass unnoticed, nor, perhaps Shervington, the Manager of Shell. As the Lufthansa offices and repair bays were adjacent, German officials and mechanics passed within feet of passengers. When Leslie reached the gangway he stopped suddenly and turned to speak to Alfred, then, beckoned to the boarding officer. He explained that he had forgotten the package of stockings which had been put in bond at the airport when they arrived from Madrid. Leslie gave him the Customs form and the man hurried back to the barrier where he spoke briefly to Van der Vliet before he vanished into the warren of the aerodrome.

He was some little time returning but as he came back he was stopped on the way by Van der Vliet. The KLM office had just had an urgent telephone call for Father Holmes of the English College. He would have to miss the flight. A message had come for him that he was to report immediately at either the British Embassy or the Papal Nunciature. As soon as Father Holmes was disembarked, the plane was to take off. The boarding officer, looking a little bewildered, hurried back to the *Ibis* carrying the package, and the laconic message. It had been a strange morning of chopping and changing – first the boy and nanny removed and now these last minute instructions for the priest.

By the time the man reached the cabin, the passengers were already fastened into their seats. He handed Leslie the package, gave Father Holmes the urgent message, then went forward to inform Tepas. When he returned Holmes explained he had a suitcase on board. Could they get it off? Impossible, said the KLM man – it was locked in the luggage bay and the plane was ready for take-off. They would send it back on the next flight, and Holmes followed him from the plane. As soon as they were disembarked, the KLM staff removed the gangway and the rear door was closed.

Holmes walked back to the barrier wondering if there had been some sudden change of plan from London. As he stopped to talk to Van der Vliet, the plane was moving towards the runway. They stood for a moment, stilled by the sound of the engines, as *Ibis* thundered past them and lifted slowly into the sky. It was odd that after all the reshuffling and passengers removed, due to shortage of seats, there was now spare capacity on the plane – and with the final removal of Holmes there were exactly thirteen passengers. *Ibis* had taken off thirty-five minutes late.

Holmes hurried away to make his enquiries, but at neither the Embassy nor the Nunciature could anyone be found who had made the telephone call that had so urgently taken him off the plane. Nor could the switch-board operators remember one being made. He rang the airport again but they could only repeat the message they had already given him. It looked like a very impractical joke – or was it? Later Father Holmes was at a friend's house in Lisbon when the telephone rang, and the friend answered it. The caller said he had just heard the news that Father Holmes had lost his life in the plane with Leslie Howard. He was soon disabused of the idea.

The mystery of the phone call at the airport was never solved –but Father Holmes owed his life to it. A parish priest, Father Joseph Phelan, who knew Holmes in Lisbon, summed it up to me in these words: 'I must admit that when I heard that no confirmation of the alleged phone call was ever forthcoming – well, I thought, that it was an addition composed by some over-religiously-minded person who wished to introduce a miraculous element of just why Father Holmes failed to take his seat on the plane.' Geoffrey Stow, the Assistant Air Attaché, recalling circumstances about the flight, wrote to me of passengers' premonitions.

A passenger who I knew on that flight was the Manager of Shell Oil in Lisbon named Bill Shervington. I learned afterwards that he told his wife that he had some sort of premonition that something dire would happen but did not want to cancel his flight because it would make him look rather foolish . . . [In fact, he had dreamt that the plane had been shot down with him on board.] With regard to Father Holmes of the English College I can only think that the mysterious telephone call was a hot line from the Almighty. It is possible that Father Holmes also had a premonition and made the call a pretext for missing the flight.

On the other hand, it is just possible that the supernatural element has obscured the fact that the unknown caller may, indeed, have had a hot line to someone who really knew what was going to happen.

*

Immediately after take-off from Portela *Ibis* signalled her departure time to Whitchurch Control Tower (Whitchurch S/S). Van Brugge made the coded wireless communication – 'G-AGBB air-borne Portela 9.35 am DBST'. Radio silence would now be kept, except for listening watch, till the routine position calls each hour of the journey. On her flight north Tepas took *Ibis* slowly up to her cruising ceiling of 9,000 feet, maintaining a speed of approximately 170 knots and setting his course on 9 degrees west. This would take *Ibis* up the coast of Portugal, for about two hours till she made her last 'land-fall' at Cape Vilano. It had been fine and sunny when they left Portela but weather reports indicated low cloud and a fairly strong wind over the Bay. Tepas would fly above cloud, and this would give him an estimated flying time to Whitchurch of seven hours.

A few minutes after *Ibis* had left Portela there was some activity at a German airfield, Kerlin-Bastard, a few miles west of Bordeaux. Along with Merignac, which operated FW200s, the long-range reconnaissance 'Condors', it was part of KG (Kampf Gruppe) 40. The shorter range Ju88 6Cs flew from Kerlin – their duties, apart from U-Boat or blockade-runner escort, to seek out and shoot down Sunderland flying-boats and C47s moving between the UK and North Africa. These ubiquitous, all-purpose machines – basically fighter-bombers – had been adapted as heavy-fighters. Their top speed was 320 mph and they cruised at 260. Powerfully armed, they had three 7.9 mm cannon and three MG17s in the wings firing forward, with two turret-mounted cannon and a machine-gun aft. They carried cameras for reconnaissance and photographic confirmation of 'kills'. Their operating radius of 600 miles took them to 14 degrees west with a range of 1,200 plus, and they could be airborne for just under five hours.

The activity at Kerlin-Bastard involved a staffel of these machines ready for immediate take-off. Each was manned by a crew of four, pilot, flight-engineer, radio-operator and rear-gunner. They were fitted with ASV radar for surface work and Lichtenstein BC sets for aircraft search in poor visibility.

The precise instructions issued to Leutnant Bellstedt, the leader of the staffel, by Major Hemm, the CO of the Junkers wing, have so far not come to light, and probably never will. Many of the crews engaged in these operations who were not shot down into the Bay later lost their lives in the final defence of Germany, and among the survivors there has been a tendency to silence over this particular operation. (Apart from an eye-witness account by one man – which tells us nothing about the orders – an advertisement placed in a journal run by an ex-Luftwaffe association failed to elicit any response from the elusive Major Hemm. Later, the Commodore of KG 40 regretted that Alfred Hemm could not be found.)

Whatever orders Leutnant Bellstedt received from Major Hemm before take-off at 10 a.m, 1st June – if they were not entirely routine – could possibly have had some bearing on what subsequently happened. They could also have come from further afield and from higher up in the German chain of command. The only evidence we have of the nature of the operation is contained in the German Atlantic Archives – and this is certainly deficient if not actually misleading. The Archives simply state that: 'Eight Junkers 88 took off at 10 am, June 1st, probably from Kerlin-Bastard airfield, *their tasks being air-sea rescue and protection of two U-Boats.*'

On the precise nature of the air-sea rescue operations to be undertaken the Archives are silent. As for the U-Boats, these were not located, and British Admiralty records on the subject state there were no U-Boats in the area at the time. Sunderlands, searching the south Biscay on 1st June in conjunction with the Navy, reported to base that they saw none in twelve hours of pattern flying. Certainly, weather conditions for sea-search were poor when Bellstedt and his squadron took off; this was confirmed by German Atlantic Archives when they stated laconically 'the weather was unfavourable for sea-search'.

However, despite conditions, Leutnant Bellstedt did not turn back to base. He flew on steadily west with his squadron towards a position approximately 46 N by 9 W, four hundred miles from Bordeaux. As search at sea level was poor, Bellstedt possibly sought other objectives – stray Sunderlands, Liberators or C 47s. Kampf-Gruppe 40 had found several profitable search areas off the north-west coast of Spain between latitudes 46-47 degrees N, 9-10 degrees W. At this distance from Finisterre conditions were better with, at times, good visibility and often quite free of cloud. Bellstedt and his squadron could position themselves very accurately through radio bearings, the operators of the staffel taking wireless fixes from

Lorient, Arcachon and the powerful De-Te* (RDF) transmitter at Cape Vilano. On reaching his selected hunting-ground, Bellstedt instituted a procedure, the German equivalent of our 'De-Range'. This was a box-system of search, not dissimilar to the one used by our Sunderlands, and was radar-assisted if conditions were cloudy. Thus, eight places, flying two miles apart, could effectively comb a series of twenty mile boxes.

Ibis, was off Cape Vilano at about eleven-thirty. Here, on high cliffs overlooking the Atlantic, the Germans had sited their powerful omni-directional beacon for radio navigation. It had an angular coverage of three hundred degrees and gave ranges up to 600 miles over land and 1,000 miles over sea by day.

> In its earlier form it was known as Elektra and, in a modified form, as Sonne. Later a method known as Consul was developed whereby the RAF was enabled to make use of enemy Sonne transmissions. It operated in 250-500 K/cs band.†

Winston Churchill made reference to this beacon (Vol IV, p 255, *The Second World War*) in these words:

> The Germans had established two long-range beam stations for enabling their aircraft and U-Boats to navigate far out into the Bay and the Western Approaches. One of these was near Brest and the other in North-West Spain. Our Ambassador at Madrid came to hear about the Spanish station, but instead of trying to get the Spaniards to close it down, which would have involved us in endless legal and diplomatic controversy, we were advised by Dr R.V.Jones to use it ourselves. By taking photographs of the equipment we were able to learn how it worked, and henceforward our aircraft and fighting ships were supplied with a first-class position-finding service which they shared happily with the enemy.

Captain Tepas, looking from the cockpit of *Ibis*, could in clear conditions easily see the masts of the 'De-Te' beacon – and Van Brugge, the radio operator, took his last positional bearings from its transmission. Not only was it possible for Tepas to position himself

---

* Decimeter Telemetry.
† Wireless Direction Finding, R.Keen 1947.

on the beacon – but the operators of the beacon could also determine the position and course of any aircraft flying through its beam. Another system the Germans used in conjunction with De-Te was the radar equipment known as 'Freya', which sent out impulses on a 240 cm wavelength and could be used for plotting air and sea targets up to a distance of 100 miles from the coast.

It will thus be seen that if the Germans wished to track the flight path of *Ibis* it presented no problems. Her position and course could be accurately monitored once radio and radar bearings had been taken. In clear conditions, flying as she did over the tip of Finisterre at roughly 8,000 feet, she could, in fact, have been observed visually through binoculars, if not with the naked eye. The KLM planes passed regularly over this point at fixed times – they did not zig-zag or vary their routes more than a few miles – and their departure times could, if required, be verified from Lisbon.

As *Ibis* flew north into the Bay, leaving Cape Vilano behind her, she was moving towards the point of interception that Parmentier, KLM's Commodore, had always feared might be repeated. He had asked for a route further west, for reasons of safety, but it had, so far, not been considered necessary. As recently as Monday, 31st May, he had had another meeting with the Superintendent of Routes to press for new routes or night-flying, but no final decision had been reached. Officially, it was still felt interception was unlikely. That meeting was to prove the turning point in official recognition of the dangers and caused some red faces among those who had delayed.

By 12 noon *Ibis* was eighty miles from Cape Vilano and on a converging course with Bellstedt's squadron searching ahead. Forty-five minutes later they would be in sight of one another. In frequent sweeps over the Bay, Bellstedt had often seen the British air-liners. He had shadowed them and, on recognising their civil markings, had turned away. As the experienced leader of a staffel, he knew well enough the difference between the military and civil machines. The civil machines were painted a kind of pale, duck-egg blue instead of the brown and green zig-zags of the war planes. The air-liners had vertical bars in red, white and blue painted on them instead of the RAF roundels or USAF stars, and the civil lettering was two feet high and boldly defined on both sides of the aircraft. Surely, no mistake could be made – no failure to identify.

Flying his boxes, with his eight planes spread two miles apart, Bellstedt combed the apparently empty sky. In or out of cloud, his radar scanners searching ahead, he flew the precise patterns, watchfully, in touch by R/T with each member of his staffel. The

question one must ask is: did Bellstedt know of the existence of the
air-liner creeping towards him at 170 knots? Whatever enigma
exists lies in the fact of whether the information available at the 'De-
Te' beacon was known to Bellstedt. He could certainly have had the
information by W/T via the German chain of communication
through Vigo, which was Gestapo HQ, back to base at Bordeaux.
With that knowledge he could position his squadron accurately. It
has always seemed to me, in view of the circumstances that
followed, that Bellstedt *was* so precisely positioned, with a very
strong chance of interception. I have discussed this with 'Anzac'
pilots and crews of Sunderlands who had no doubt that enemy
squadrons could be homed onto them through wireless fixes and
radar. Whatever the circumstances of Bellstedt's search, when his
squadron broke cloud at 12.45, there, flying a northerly course in
the sun a few miles away, was *Ibis*, clear to the naked eye.

Referring to Bellstedt's squadron at this precise moment, German
Atlantic Archives state: 'They *may* have been on their way back to
base when at 12.45 a transport aircraft' – described in the German
report as a DC 3 – 'was sighted on a N/E course.' At this moment
Bellstedt, followed by his squadron, closed in on the air-liner,
narrowing the range. If the sighting time, 12.45, is correct (and this
was confirmed by van Brugge's final signal at 12.54) then Bellstedt
flew towards *Ibis* for no less than nine minutes. Ample time, one
would think, to communcate the sighting to base, and, certainly, to
identify the airliner. In that time, he could have closed to one
hundred yards to scrutinise the DC3. He could have read her
markings easily and reported them back.* He waited no longer. On
the ninth minute he turned towards *Ibis* and opened fire, raking her
with cannon and machine gun bullets. His squadron followed suit,
taking turns, one after the other, at what amounted to target
practice. There was no danger that the airliner would fire back.
Unlike a C47 she was completely unarmed.

As Tepas put her into a dive, seeking the cover of clouds, 3,000

---

* Referring to the time element from sighting to shooting down, Ian Colvin,
writing to my aunt, said: ' . . . on coming to compare that with the one German
document of that time, I find that the German flight . . . must have had time to see
its civilian markings, and once more I am bound to accept the probability that the
shooting down was deliberate.' Arthur Howard, my uncle, who served in the RAF
during the war, remembering the interrogation of German pilots who recollected
the incident on 1st June, told Colvin: 'These German pilots said that day after day
they had spotted our air-linerrs on the Lisbon route over the Bay of Biscay and
reported them to base. But on this occasion, when they reported it, the instructions
came back – "Shoot it down!" '

feet below, van Brugge tapped out a desperate signal to Whitchurch control: 'Am being attacked by enemy aircraft.' It was the last signal *Ibis* was ever to make. The shelter of the cloudbank was too far away. As the sixth of the Junkers went in, spraying her with cannon and machine gun bullets, her wing tanks caught fire – followed by an explosion. Like a flaming torch *Ibis* dived on out of control till, piercing the clouds, she disappeared from sight on her way to extinction in the sea.

'She was attacked . . . ' says the German report, 'with six attacks, caught fire and dived into the sea. Four men were observed to jump from the aircraft but no mention is made of any search for survivors.' In fact, no men jumped from the aircraft either, as later reported, 'in desperation' or 'in parachutes': they were simply four passengers hurled from the cabin by the force of the explosion as the plane broke up. The last thing Bellstedt did, with commendable German thoroughness, was to follow what was left of the blazing plane down to the surface of the Bay – not to search for suvivors or, even, dip his wing in salute to a vanquished opponent – but simply to photograph the smoking wreckage on the water for posterity, and confirm his kill. Then, the squadron formed up and returned to base.

CHAPTER FOURTEEN

Reactions, Evidence and Theories

The last wireless communication from *Ibis* – 'From G-AGBB to GKH. Am being attacked by enemy aircraft' – was received by Whitchurch S/S at 12.54 p.m. Whitchurch continued to send out signals to the plane, but no reply was received, and at 1705 LST (1505 GMT) she was reported overdue to the Traffic Control Officer. It was still hoped she might have survived the attack and landed elsewhere. Ops Room at the Air Ministry was notified and Traffic Watch was alerted. There were two Sunderlands of 461 – the 'Anzac' – squadron in the Biscay area, both from Pembroke Dock, Milford Haven, and they were diverted from anti-U-boat patrol to search for survivors. One was only fifteen minutes from *Ibis*' last reported position, the other one hour. Both did a square search north of Finisterre for three hours, but as one of the Sunderlands' Australian skippers said: 'Conditions were very bad, cloud base down to under a thousand feet with heavy swell and white caps' – and they saw absolutely nothing of either wreckage or survivors, and as darkness fell the search was called off. The following morning another Sunderland of 461 made a final search of the area. It is possible this was the Sunderland, manned by an Australian crew of twelve, that fought a hectic battle with eight Junkers 88s while in the search area. A Spanish-destroyer also left El Ferrol and joined in the search for twenty-four hours. But nothing was sighted by either air or sea-search – a report that the crew had been picked up by a Spanish trawler proved abortive – and by the afternoon of 2nd June the plane was listed as officially missing, all on board presumed dead.

The first public announcement of the disaster came from Berlin. The German High Command communiqué stated that their reconnaissance planes had 'shot down three enemy bombers and one transport plane'. This was followed by a German news bulletin picked up in England the evening of 1st June from Radio Zeesen in Holland – which 'was frequently interrupted by a ghost voice saying that the KLM plane had been shot down by the Luftwaffe'. Certain names had been reported by a German news agency – those of Leslie Howard, Alfred Chenhalls and Kenneth Stonehouse. Berlin radio added that 'some prominent British economists were on board.'

Reactions to the shooting down made headlines across the world. News of the death of Leslie Howard was given special prominence in Goebbels' newspaper *Der Angriff*. It was celebrated almost like a victory. Under banner headlines, larger than those accorded 'the strategic withdrawal' of Hitler's armies in Russia, the front page bore the words: 'Pimpernel Howard has made his last trip!' It was a pathetic victory to crow about, but Goebbels probably enjoyed it. The Germans also got off the mark quickly with excuses and justifications. Herr Klein, the Press Counsellor in Lisbon, persuaded the *Diario de Noticias* and the *Diario de Manha* to mention that the plane had been escorted by British bombers and that there had been an air-battle. After the British Embassy and Dutch Legation had denied the allegations, the Germans stated that the crew had baled out, presumably to make the air-liner look to the world like a fighting machine. Another communiqué was then issued to all papers by the Dutch and ourselves that no parachutes had been carried. Further statements by the Germans insisted that *Ibis* was 'a DC fighting machine' – 'that it was escorted by fighters' and that 'it carried contraband'. Clearly the Germans wished to find any means to justify and legitimise their actions, and were prepared to tell all sorts of lies. But were these the real reasons – or simply the cover reasons? Later, they were to deny all this and dismiss the shooting down as an error of judgement.

The British Press reported the facts – alongside the German excuses. 'Lost airliner had no escort', stated *The Daily Telegraph* – 'German excuse exposed'. And under the headline 'Leslie Howard's plane "like bomber" say Germans', Basil Cardew of the *Daily Express*, quoting the German overseas radio, reported: 'The machine was a Douglas DC 3 . . . and the Germans stated it had camouflage paint in no way distinguishable from a war-plane and that the British and Americans are using this type of aircraft as bombers'. Describing the attack, which Cardew remarked was contrary to International Air Law, the German radio said: 'When the German machine opened fire destroying the right wing and fuselage . . . four men of the crew baled out without making any attempt to save the machine. Only two parachutes opened. One collapsed in mid-air, while the second disappeared after hitting the sea.' Well, that certainly disposed of the

evidence for the parachute story! 'Why not a fighter escort?' said the
Evening Standard a little belatedly, ' . . . our long-range fighters –
Mosquitoes and Beaufighters could easily escort the passenger
liners as far as the coast of Spain.' Airline experts in London said the
Germans must have known they were attacking a civilian plane
because of its entirely different markings.

Very quickly the disaster became a mystery. Under the headline.
'The mystery of the Leslie Howard plane. Why did the Germans go
for it?' G.Ward Price of the *Mail* said:

> It is conceivable that the Germans were making some special
> effort to intercept that particular aeroplane. Their spies in Lisbon
> may have reported that some particular document of high
> military importance was being sent to this country by it.

And Ward Price added: 'An incident such as that . . . leads people to
think of Mr Churchill and his safety. But the Prime Minister on a
journey by air would be in the trusty keeping of the Royal Air
Force.'

Questions were asked in the House of Commons (*Hansard* – 'Lost
Air Liner' – Oral answers, 10.6.43). The Under Secretary of State for
Air (Captain Balfour) was asked 'Whether, in view of the harmful
effects of the German radio version . . . suggesting that the machine
was to all intents and purposes a Douglas fighting machine and that
the crew baled out leaving the passengers to their fate, he proposed
to deal with these allegations . . . '

Captain Balfour, in reply, said: 'The statements made by the
German radio were, as usual, completely untrue. As my Rt Hon
Friend stated in the House yesterday the aircraft plainly bore
international civil aviation markings. The registration letters were,
in fact, two feet high. The aircraft was, therefore, readily
distinguishable from a military aircraft, apart from other differences. For technical reasons concerned with exits, the allegations
that the crew abandoned the aircraft leaving the passengers to their
fate, is just a despicable lie.'

In reply to questions from Wing Commander Hulbert and Sir
Malcolm Robertson, the Secretary of State for Air, Sir Archibald
Sinclair, replied: 'That only one accident has occurred during the
period shows that no undue risks have been taken.' And he went on
to say ' . . . certain further steps have been taken to reduce the
chances of interception, but it would not be in the public interest to
give details.' Mr Emanuel Shinwell (Seaham, Labour) seemed

interested in this point and asked, in view of the improved methods of protection: 'Were those decided on since the accident or before?' To this specific question on timing the Minister gave a somewhat evasive reply: 'It is a question of the methods of routing or avoidance. The best methods of avoidance are under constant review and the question of routing is under constant study. Certain steps have been taken quite recently.'

Well, certainly, the questions had been both under review and study for some time, and 'certain steps' *had* been taken 'quite recently'. Since the accident KLM had gone over to night-flying – but for months prior to the loss of *Ibis* nothing had been done – except to study and review the methods of routing and avoidance. Parmentier had badgered the Air Ministry, the Ministry of Civil Aeronautics and the Superintendent of Routes with his recommendations for routes further west or, alternatively, night flying – but they had turned a deaf ear. Only a disaster had made them listen and take action.

At this early moment after the disaster it was generally believed that the attack on *Ibis* had been carried out by one isolated German warplane, flown by a trigger-happy pilot returning from a long-range reconnaissance mission. It was only much later that it became at all widely known that a squadron of Ju88s was involved. Ian Colvin, in his researches into the loss of *Ibis* some years after the war, interviewed a member of the staffel engaged in the attack. His name was Peter Friedlein, the radio-operator in the sixth aircraft of the Junkers squadron, and the 'eye-witness' to whom I earlier referred. Colvin went to see him in Franconia in southern Germany. Before he replied to any questions, Friedlein said immediately: 'I would like to get in touch with my CO, Major Hemm. Do you know where he is?' Unfortunately, as the Commodore of KG 40 admitted, Alfred Hemm – the man who issued the orders to the squadron – had vanished, never to be found. It was clear to Colvin that he was not dead – he had simply disappeared.

'I'm not sure what instructions Leutnant Bellstedt had when he attacked the aircraft,' Friedlein told Colvin. 'Leutnant Bellstedt is dead now. All the officers of that flight were killed. But there was no disciplining of Leutnant Bellstedt.' Friedlein remembered the occasion with great clarity. 'The time was about noon – the position about 46 N, 09 W. The Bay was rough – there was high wind, low cloud. Leutnant Bellstedt sighted the aircraft in the sun flying a northerly course. Bellstedt went into the attack at once. My aircraft, the second in the third pair, did not have time to attack. By then the airliner was diving steeply and in flames. All sorts of stuff was thrown out. I remember people jumping in desperation. I think there was a parachute. She dived through the cloud, but I did not see her hit the sea.'

'Didn't you look for survivors?' Colvin asked.

'We'd been out a long time and were not minded to stooge about.'

'Didn't you follow down through the cloud?'

'Well, we followed down but there was bad visibility and we saw nothing.'

But this was not true. Somebody did see something – and recorded it as evidence – because photographs were taken of the floating wreckage of *Ibis* and a cloud of black smoke over the sea. These photos were inserted in an album, along with a German newspaper report and some personal notes, kept by a pilot or crew member of the flight. Some years later copies of the photos and an extract from the album were sent to me under cover of a letter from the Personal Services Dept, Ministry of Civil Aviation, dated 10th September 1945. The letter reads:

Dear Sir,

I am directed to forward herewith translated extract from captured German documents relative to a Douglas DC 3 aircraft shot down over the Bay of Biscay on 1st June 1943. The document in question was a photo-album compiled by a member of a long range 'Ju 88' squadron (Letter Y) operating from Bordeaux, then Lorient, in 1943. This album was captured by the 5th Battalion, the Dorsetshire Regt at Rockwinkel, near Bremen, in April 1945 and is now held by them at Dorchester. The location of the crash of the above aircraft according to a map at the end of the album is 10.15 W – 46.07 N., 750 kms from Bordeaux,

I am etc

(For Director of Personal Services)

The photos told me little, except as corroboration of the plane's destruction, for both of them were fuzzy and unclear, and the newspaper cutting pasted in was based on the German news agency report describing the shooting down of the plane, mentioning the names of Leslie, Alfred Chenhalls and Kenneth Stonehouse. But the compiler's notes were interesting, and told me something more.

They drew a different light on the operation and the possible motives for the attack. These handwritten pilot's or crew member's notes, recorded after the operation, gave an insight into German thinking, possibly a justification for the assassination of the aircraft, even a reason for the orders Bellstedt had from the elusive Major Hemm. The translated words read:

> Leslie Howard was not only a film actor but a manufacturer of aircraft parts and a member of the Intelligence Service. Further, the Director of Shell Co of Lisbon (Shervington), who was at the same time Chief of Secret Service in Lisbon, was on board. The casualty to this aircraft necessitated the cessation of Lufthansa Section, Berlin-Madrid and caused a great sensation.

It seems clear from the compiler's notes that both Leslie and Shervington, mistakenly or not, were listed by the Germans as British agents. If the Germans believed this, it of course gave them a motive, and it certainly is in line with German suspicions about Leslie from the moment he arrived in the Iberian peninsula. They had had him under surveillance both in Lisbon and Madrid. As to Shervington I can only submit the following evidence. The Shell company had been suspected by the Germans of espionage activities since early in the war – probably because they had been handling propaganda material through their branches – and two of their representatives had been imprisoned by the Salazar regime on charges laid by the German Legation. A report by our Ambassador in Lisbon, Sir Ronald Campbell, to Anthony Eden in February, 1943, throws some light on this:

> It was highly unfortunate that in January the International Police (the branch of the Portuguese administration responsible for visas, permits and the control of foreigners) should have discovered a secret British organisation and should have at once jumped to the conclusion that it was lending itself to subversive agitation, and that our propaganda machine was being used as a cloak to cover its activities. Their subsequent investigations . . . resulted during the months of January to May inclusive (as part of a whole series of arrests following upon one another at intervals) in the imprisonment of two British subjects, Mr H. Brown and Mr T. Booth, and a number of Portuguese nationals employed in different parts of the country by the Shell Co and our propaganda service. Successive protests of HM Ambassador . . . included a

strong personal remonstrance to Dr Salazar at an abuse of
diplomatic privilege by the German Legation which announced
that investigations had brought to light an association between
the British Secret Service and the Portuguese Communists and
praised the International Police for their vigilance.

(This was described as 'the first fruits of the Seville meeting' between
Franco and Salazar).

These actions by the Salazar regime, on the instigation of the
Germans, however unreasonable and far-fetched to us, seemed
more than just a storm in a tea-cup. If they indicated German
suspicion of the Shell Co, as a whole, they also doubtless implied
suspicion of its Chief, Shervington. Rightly or wrongly, they had
him listed as Chief of British Secret Service. As far as Leslie was
concerned our departments have always dismissed any idea that he
was a secret agent as so much moonshine and wishful German
thinking. But it *is* the German state of mind that one is concerned
with. In both the case of Leslie and Shervington I have presented it
as an example of what Germans were led to believe by Germans. If
the pilot or crew member engaged in the attack had this information,
it was obviously information he had been given. He had no reason
to invent it and it was more than likely believed by others in the
attack – and had been put about at the Bordeaux base from which
they flew. I can only suggest that the probability is that it came from
higher up in the chain of German command, and that the presence
on the plane of Leslie Howard and T.M.Shervington may well have
been the main motive, the basis for the search and final interception
of *Ibis*.

Earlier the Germans had been quick to put out a variety of
excuses for the shooting down, but as the arguments proved too
feeble to be believed they soon settled for 'error of judgement'. It
certainly put an end to further speculation. However, the
information contained in the photo-album has never, to my
knowledge, been admitted by the Germans. It could well have been
a closely guarded secret – for agents are liquidated quietly, without
fuss – and frequently as the victims of unfortunate accidents. One
cannot gun down well-known and respected personalities in a
neutral capital without causing protracted and unpleasant public
investigations – yet if the plane is destroyed over the sea, as 'an error
of judgement', it washed all hands of responsibility. If the orders
came from higher up by people who did not want themselves
names – say the Gestapo or even Goebbels himself – then an

'accident' was the simplest way out. To make too clear one's reasons would look like an admission of intent. To sweep it under the carpet marked 'error of judgement' gave the whole operation an impersonal anonymity. Besides, had they claimed Leslie or Shervington or anyone else were agents and been proved wrong it would have made them look not only irresponsible and stupid but, possibly, culpable of crimes against humanity. The shooting down of a civil airliner could have brought the instigators, and perpetrators, before a War Crimes Tribunal. But the evidence for that had been sealed off. According to the Commodore of KG 40 a report on the shooting down went up to Air Fleet III in Paris but it went no further: there the 'buck' stopped. 'As the crews were young and inexperienced there was no official court of inquiry and the incident was booked as an error of judgement.' The Commodore had been unable to find Major Alfred Hemm so there was nothing more he could do. His final remark was: 'I couldn't answer for everything that happened at KG 40 while I was Commodore.'

In the search for motives one is drawn back to the VIPs on board the plane who might have been acting against German interests. I have always felt that only four passengers meant anything to the Germans: Leslie, Shervington, Wilfred Israel and possibily Ivan Sharp, the Wolfram man.

In Leslie's case, I have quoted the possibility that under the guise of propaganda he was serving the interests of the secret service. He had played the part of a man who was tricking the Germans in *Pimpernel Smith*. Possibly he was doing the same thing in real life. Was he carrying a secret report back to Eden – perhaps about the Schwarze Kappelle, the activities against the Hitler regime, or some evidence of the German rocket programme which trickled from Switzerland via Lisbon in 1943? This charming, apparently, vague actor might, indeed, be more than he appeared – a kind of carrier pigeon, storing information in his actor's memory for the use of British intelligence. If that was a long shot, the Germans had good reason to believe he had been trying to subvert one of their women agents in Madrid. These are possible speculations sown in suspicious minds.

Then, there is the other – more emotional – theory: Goebbels' hatred of him for making fools of the Germans in *Pimpernel Smith* and for his truculent, anti-*Herrenvolk* broadcasts. He was, after all, Goebbels' principal propaganda opponent in Britain. And to this the insidious Goebbels would not be slow in adding the racial element, perhaps the lynchpin of his hatred. The little Doctor was a frenetic anti-Semite and to international Jewry he attributed all the ills of the world. Though Leslie's point of view was scarcely predominantly Jewish he was tainted, in Goebbels' eyes, by the fact that he had a Hungarian-Jewish father.

On a more simplistic, more obvious level there was the incident at the airport – the last minute collection of the package of presents. To a German observer, say one of the Lufthansa people, perhaps the package contained valuable contraband – industrial diamonds, a secret device, documents of importance. Such an innocent item, a trifle almost forgotten twice, could be misinterpreted and assume the proportions of something vital.

Of Shervington I know nothing save the evidence submitted that the Germans suspected him of being Chief of Secret Service in Lisbon. I am convinced that the Germans fully believed in the rightness of their evidence against the Shell Company – the investigations into which our Embassy had treated as 'an abuse of diplomatic privilege' and dismissed as 'worthy of a better cause'. Whether Shervington was on his way to London to report to the Foreign Office – or simply to Shell on routine matters and to see his son – no one will, I suppose, ever be the wiser. The silence with which he met his death has been preserved, yet at the time he had been afflicted with a premonition, a sense of impending disaster, which he not only admitted to his wife but to a friend at the airport. We may ask, why? He was not the kind of man normally a prey to forebodings and had travelled to and fro between Lisbon and the UK many times by air without alarm. In fact, his wife, who was awaiting him in England, wrote shortly after the disaster:

> One has always felt so safe travelling to and from Lisbon that it was a most terrible and totally unexpected shock. Knowing the journey I never had the slightest hope but it would be a very small comfort if we could ever hear that wreckage had been found or some trace – but this I suppose will never be.

Perhaps Tyrrel Shervington's forebodings about the journey sprang from more practical sources and his fears, perhaps, from a more real evaluation of German hostility towards him. The question one must ask about Shervington is did he know more about German activities, or carry more in his briefcase, than met the eye? Was he concealing something the Germans suspected? To look at Shervington was to see a large, resolute bear of man – both amiable and, normally, sanguine. But on this occasion, as he waited at the airport, he seemed a lot less than his cheerful self. Certainly, there had been infuriating delays due to the reshufflings of the passenger list – but this would not have accounted, I think, for his apparently dire forebodings. It would seem, unlike Father Holmes, that he felt no occult or divine inhibitions. Yet had he not felt his fears rather foolish he might well have acted on his instincts and not flown.

Towards the third passenger, Wilfrid Israel, the German intentions may have been more malign. He was working very positively against what the Hitler regime called 'the final solution' of the Jewish question. He had been actively rescuing Jews over the years from concentration camps and extermination centres. He was instrumental in helping set up the Jewish State in Palestine, which was to become, like his name, Israel. This risky, dedicated work of salvation – far more effectively damaging than the filmic rescues of Professor Horatio Smith – was confronted by the implacable hostility of the Nazis. I think this slight, pale man, with the high forehead and sensitive face, was greatly at risk himself at this time. Should the war go against the Nazis and they lose, Israel had a secret dossier compiled from records in Poland and Germany of all the principal Jew-baiters, extermination 'doctors' and gas-camp commandants. This document, and his knowledge of the people concerned, would be available at subsequent War Crimes Tribunals, and Israel himself would be a leading witness for the prosecution. Understandable that the Germans would like to be rid of him – if a favourable opportunity occurred. As he boarded the plane that 1st June morning with Howard and Shervington, I am sure the Germans in Lisbon had not only noted his name – which had been listed in the Wehrmacht Confidental Book since 1938 as a British agent – but, probably, marked it with a star.

The fourth name on the German list, though not quite such a VIP from their point of view but, certainly, important, was possibly Ivan Sharp of the UKCC. He was carrying home a list of negotiations with the principal wolfram producers in Spain and Portugal, mine owners of this precious tungsten mineral over which he had been in such fierce competition with the Germans. If these new allocations could be agree by contract in London with UKCC, we would, by outbidding the Germans, considerably reduce their supply. It was a tricky question for Franco and Salazar, but money certainly talked in these negotiations. Sharp had all the arrangements at his fingertips. But the time element in speedy negotiation was vital. To interrupt his arrival home would cause great inconvenience and delay for his lists contained important details. Such a thought may well have occurred to the Germans as they watched Ivan Sharp walk towards the plane with his heavy briefcase.

This cargo of interesting passengers – all valuable, all working against the Germans in their separate ways – when added up had distinct possibilities if total liquidation could be achieved quietly and without fuss, over the sea, outside the territorial waters of Spain and Portugal. And the plane would simply be sucked down into the ocean, leaving no trace, involving no investigations – neatly dismissed as an unfortunate accident.

A theory that was pursued shortly after the loss of *Ibis* was the Chenhalls-for-Churchill one. Some people believed – and may still believe – that this was a deception plan circulated by the War Office to cover the Prime Minister's return from Gibraltar. The essence of the scheme was to persuade the Germans that Chenhalls, boarding the plane, was, in fact, Churchill. Other people, not wholly accepting this theory, believed the Germans genuinely mistook Chenhalls for Churchill at the airport. It remains to this day a popular fallacy not easily discredited.

There was, in fact, only the most superficial resemblance between the two men. Churchill was a lot smaller and stockier than Chenhalls, he was also twenty years older and didn't really resemble him facially – unless one was rather short-sighted. Perhaps, from behind – and at a distance – they could have been confused. But, of course, they both smoked cigars – and this fact was battened onto and seems, on reflection, the only concrete evidence presented. However, the 'connection' was pursued with zeal in the journalistic vacuum following the unexplained disaster and, if it was naive, the mysterious, unresolved nature of the tragedy – apparently motiveless – cried out for invention.

The first mention of the mistaken identity theory occurred in a London newspaper a few days after the disaster. In the 'it is suggested' nature of such inventive journalism, the columnist put it this way:

We may never know whether the Nazi attack upon the British plane carrying Leslie Howard . . . was deliberately planned. At the time, I referred to the suggestion that the Germans may have been 'out to get Howard'. Today I heard another story. It is, briefly, that the German spies in Lisbon reported that Mr Churchill was aboard. There was, indeed, a passenger who very much resembled the Prime Minister in the plane. His name was

Alfred Chenhalls . . . When last seen on Lisbon's civil aerodrome he was smoking a long cigar. It is suggested that enemy observers there saw him and mistook him for Mr Churchill.

When Leslie and Alfred boarded the plane on 1st June, Mr Churchill, who had been joined by Eden, was in conference with his staff and military commanders in Algiers. He had left Washington on May 26th in a Boeing – arriving at Gibraltar at 5 p.m. On the 27th he flew on to Algiers in a York aircraft of the RAF – as he wrote, 'with a dozen Beaufighters circling above us.' Mr Churchill spent some time conferring on the next Allied moves and for this purpose remained nine days in the area of Algiers and Tunis. 'I propose to stay here, or hereabouts, till about the 6th (June) as I need some rest after the hustle of Washington.'

It will be seen that there was, thus, a gap of at least five days after the shooting down of *Ibis* before Winston Churchill flew home. His departure from Algiers and his stop in Gibraltar about 6th June would presumably have been specially watched for by the Abwehr and their agents. They must have known he would fly escorted a great part of the way. In any event, his course home would have taken him – in the interests of safety – a considerable distance out into the Atlantic. It must have seemed highly improbable – even to the dimmest German mind – that he would arrive in his Boeing at Lisbon and transfer to a KLM civil machine and risk flying home unescorted in broad daylight within easy range of German squadrons.

As far as Leslie and Alfred were concerned, they had clearly been observed together in Lisbon since 21st May and their movements reported by German intelligence. They were seen boarding the plane together on 1st June. It would seem that only the most short-sighted, possibly one-eyed, German agent could have mistaken Chenhalls, seeing him at such close range at the airport with Leslie Howard, for Winston Churchill.

However, Winston Churchill gave further credence to the mistaken identity theory when he wrote in his history of the Second World War (Vol IV, *The Hinge of Fate*)

Eden and I flew home by Gibraltar. As my presence in North Africa had been fully reported, the Germans were exceptionally vigilant, and this led to a tragedy which much distressed me. The regular commercial aircraft was about to start from the Lisbon airfield when a thickset man smoking a cigar walked up and was thought to be a passenger on it. The German agents therefore signalled that I was on board . . .

Now this seems odd because the first announcement of the loss of *Ibis* came from Berlin and the Germans knew from their own sources that Chenhalls was a passenger – for they announced the fact – and not Churchill (the German News Agency gave the names of Howard, Chenhalls and Stonehouse immediately following the disaster). So the Germans were apparently not mistaken – or deceived – yet for some reason, for which no evidence has ever been forthcoming, Winston Churchill insisted that the Germans thought he was on board – and that their agents signalled the information to them from North Africa. Perhaps, when Churchill wrote his description eight or nine years later, he had at the back of his mind the journalistic 'version' which had appeared in the London newspaper. There does seem to be a marked resemblance between them – even to the phraseology. I suppose it is possible that Churchill was so impressed by the story that he used it in his own version.

Mr Churchill's version of the disaster went on: 'Although these passenger planes had plied unmolested for many months between Portugal and England, a German war plane was instantly ordered out, and the defenceless aircraft was ruthlessly shot down.' In this Mr Churchill was in error. The truth was the *Ibis* had been severely attacked the week before Leslie flew to Portugal – and not *one* warplane but a squadron of eight had eventually shot it down. Finally, Mr Churchill seems to have dismissed the idea of his presence on the plane as far-fetched and ridiculous, with the words:

The brutality of the Germans was only matched by the stupidity of their agents. It is difficult to understand how anyone could imagine that with all the resources of Great Britain at my disposal I should have booked a passage in an unarmed and unescorted plane from Lisbon and flown home in broad daylight. We of course made a wide loop out by night from Gibraltar into the ocean, and arrived home without incident. It was a painful shock to me to learn what had happened to others in the inscrutable workings of Fate.

Epilogue

When I began this memoir I had not intended to become so
involved in Leslie's journey to the Iberian peninsula, with all its
initial uncertainties and prevarications. It was simply meant to be
an intimate record, in sequence, of the events that shaped the final
four years of his life. Nor did I intend to probe at such length into
the possible motives for the return journey's sudden termination.
Perhaps, in my search for truth, I have over-reacted, whereas for
want of better evidence, I should simply have put down those
events to 'the inscrutable workings of Fate'. Perhaps, in the widest
sense, those have been my perspectives.

Yet, like Hamlet's search for truth into his father's untimely
death, I have become caught up in the events, despite the obscuring
distance of time. Certainly, the reasons for Leslie's death have
nagged at me for years and I have, in the Iberian journey, sought a
motive for murder – for murder I believe it was – of all those who
died that day in *Ibis*.

I only regret that despite my researches and those of others, I am
still no nearer a positive solution. The shooting down of the plane
remains an unresolved mystery because the last piece of the puzzle
is still missing. So far no further German evidence has been made
public, nor has any German come forward to clarify the precise
orders issued at Bordeaux if, as I suspect, they were other than
routine.

By now, of course, in terms of time many lips will have been
sealed – and maybe for other reasons – but it seems unlikely at this
range from events that one will hear from the elusive Major Hemm
or any other of the thirty-two men engaged in the attack. Besides it
seems probable that those engaged in the operation, or those who
issued the orders might still feel a sense of guilt or shame for what
they did. The destruction of that undefended plane, containing
women and children, may shock them into silence still. More than
that there may be the underlying uneasiness that their actions might

yet be subject to War Crimes, or some other, Tribunal. Perhaps
with the lifting of relinquishing of such tribunals – already under
discussion in Germany – something more may yet be forthcoming.
But I somehow doubt it.*

Earlier I mentioned the element of risk attached to Leslie's trip.
There were, of course, always risks connected with the movements
of VIPs in war-time. Perhaps, in Leslie's case, the risk was not
thought to be serious enough to outweigh the advantages. Yet the
week before he flew there was the sudden, unexpected attack on the
KLM service – in fact, on the very plane in which Leslie flew. So, if
this was no more than coincidence, it would appear the risk had
palpably increased.

Leslie's 'sponsor' at the Foreign Office was Mr John Ward. Later,
as Sir John Ward, GCMG, he had a distinguished career in the
diplomatic service, becoming British Ambassador to Argentina,
and finally, Ambassador in Rome. Sir John was kind enough to pass
to me his few memories of Leslie and the Iberian journey. He wrote:

> I had a many-sided job in those days and I cannot remember
> now what exactly the Foreign Office interest was in your father's
> mission to Spain. I do remember, however, feeling that it was
> taking a big risk. The answer was that the Germans had given the
> Franco Spanish authorities a secret promise that they would not
> attack the weekly British civil aircraft service between England
> and Spain (in fact, the service flew every day of the week) since
> they were anxious to appease the Spanish complaints that the
> German occupation of Vichy France had cut them off . . . It was
> much discussed in 'official circles' but no conclusion reached . . .
> I certainly recall that the the circle in which I moved in Whitehall
> thought that your father's valuable life had been thrown away.
> The risk would have been infinitely less if he had been flown back
> secretly by night in a military airplane from Portugal (or even
> Gibraltar through which I went several times).

Later I received another letter from Sir John regarding the
invaluable nature of any report Leslie might have brought back
from Spain and Portugal. Sir John said:

---

* In a recent vote in the West German Parliament it was decided to retain the
legal procedures for prosecution under War Crimes tribunals. As people will,
thus, be still liable to trial and possible conviction the ruling will, I think, enforce
secrecy rather than reduce it.

As we were so cut off from those countries it is true that the Government welcomed any impartial report on conditions, specially coming from a man of the intelligence and experience of your father with contacts with 'intellectuals' outside the minions of the dictatorships that were ruling Spain and Portugal in those years. So I can understand how Eden wrote to your father to encourage him to make the trip – something I would not have done in the circumstances of the time, but politicians are a hardboiled lot to get where they do and it was a period of death and destruction.

My own 'guess' is that the German deliberately shot down the civil air-liner to put Franco on notice that they would not allow these increasing cultural-political contacts with the Allies to build up.

In the introduction I suggested that there was an element of destiny in Leslie's life – as if he had reached the apogee, the high, final point of his destiny. I suggested the war had forged his life for a final achievement and purpose – then, snuffed it out. This was not meant to sound grand or theatrical, as special pleading for a thespian farewell. Many died during the war far from the zenith, unspectacularly, and in squalid circumstances. Death was not particular in war whom it sought out – or where. It cut with a universally careless and casual blade. A man's destiny – his 'To be or not to be' – may simply be an incalculable hazard, a game of chance based on a mathematical law of averages like some cosmic 'Bingo'. Whether the bullets that ended Leslie's life were fired haphazardly or by more predictable decision may, indeed, never be proved. I can only say that I have always felt an instinctive sense of destiny terminating Leslie's life at a given or preordained point. And that may be pure conjecture in the light of hindsight.

All one really knows is that physically he vanished, disappeared that first day of June 1943, leaving no evidence, no trace – leaving no body, no call for obsequies. He simply vanished into the blue. In a sense, it was almost typical of Leslie, his way of doing things, for in the most ordinary, mundane way he had the ability to vanish, to disappear – from a crowded room, a gathering of friends. One moment he was there and the next, when one looked around, he was gone. He would be found in his room quietly reading a book, doing some work on a script. He would be upbraided by my mother and dragged back, full of apologies for his absent-mindedness. But this time, in his quietly self-effacing way, he would not be found. He had vanished for good.

It was so like him. I always thought his exits
Had a ghost-elusive touch; he left the stage
Before one was aware that he had gone . . .
The sort of touch that turned plays into hits;
He knew the quality, seemed to gauge
Its value, as if he thought: 'This I have known,
I rather fancied it would go like this.'
And where the eyes were his defiance shone,
That always seemed much more than artifice.

Beauty he taught me, yet his presence
Near me was a teaching, an unspoken thing
That sprang between us, voice within my blood,
Consanguine music both our hearts could sing.
He gave me eyes to see as his eyes saw
The sunlight in the darkness of a wood,
Beyond the brief horizons of the war.
He gave me hope to know that he was there
Beside me, making sorrow easier to bear.

He did not fail, his life-fire was not spent;
Nor did he weary of the years that steal
Away the spirit. He simply went
Between the barriers of time as through a door
Unbolted on a new experiment,
Inquisitive to seek a life more real
Than he had known, to find his answer there
Beyond the furthest pinnacles of air.

When I wrote that I was twenty-five, serving in a cruiser in the
Indian Ocean. I wrote it a few days after I was certain that Leslie had
gone. It was not typical of my first reaction – which was one of shock
and horror. I certainly did not believe, then, in the possibility of
destiny – nor thought about it in that way. After the first shock of
separation I simply accepted the fact that his plane had been
destroyed as a consequence of war – the risks we all took. Later,
when I heard the details, I despised the Germans for destroying
innocent people in a defenceless plane and my pity spilled over into
somewhat more hectic poems of protest and sense of loss. I actively
wanted to revenge myself on Germans, to kill them as they had
killed him. But I soon realised that sort of revenge was not going to
solve anything – and it would certainly not bring Leslie back.

Now, thirty-eight year later, my feelings have solidified and the wound is an old scar long-healed. In the process of time the reactions of youth have become the reflections of middle age. My initial beliefs haven't changed. I still believe Leslie's death was an act of intent and not an accident. I still identify myself with Hamlet's dilemma, but without desire for revenge, only for clarification which is unlikely. I doubt very much if the ghost of my father will appear – on some spatial rampart of the mind – to explain, like Hamlet's father, the circumstances of his murder. With the passage of time, and the perspective that it gives, I have grown ever closer to the idea that Leslie's death was the final act of destiny – at the moment his star was at zenith.

When the ghost of Hamlet's father cried 'Adieu, adieu! Hamlet, remember me,' Hamlet replied:

Remember thee!
Ay thou poor ghost, while memory holds a seat
In this distracted globe. Remember thee!
Yea, from the table of my memory
I'll wipe away all trivial fond records,
All saws of books, all forms, all pressures past,
That youth and observation copied there:
And thy commandment all alone shall live
Within the book and volume of my brain . . . '

Well, there is no final commandment for me, no vengeful swearing on a sword – nor 'from the table of my memory' would I ever wish to 'wipe away all trivial fond records . . . that youth and observation copied there'. Quite the reverse. I would forswear nothing of those years, wishing only to preserve and remember with affection both the 'trivial' and the 'fond' – the small, the light-hearted, the unimportant things that formed familiar boundaries, strongest links. Looking back on those fractured war years I realise that 'youth and observation' copied much more of him than I suspected not only in my memory but in my heart. And that is how I shall remember him. When we were both extraordinarily young – for there was something extremely youthful and unpragmatic about Leslie's fatherhood, and when we were together it was more like brothers than father and son. I shall always remember with affection and gratitude those disconnected, dangerous days – 'magnetic' meetings that always drew bombs, crammed moments of communion, shared pints of beer and jokes and laughter in that far-off battle through which we oddly lived and oddly died. And if it is 'Adieu, adieu' I feel, somehow, it is not goodbye – but simply *au revoir*. And if it is 'Remember me', then, I'll remember him for what he unstintingly gave – swearing never to forget – companionship, friendship, love.

LESLIE HOWARD'S
FILMS AND PLAYS

Films

1917   Rollo in *The Happy Warrior*
1919   Tony Dunciman in *The Lackey and the Lady*
1920   Tony Marchmont in *Five Pounds Reward*
        Richard in *Bookworms*
1930   Tom Prior in *Outward Bound*
1931   Dan Pritchard in *Never the Twain Shall Meet*
        Dwight Winthrop in *A Free Soul*
        Berry in *Five and Ten* (Released in GB as *A Daughter of Luxury*)
        David Trent in *Devotion*
1932   Max Tracey in *Service for Ladies* (Released in US as *Reserved for Ladies*)
        John Carteret in *Smilin' Through*
        Tom Collier in *The Animal Kingdom* (Released in GB as *A Woman in his House*)
1933   John Carlton in *Secrets*
        Captain Fred Allison in *Captured*
        Peter Standish in *Berkeley Square*
1934   Albert Latour in *The Lady is Willing*
        Philip Carey in *Of Human Bondage*
        Stephen Locke in *British Agent*
1935   Sir Percy Blakeney in *The Scarlet Pimpernel*
1936   Alan Squier in *The Petrified Forest*
        Romeo in *Romeo and Juliet*
1937   Basil Underwood in *It's Love I'm After*
        Atterbury Dodd in *Stand-In*
1938   Professor Higgins in *Pygmalion*
1939   Ashley Wilkes in *Gone with the Wind*
        Holger Brand in *Intermezzo* (Released in GB as *Escape to Happiness*)
1940   *From the Four Corners*
1941   Philip Armstrong Scott in *49th Parallel* (released in US as *The Invaders*)

Professor Horatio Smith in *Pimpernel Smith* (Released in US as *Mister V*) Also directed and produced.

1942   R.J. Mitchell in *The First of the Few* (released in US as *Spitfire*) Also directed and produced.

1943   *The Gentle Sex*; co-directed and co-produced.
The Lamp Still Burns: produced.

Plays

1917   Jerry in *Peg O' My Heart*
Charley Wykeham in *Charley's Aunt*
Monty Vaughan in *Under Cover*
1918   London: Ronald Herrick in *The Freaks*
          John Culver in *The Title*
1919   London: Lord Bagley in *Our Mr Hepplewhite*
1920   London: Brian Strange in *Mr Pim Passes By*
          Lord Stevenage in *The Young Person in Pink*
          Billy Benson in *East is West*
       USA: Sir Calverton Shipley in *Just Suppose*
1921   USA: Roddy in *The Wren*
          Percy Sturgess in *Danger*
1922   USA: Oliver Blayds in *The Truth About Blayds*
          Jerry Middleton in *A Serpent's Tooth*
          Gervase Mallory in *The Romantic Age*
          Martini in *The Lady Cristilinda*
1923   USA: Hal Turner in *Anything Might Happen*
          The Hon Willie Tatham in *Aren't We All?*
1924   USA: Henry in *Outward Bound*
          Pablo Moreira in *The Werewolf*
1925   USA: Peter Graham in *Isabel*
          Mr Preen in *Shall We Join the Ladies?*
          Napier Harpenden in *The Green Hat*
1926   London: Bobby Rendon in *The Way You Look At It*
1927   USA: Andre Sallicel in *Her Cardboard Lover*
          Wrigley in *Murray Hill*
          Matt Denant in *Escape*
1928   London: *Her Cardboard Lover*
1929   London: Peter Standish in *Berkeley Square*
       Southampton: Joseph in *Candlelight*
1929   USA: *Candlelight*
          Berkeley Square

1932   USA: Tom Collier in *The Animal Kingdom*
1933   London: William Shakespeare in *This Side Idolatry*
1935   USA: Alan Squier in *The Petrified Forest*
1936   USA: Hamlet in *Hamlet*

INDEX

Index